Negative Theology and Modern French Philosophy

Negative theology is a premodern theological discourse but the questions it poses about the relationship between the known and unknown, the finite and the infinite and the immanent and the transcendent echo throughout secular postmodern philosophy.

The philosopher Jacques Derrida speaks of a deeply ambiguous desire to 'save the name' of God in his work on negative theology, and this desire resonates in different ways in the work of his contemporaries. This turn to religion within the work of a group of thinkers who have been stereotypically identified as relativists or nihilists prompts a series of questions which form the backdrop to this study:

- Who precisely do Derrida and his contemporaries want to 'save the name' of negative theology for and/or from?
- What exactly is the relationship between their – often so very different – readings of the negative way?
- Why does this comparatively obscure Christian tradition remain a significant resource for a group of thinkers who range from committed believers to agnostics or atheists?

Negative Theology and Modern French Philosophy advances a reading of negative theology as an ancient name for something that is essential not simply to modern French thought but to all responsible thought and action whatsoever. It will be essential reading for theologians and philosophers and will also interest those concerned with the work of Derrida and his contemporaries.

Arthur Bradley is a lecturer in the Department of English at University College Chester. He has published on religion and nineteenth- and twentieth-century philosophy, particularly romanticism, phenomenology, genealogy and deconstruction.

Routledge Studies in Religion

1 **Judaism and Collective Life**
   Self and community in the religious kibbutz
   Aryei Fishman

2 **Foucault, Christianity and Interfaith Dialogue**
   Henrique Pinto

3 **Religious Conversion and Identity**
   The semiotic analysis of texts
   Massimo Leone

4 **Language, Desire and Theology**
   A genealogy of the will to speak
   Noëlle Vahanian

5 **Metaphysics and Transcendence**
   Arthur Gibson

6 **Sufism and Deconstruction**
   A comparative study of Derrida and Ibn 'Arabi
   Ian Almond

7 **Christianity, Tolerance and Pluralism**
   Michael Jinkins

8 **Negative Theology and Modern French Philosophy**
   Arthur Bradley

Negative Theology and Modern French Philosophy

Arthur Bradley

LONDON AND NEW YORK

First published 2004
by Routledge
11 New Fetter Lane, London EC4P 4EE

Simultaneously published in the USA and Canada
by Routledge
29 West 35th Street, New York, NY 10001

Routledge is an imprint of the Taylor & Francis Group

© 2004 Arthur Bradley

Typeset in Baskerville by Wearset Ltd, Boldon, Tyne and Wear
Printed and bound in Great Britain by MPG Books Ltd, Bodmin

All rights reserved. No part of this book may be reprinted or reproduced or utilized in any form or by any electronic, mechanical, or other means, now known or hereafter invented, including photocopying and recording, or in any information storage or retrieval system, without permission in writing from the publishers.

British Library Cataloguing in Publication Data
A catalogue record for this book is available from the British Library

Library of Congress Cataloging in Publication Data
Bradley, Arthur.
 Negative theology and modern French philosophy / Arthur Bradley.
    p. cm.
 Includes bibliographical references and index.
 1. Negative theology—Christianity. 2. Philosophy and religion—France. 3. Philosophy, French. I. Title.
 BT83.585 .B73 2004
 194—dc22   2003024364

ISBN 0-415-32903-5

For my parents

Contents

Acknowledgements ix
A note on texts xi

Introduction 1

PART I
Histories 9

1 Derrida and 'saving the name' 11

PART II
Theologies 47

2 Certeau's 'Yes, in a foreign land' 49
3 Marion and 'a paradoxical writing of the word *without*' 81

PART III
Atheologies 113

4 Foucault and 'the thought from the outside' 115
5 Kristeva and 'the original *technē*' 150

PART IV
Futures 187

6 Derrida and the 'passage to the totally other' 189

7 Conclusion: negative theology after modern French
   philosophy   216

   Notes   220
   Bibliography   227
   Index   238

Acknowledgements

I would first of all like to thank a number of friends, family and colleagues who have helped me in large and small ways with this book: Brian Baker, Bernard Beatty, Michele Desmond, Melissa Fegan, Sara Haslam, Sue and Brian Holmes, Shane Johnson, William Large, Jen Mawson, Martin McQuillan, Caroline Middleton, Alan Rawes, Andrew Tate, Marion Williamson and Eric Woehrling. My deepest gratitude goes to Anne and John Bradley.

I would particularly like to thank Chris Walsh and the English Department at Chester College who gave me a period of research leave in order to complete the book. I must also thank Joe Whiting, Amritpal Bangard, Susan Dunsmore and the rest of the editorial team at Routledge for their invaluable help in guiding this book through the different stages of production. I would also like to thank the anonymous readers at Routledge for their encouraging and constructive responses to my work. My gratitude also goes to audiences at Chester College, Staffordshire University, St Martin's College, Lancaster, the College of St Mark and St John, Plymouth, and the University of Greenwich on whom I tried out earlier versions of the material presented here.

I would also like to thank the editors and publishers of a number of books and journals for their permission to reprint material here. Quotations from Jacques Derrida, *On The Name* edited by Thomas Dutoit © 1995 by the Board of Trustees of the Leland Stanford Jr. University English translation are used here with the permission of Stanford University Press, www.sup.org. Chapter 3 of this book was originally published in an abridged form as 'Without Negative Theology: Deconstruction and the Politics of Negative Theology' in *The Heythrop Journal: A Quarterly Review of Philosophy and Theology*, 42 (2001), pp. 133–47. Chapter 4 was published in an earlier form as 'Thinking the Outside: Foucault, Derrida and the Thought of Negative Theology' in *Textual Practice*, 16 (2002), pp. 57–74.

Finally, I would like to thank Rebecca Smith for her love, support and constant belief in me over the years.

A note on texts

This book refers to English translations of French texts where available. The original date of publication in French is given in square brackets, followed by the date of the English publication, on its first appearance. Occasionally existing translations of the primary texts have been modified in the interests of consistency. If there is no indication to the otherwise, translations are my own.

Introduction

This book attempts to explore the treatment of negative theology in modern French philosophy. It is now surely incontestable that we are in the midst of a 'theological turn' in continental thought to rival the much-vaunted ethical and political shifts of the 1980s and 1990s (de Vries 1999). Religious themes, questions and problematics abound in current continental thinking from deconstruction to phenomenology and from genealogy to psychoanalysis in a way that would have been thought unimaginable even a decade or so ago. To speak of the 'faith', the 'religion' or even the 'prayers of tears' of Jacques Derrida – or Jacques Lacan, or Michel Foucault, or Gilles Deleuze or indeed almost any major continental thinker of the past 30 years – is no longer to invite scorn or ridicule.

If this theological shift takes many forms – many of which are still only beginning to be glimpsed – perhaps its most obvious and yet no less enigmatic and surprising manifestation is an interest in what is called negative theology, apophatic theology or simply the *via negativa*. Negative theology has been identified by numerous recent critics (Hart 1989; Caputo 1997; de Vries 1999; Carrette 2000) as one of the key sites of engagement – in the double sense of *both* commitment *and* confrontation – between theology and contemporary philosophy. Michel Foucault's early attempts to formulate archaeologies of madness, illness and knowledge, to take just one obvious example, frequently take the form of something very close to negative theology even if he rightly denies that they have any theological content whatsoever. Michel de Certeau's monumental but still perhaps neglected text *The Mystic Fable* ([1982] 1992) represents the culmination of a career-long exploration of the linguistic, historical and political implications of the *via negativa*. Jean-Luc Marion's *God Without Being* ([1982] 1991) identifies the *via negativa* as a means of circumventing what he sees as the idolatrous God of metaphysical theology and ontotheology. More recently, Julia Kristeva and Catherine Clément's *Le féminin et le sacré* (1999a) has seen the discourses of female mystics such as Angele de Foligno as anticipating the psychoanalytic critique of religion developed by Freud and Lacan. Perhaps the most famous example of this curious phenomenon is Jacques Derrida, however, whose fascination with negative theology stretches across three decades from early essays like 'Différance' ([1967] 1982c) to comparatively late texts like 'Sauf le nom: (Post-Scriptum)' ([1993] 1995a) which even speaks of a deeply ambiguous desire to 'save the name' of the *via negativa*.

The striking interest in negative theology among selected thinkers such as these – not to mention such massive and varied figures as Georges Bataille, Emmanuel Lévinas, Jacques Lacan, Luce Irigaray, Hélène Cixous, Michel Henry, Jean-Louis Chrétien – is the subject of the following study. This theological turn within the work of a group of philosophers who have been journalistically or stereotypically identified with positions of relativism or nihilism since their emergence on the popular stage prompts a series of critical questions that form the backdrop to my work. Who precisely do Derrida (and his contemporaries) want to 'save' negative theology for and/or from? What exactly is the relationship between their – often so very different – readings of the negative way? And why does this comparatively obscure Christian tradition remain a significant resource for a group of thinkers who range from committed believers to agnostics or atheists? In this Introduction, I would like to briefly sketch the argument of my work.

Part I: Histories

First, I offer a brief sketch of the history of negative theology as a theological tradition from the Neoplatonists onwards. It is, as we will see, an open question as to whether there is such a thing as 'negative theology' at all in the sense of a self-identical corpus, tradition or movement that stretches all the way from Neoplatonism through Thomism to the Renaissance mystics. The discussion identifies some of the theological, philosophical and historico-political factors that inevitably problematize any discussion of the negative way. This Part continues by arguing that Jacques Derrida's surprisingly generous and affirmative reading of negative theology turns this problematic into an opportunity to reconceptualize the *via negativa*. In Derrida's account, the *via negativa* needs to be 'saved' – in a sense that requires careful definition – from its own historical fate.

Jacques Derrida's reading of negative theology, then, is the subject of Chapter 1. It is Derrida's critique of negative theology that provides the critical lens through which we will view the relationship between the *via negativa* and modern French thought more generally. His attempt to 'save the name' of the *via negativa*, as he puts it in the essay 'Sauf le nom' (1995a), has been interpreted as everything from a nihilist critique to a neo-Christian apologia but I want to suggest that both interpretations are mistaken. My guiding argument will be that Derrida neither simply attacks nor defends negative theology but attempts – in an apparently paradoxical fashion that will again need to be defined carefully – to repeat it differently. Derrida demonstrates that negative theology's identity depends, to put it in less paradoxical terms, on its ability to be repeated as such outside its apparently original theological context. Derrida's repetition in alterity results in a situation whereby it becomes more and more difficult to define, limit or even *conceive* an idea of what negative theology actually is in itself. Negative theology becomes a privileged name for a linguistic force, excess or opening in the direction of the other – traced in other contexts under the figure of the messianic (Caputo 1997) or the adieu (de Vries 1999) – that refuses to be locked within any particular theological or philosophical determination. Negative theology's ambiguous status thus exceeds the distinctions between the Christian and the non-Christian, the theological and the secular and the transcendental and the empirical. The paradoxical upshot of this situation is that the canonical negative theological texts can never be completely theological and – by the same token – secular or atheist texts cannot wholly escape contamination by negative theology either. This leads to a situation whereby negative theology's identity is essentially undecidable but – as we will see at length – this undecidability calls for a series of decisions that do the least possible violence to its irreconcilable imperatives and injunctions. For Derrida, then, negative theology has important implications both for committed theologians and those apparently secular thinkers who do not believe they have any relation with theology whatsoever and the remainder of the book seeks to put this thesis to the test.

Part II: Theologies

Second, I move on to consider the implications of Derrida's thesis on negative theology in the work of two quite distinct French thinkers who are explicitly concerned with, or particularly influenced by, the question of negative theology in their theological and ostensibly non-theological writings: Michel de Certeau and Jean-Luc Marion. Michel de Certeau's work on the social, political and psychological status of mystic speech acts in the seventeenth century, for example, seems to spill over into his secular writings on tactics and strategies of resistance and belief in the secular twentieth century such as *The Practice of Everyday Life* ([1980] 1984). Jean-Luc Marion's reading of Pseudo-Dionysius's *Celestial Hierarchy* and *Mystical Theology* prefigures and – some would argue – remains discernible within his later development of a phenomenology of givenness beyond all intention in texts such as *Etant donné* (1997a). The two chapters that comprise this Part demonstrate how Certeau and Marion advance a reading of negative theology from within the boundaries of Christian orthodoxy but – as Derrida hypothesizes – in each case such boundaries can never be rendered absolutely secure. This Part argues that Certeau and Marion's attempts to police the theological space around negative theology, so to speak, depend on more or less dogmatic or political decisions that arbitrarily limit the identity of the *via negativa*. In both cases, negative theology needs to be saved from Christian theology.

4 *Introduction*

Michel de Certeau's still little-known and untranslated Christian theology is, then, introduced in Chapter 2. It is the argument of this chapter that the study of belief – what belief consists of, why people believe or disbelieve in something, whether belief itself is still believable or is now somehow *beyond* belief – constitutes the single most abiding theme of his body of work. My argument traces Certeau's shifting analysis of belief from his early texts on Catholic theology through his famous analysis of Renaissance mysticism to his last uncompleted project to formulate an anthropology of belief. The main body of the chapter compares Certeau's theological concept of the mystical speech act of saying 'yes' to God in Angelus Silesius with Derrida's own analysis of the 'yes, yes' that precedes all discourse altogether in 'A Number of Yes' ([1987] 1988a). There is a radical undecidability or foreignness at the heart of Certeau's analysis of mystic speech acts, Derrida demonstrates, that makes it *a priori* impossible for us to determine who or what these acts are giving assent to. This chapter concludes by imagining what role Certeau's Christian theology might play in his later work which, as we will see, is characterized by a deep scepticism about the possibility of belief in general.

Jean-Luc Marion's increasingly influential theology and phenomenology of donation is the subject of Chapter 3. It focuses on Derrida and Marion's now well-known debate about the metaphysical or counter-metaphysical status of negative theology. My argument is that the Derrida/Marion debate partially hinges upon their conflicting interpretations of a key concept in Dionysius's theology – '*hyperousios*' – which is variously translated into English as 'hyperessential', 'superessential' and perhaps most ambiguously as 'without being'. The chapter attempts to mediate between the conflicting interpretations of '*hyperousios*' advanced by Derrida and Marion by putting them in the context of Derrida's complex and aporetic uses of the word 'without' in his essays on Pseudo-Dionysius, Angelus Silesius and Maurice Blanchot. This 'paradoxical writing of the word *without*' indicates an ambiguity or aporia 'within' the *via negativa* that has important implications for Marion's reading of negative theology and the chapter concludes by pursuing some of the political dimensions of this situation.

Part III: Atheologies

Third, I pursue Derrida's reading of the *via negativa* in the work of two very different thinkers who are united by an understandable eagerness to distinguish their work from any charge of negative theology, and indeed, theology in general: Michel Foucault and Julia Kristeva. Michel Foucault is understandably interested in distinguishing his own attempts to develop an archaeology of negativity, repression and deviance in texts like *Folie et déraison: Histoire de la folie* (1961) and *The Archaeology of Knowledge* ([1969] 1972) from any kind of negative theological movement. Julia Kristeva's

Introduction 5

psychoanalysis of the sacred in *Le féminin et le sacré* (1999a) has its roots in the ineffable experiences of the female mystics but, despite this, she maintains that it is emphatically an atheist and immanent project at all times. The two chapters that comprise this Part thus demonstrate how – in their very different ways – Foucault and Kristeva attempt to develop what might be called an immanent or secular negative theology that seeks to collapse the transcendental appeal of apophasis into the empirical mix of history, politics or the body. If Marion and Certeau are unable to maintain an exclusively theological reading of the *via negativa*, however, I will argue that Foucault and Kristeva find it equally impossible to make good a non-theological one because their critique of negative theology just as inevitably reproduces what they are criticizing. In this Part, then, we find that negative theology also needs to be saved from atheism or secularism.

Michel Foucault's famous archaeologies of madness, illness and knowledge are discussed in Chapter 4. It begins by noting a number of parallels between Foucault and Derrida's readings of negative theology in their early work. It shows how the two philosophers both criticize negative theology as a 'thought from the inside' that can be opposed to their respective attempts to develop a 'thought from the outside' in deconstruction and archaeology. My argument here is that – despite these apparent similarities – Foucault's and Derrida's understanding of exteriority remains fundamentally different. The chapter argues that in their famous debate on Descartes and madness Foucault develops a historicist account in which the difference between the interior and the exterior emerges at a particular historical point whereas Derrida substitutes what would now be called a quasi-transcendental reading in which the outside is *already* inside. This results in a situation where Foucault's attempt to develop a thought from the outside has a tendency *to turn into* a thought from the inside and the chapter pursues the implications of this position with a revisionist reading of Foucault's critique of the *via negativa* and, in particular, Christian confession.

Julia Kristeva's psychoanalytic concept of the sacred is addressed in Chapter 5. It examines Kristeva's attempt to articulate a concept of the sacred as a kind of 'secular mysticism' within the experience of the feminine. It also considers the opposition Kristeva draws between the sensible, immanent work of the sacred, on the one hand, and the dogmatic, transcendental projects of what she calls 'belief and religion', on the other. My contention, however, will be that Kristeva's concept of the sacred is above all a form of resistance to what she sees as a valorization of *technology* that stretches from Christian doctrine to contemporary bio-technologies and genetics. The chapter compares Kristeva's sacred critique of technology in *Le féminin et le sacré* with Derrida's analysis of a constitutive or originary technicity that lies at the heart of all being in such texts as 'The Mystic Writing Pad: Freud and the Scene of Writing' ([1967] 1978b). This logic of originary technicity produces a situation wherein Kristeva's concept of the sacred itself becomes indebted to the very technology it seeks to oppose and so the chapter concludes by imagining what a concept of 'theology after technics' might look like.

Derrida's reading intimates that the 'salvation' of negative theology is a matter for everyone, then, and this book puts this hypothesis to the test with a series of essays or case studies on selected figures who, crudely speaking, position themselves 'outside' or 'inside' the *via negativa*. It goes without saying that the choice of subjects here is not intended to be comprehensive and the particular figures under discussion have been chosen simply because they best demonstrate the range of Derrida's critique. My choice of subjects do nonetheless amount to quite a representative sample of the major trends in continental philosophy over the past 30 or 40 years – including deconstruction, genealogy, psychoanalysis and phenomenology – and the wider implications of the discussions will hopefully be apparent. More strikingly, however, it will become clear by the end of the book that each of the chapters in Parts II and III ultimately *says the same thing*, albeit each time slightly differently. First, each discussion begins with what is naïvely intended to be a fairly neutral *description* – if there is one – that presents the question at issue in as accessible a way as possible. If the discussions begin with a description, however, they continue with a very particular act of *intervention* into one area of the work of their subject. The interventions consist of locating a specific concept, gesture or movement within the readings of negative theology at hand – Certeau's 'yes', Marion's 'without', Foucault's 'outside' and Kristeva's 'beginning' – and trying to pursue its logic straight through the particular decisions, traditions or contexts that have accrued to it. This now classic deconstructive gesture is neither an attempt to reproduce the internal arguments of their texts as faithfully as possible nor to criticize them from some spuriously detached or external stance – what would be the point of that? – but what I hope is a more affirmative attempt to *repeat* what they say about negative theology *differently*. In this spirit, each chapter concludes with what we might simplistically call an 'experimental' reading of negative theology that necessarily exceeds the animating intention of its author and the philosophical context in which he or she writes while still hopefully remaining faithful to a certain spirit within their thought.

Part IV: Futures

Finally, and perhaps most importantly, however, I try to sketch some of the possible *futures* modern French philosophy imagines for the *via negativa*. It is my larger contention that Derrida's reading of negative theology does enable us to imagine a certain concept of the *via negativa* at the heart of modernity without, however, succumbing to the twin dangers of attempting to re-theologize secular society or simply co-opting theological concerns to secular interests. Negative theology is not simply a theological concept or tradition we can use or drop at will, in Derrida's account, but a privileged name for something that might actually be central to any act of responsible thought or action whatsoever. If it obviously has a very specific theological history, it is a form of thought whose characteristic feature is to move beyond itself, to transgress the limits of the thinkable and – however impossibly – to think the other as absolutely and unconditionally other. The ancient experience of the impossible that passes under the name of the *via negativa* overlaps, as a number of critics have recently suggested, with the modern experience of the impossible that goes under the name of deconstruction (Hart 1989; Caputo 1997; Carlson 1998). This Part argues that negative theology enables a reinvention of ethico-political responsibility, judgement and decision-making in an increasingly technocratic society that wants to reduce such questions to matters of bureaucratic administration. In this final Part of the book, then, it becomes a question of how negative theology could be saved for the future.

Jacques Derrida's reading of negative theology concludes the book in Chapter 6. It is impossible to predict the future of negative theology without betraying the unconditional appeal to the other that constitutes it, but this chapter explores Derrida's enigmatic claim that the *via negativa* might represent a new form of hospitality. Derrida has recently developed a concept of unconditional hospitality to the other – regardless of who or what they might be, where they come from or whether they even deserve it – but little or no work has been done to elaborate on this link between hospitality and the *via negativa*. My contention here is that Derrida's reading of negative theology successively represents an *act* of hospitality, a *critique* of dominant theologico-political concepts of hospitality as fraternity, community or cosmopolitanism and an *example* of this new concept of unconditional hospitality to every other as absolutely other. The argument shows how negative theology also represents one model for the inevitable negotiation between this unconditional welcome to the other and the conditional juridical and political contexts in which it must take place. This chapter concludes by speculating that one way of saving the name of the *via negativa* for the future could be to translate its appeal to unconditional hospitality into the juridical and political fields of asylum, immigration and more generally human and non-human rights.

So my argument seeks, then, to imagine the future of negative theology as it emerges through a close engagement with modern French philosophy. I obviously could not have written this study without the remarkable work of Jacques Derrida on theological questions over the past 20 years or so and the traces of his thought mark every page. I am also greatly indebted to the work of Derrida critics such as Kevin Hart, John D. Caputo and Hent de Vries and my book is, at best, merely a supplement to their pioneering work in this field. Its focus is not so much on negative theology's *past* as on its *future*, however, because my wager is that the *via negativa* does indeed have a future in what we too simplistically call postmodernity. Negative theology is not simply a theological concept to be valorized or dispensed with at will – to repeat – but a historical name for the impossible experience of the other as absolutely other that is central to all thinking worthy of the name. The negative theology I have in mind is neither a business-as-usual repetition of an ancient theological idiom nor a distortion or appropriation of that idiom for secular ends, then, but hopefully a more surprising, original and pluralized force that is integral to any thought even or especially those that imagine they have no relation to it whatsoever. This book imagines many alternative futures for negative theology in postmodernity, of course, and political theologies, historical theologies, cultural theologies and even technological theologies can all be found within the pages that follow. My intention is not so much to *predict* the future of negative theology, however, but to affirm a future for negative theology that is essentially *un*predictable and must be judged on its own terms as it arrives, here, now. In other words, I argue that the future of negative theology remains to be *decided*. Let the reader be the judge.

Part I
Histories

This opening Part explores Jacques Derrida's reading of negative theology. It begins with a brief history of the *via negativa*. It goes on to argue that Derrida's reading of negative theology is neither a theological extension nor a secular demolition of the historical identity of negative theology but an attempt to affirm a certain plurality within that identity that resists appropriation by any one tradition. The chapter argues that Derrida's reading of negative theology canvasses for a concept of the *via negativa* as something that is central to all thought – whether theological or non-theological – that seeks to responsibly address the other. In Derrida's view, negative theology is a name worth saving for the future and this thesis will be put to the test in the chapters that follow.

1 Derrida and 'saving the name'

– [O]f him there is nothing said that might hold . . .
– Save his name [sauf son nom] . . .
– Save the name that names nothing that might hold, not even a divinity [Gottheit], nothing whose withdrawal [dérobement] does not carry away every phrase that tries to measure itself against him. 'God' 'is' the name of this bottomless collapse, of this endless desertification of language.
(Derrida 1995a: 55–6)

Jacques Derrida speaks of a paradoxical desire to 'save the name' [sauf le nom] of God in his essay on negative theology 'Sauf le nom (Post-Scriptum)' ([1993] 1995a). Derrida's reading of negative theology is the starting point for this book. It stretches over almost four decades of texts from seminal early works like 'Différance' ([1967] 1982c) to comparatively later studies like 'Faith and Knowledge' ([1996] 1998a). More importantly, it has been almost single-handedly responsible for bringing about the much-vaunted 'theological turn' in contemporary critical theory over the last decade or so with the corresponding weight of ongoing work on religion in thinkers such as Certeau, Foucault, Kristeva, Deleuze, Marion, Lyotard and others. But Derrida's reading of negative theology remains – despite its relative fame or notoriety – a deeply controversial and misunderstood theological engagement that has prompted wild critical allegations comparing its author to everything from a mystic *manqué* to a modern 'death of God' atheist or nihilist. The primary aim of this opening chapter is simply – though it is in fact anything but a simple task – to describe and assess Derrida's reading of negative theology in as clear terms as possible. This chapter will go on to argue that Derrida's attempt to 'save' negative theology is neither the theological recuperation of an unlikely born-again Christian nor a secular appropriation or demolition job on the *via negativa* by a polemical atheist or nihilist but an *attempt to repeat it differently*. Finally, I want to pave the way for the chapters that follow by suggesting that Derrida canvasses for a reading of negative theology as a mode of what he calls 'paradoxical hyperbole' (Derrida 1995a:

63) that is central to all thinking worthy of the name, whether it is theological or non-theological, secular or sacred. To begin this enquiry we need to ask three basic questions. What is Derrida's reading of negative theology? Why exactly does he want to 'save the name' of the negative way? And who precisely does he want to save the *via negativa* for and/or from? In this introductory chapter, I will show how Derrida argues that negative theology's meaning *remains to be decided* and that this ambiguous fate means that it increasingly assumes a central place both in his thought and modern French philosophy more generally.

Negative theology

I would like to begin with a brief history of negative theology in its various forms. It is, as we will see, extremely difficult to identify any consensus view about exactly what 'negative theology' is or even whether such a thing actually exists. My intention here is to provide a very basic working definition of the negative way that – for all its inadequacy – will hopefully provide a valid point of departure for the more detailed discussions that follow. The negative way names a theological tradition that insists that the divine cannot be understood in human terms because it is radically transcendent. This leads the *via negativa* to approach the divine not by positive or anthropomorphic language but by negative language, by paradoxical or contradictory language, or by insisting on the inadequacy of all language to describe His transcendence. In simple terms, then, negative theology is a theology that says what God is not rather than what He is; that insists on His radical otherness from all human images of Him and that affirms His absolute unknowability, incomprehensibility and irreducibility to human thought (Louth 1980; Mortley 1986; McGinn 1991; Bulhof and ten Kate 2000). Let me identify some of its main theological phases.

Neoplatonism

Negative theology's origins lie in late antiquity. Its philosophical roots go as far back as pre-Socratic notions of the divine but it first comes to prominence with the Neoplatonic tradition. Plato arguably inaugurates the tradition of thought that will lead to the negative way in the *Phaedo* with the concept of philosophy as the soul's desire to ascend to its divine origin through the *theoria* or contemplation of the Ideal Forms. Plato's *Seventh Letter* states that the act of *theoria* cannot finally comprehend the Ideal, however, because the Form of the Good is unknowable and this emphasis on the incomprehensibility of ultimate reality resonates in Neoplatonism (Plato 1967: 476–565). Platonism introduces some key elements into the philosophy of negation (such as the concepts of knowledge by abstraction or purification) but it is with Neoplatonism that the negative way to knowledge of the transcendent is articulated most explicitly.

Plotinus intensifies the Platonic notion of the transcendence of the Forms by introducing the concept of an absolutely transcendent origin called the One. It is Plotinus's position that the One extends itself by the famous process of emanation into various lower levels of being in which each lower level is a weaker extended expression of the level immediately above it. He emphasizes more strongly than Plato that the One transcends all being, is not itself a being, and that all beings owe their existence to the contemplation – however imperfect – of it. Plotinus's thought also introduces the idea that negative formulations constitute a superior form of knowledge than positive ones and can be used to affirm the transcendent status of the One by negative example (Plotinus 1991). Plotinian thinking on negation is followed by a further development in the Neoplatonic tradition, which is often seen as a critique of its emphasis on negativity, but which, in a more profound sense, constitutes a continuation and radicalization of that tradition through the *negation* of its negations.

Proclus, for example, pursues the Plotinian model of hyper-negativity to a more radical conclusion by insisting that even the negations themselves ultimately have to be negated because as products of logic and language they ultimately reveal nothing about the One. Proclus's thought concludes that, since neither affirmations nor negations give us any access to reality, they must ultimately give way to silence. Damascius pursues an even more uncompromising line that insists that affirmation and negation are both simply products of an emotional or psychological desire for knowledge on the part of the knower and provide no ontological understanding whatsoever of the transcendent status of the One. Damascius concludes that the real point is not to profess knowledge or ignorance of the One's Being but to attain a state of epistemological 'hyperignorance' where the subject recognizes the limits of what he or she can possibly know and not know (Damascius 1987; Carabine 1995).

Christianity

Negative theology's emergence as a distinct theological tradition, however, occurs in the cross-fertilization between Greek Neoplatonism and Christian revelation in the first centuries of the new millennium. It is plausible to argue that the *via negativa* is above all the product of this intellectual dialogue between Neoplatonist and Christian concepts of the relationship to ultimate reality. Negative theology, as we understand the term today, is the result of an imaginative philosophical synthesis between the Christian concept of the revelation of Christ and the Neoplatonic concept of the transcendence of the One.

Christian Neoplatonism strikes a balance between a Christian God who is absolutely revealed to Man through scripture and the doctrine of the incarnation and a Neoplatonic God who is beyond all being and who flows out into being hierarchically according to the theory of emanation. God in Christian Neoplatonism, to put it another way, is *both* revealed as visible, legible and iterable through Christian scripture and liturgy, on the one hand, *and* transcendent, ineffable and incomprehensible according to the Neoplatonic tradition of transcendence on the other. If God is both revealed and transcendent, so to speak, then it becomes clear that there needs to be (at least) two different ways of talking about Him and so the negative theological tradition develops the dual approach of what are called *kataphatic* and *apophatic* theologies. Kataphatic theologies are positive in approach and concentrate on what can be said about God as His nature is voluntarily revealed to us by Him through Christian scripture and liturgy or on what can be gleaned about Him from the study of His creation. Apophatic theologies are negative in orientation and emphasize God's absolutely transcendent nature with respect to being and creation along the lines suggested by Neoplatonic theory.

Pseudo-Dionysius the Areopagite is the pivotal figure in Christian Neoplatonist negative theology. It has been argued by a number of leading commentators – Andrew Louth, Raoul Mortley and Denys Turner among others – that Dionysius is perhaps even the single most important figure in the history of Christian negative theology whose work influenced Maximus the Confessor, Gregory Palamas, Bernard of Clairvaux and Thomas Aquinas amongst others. His decision to write under the name of an Athenian convert of St Paul was once derided as an act of forgery but is now thought to be a strategic move that advertises his audacious attempt to synthesize Judaeo-Christian theology and Neoplatonic philosophy. Dionysius stitches together the Christian doctrine of the world as God's creation *ex nihilo* and the Neoplatonic philosophy of the world as a progressive emanation from an ultimate reality. Dionysius's work can be divided into kataphatic and apophatic approaches although recent criticism suggests he also posits a 'third way' that exceeds both affirmation and negation. On the one hand, *The Divine Names* (1980) progressively affirms a series of names for God culminating in the primary nomination of His Goodness. *The Divine Names* elegantly combines the Plotinian concept that creation exists in a hierarchy wherein each lower level is a weaker extended expression of the level just above it with the Christian creationist doctrine that every creature in that hierarchy receive its beings not from the being above it in the order but immediately from God Himself as a manifestation of His glory in accordance with the particular role He has given it. If Dionysius insists that it is possible to affirm God on the basis of His manifestation in what He creates, however, he also stresses that on a much deeper and more fundamental level God is not simply the highest part of man but something that absolutely transcends Him. On the other hand, *The Divine Names* and the shorter and more enigmatic text *The Mystical Theology* progressively negate all names for God as well, culminating in the Neoplatonic assertion that God is '*hyperousios*' or absolutely beyond being. *The Divine Names* and *The Mystical Theology* do not contradict the earlier claim that God manifests Himself immediately in creation but complement or supplement it with the insistence that the One who manifests Himself still absolutely exceeds His manifestation. For Dionysius, however, both kataphatic and apophatic theology are themselves superseded by a Proclean or Damascean negation of the negation that denies that anything predicative can be said of God whatsoever (Pseudo-Dionysius 1980). (See Chapter 3 for Derrida and Marion's discussion of Dionysius's third way.)

Medieval theology

Negative theology's position becomes increasingly complex and difficult to track on both a theological and an institutional level in the medieval period. It is clear that Neoplatonism is the main influence on Christian negative theology from the second to the eleventh centuries but the beginning of the twelfth century sees the reintroduction of the *Corpus Aristotelicum* into Western culture. If Aristotelian philosophy is undoubtedly highly influential upon medieval apophaticism, Christian Neoplatonist assumptions about the transcendence and unknowability of God and the existence of finite things by way of their degree of participation in the existence of God persist in such massive figures as Aquinas and Eckhart.

Thomas Aquinas famously provides the first synthesis of Christian doctrine and Aristotelian philosophy but Christian Neoplatonism endures in his corpus through the influence of, most notably, Pseudo-Dionysius. Aquinas reconfigures the distinction between apophasis and kataphasis in Dionysius by identifying two complementary approaches to understanding the nature of God, namely, the *via remotionis* or way of removing and the *via affirmationis* or way of affirmation. On the one hand, the *via remotionis* emphasizes that God must be approached negatively because in Aristotelianism all knowledge proceeds from sensory experience and, for Aquinas, God absolutely exceeds sensory experience. God is not an object of sensory knowledge; He lacks the composition that characterizes finite beings; He is not a composition of spatial and temporal parts because He is immaterial and timeless; He is not a composition of actuality and potentiality because He is wholly immutable, and He is not a composition of essence and existence because, famously, His essence is His existence. If sensible knowledge does not provide any direct knowledge of God, however, Aquinas's proof of God's existence from motion insists that sensible things are still effects of God and thus can be used to elicit knowledge of Him indirectly or analogously as their first cause. On the other hand, then, the *via affirmationis* concentrates on what can be positively affirmed of God on the basis that God as first cause possesses in an unlimited sense all the perfections that finite creatures possess as His effects. He can be affirmed through the famous theory of analogy as *pure* perfection (wise, good, intelligent, and so on); He is affirmed as *pre-eminent* in perfection (first cause, unmoved mover, and so on), and He is affirmed as perfect in a *wholly simple* manner (wisdom itself, goodness itself, and so forth) (Thomas Aquinas 1964–75). (See Chapter 3 for Marion's critique of Thomas Aquinas.)

Meister Eckhart is another massive figure working in the negative theological tradition in the medieval Church. It is impossible to reduce Eckhart's radically diverse and pluralized body of work to simple positions but the emphasis on apophasis remains constant. He takes a range of different and apparently contradictory approaches to discourse on God. God is described as exceeding all human predicates whatsoever; He is affirmed as *esse simplicitus* or undifferentiated existence, and He is also said to be beyond all concepts of existence, goodness, and so on (see the remainder of Chapter 1 for a discussion of Derrida's reading of Eckhart on *esse*). Eckhart was famously indicted for heresy in 1329 and one of the charges against him was related to his radically apophatic claim that we speak as incorrectly when we call God 'good' as we do when we call white 'black'. Eckhart's paradoxical argument about God's being is sharpened by a more uncompromising concept of analogy than is found in Aquinas that prefers to posit an absolute opposition rather than a relation of proportion or extension between the respective analogates. To argue that God is properly understood as *esse* is to deny that creatures can also possess such a value in themselves and – by the same token – to attribute the value of *esse* to creatures is to deny that value can be properly applied to God at all. If we want to figure out exactly what Eckhart is saying and not saying about God, Bernard McGinn argues that we need to place his myriad local arguments within the larger context of his notion of God as Absolute Unity or *unum* (Meister Eckhart 1981). Absolute unity or *unum* reconciles the kataphatic and apophatic aspects of Eckhart's discourse on God because it enables him to posit God as simultaneously transcendent and immanent with respect to His creation. The key to the matter is Eckhart's ingenious argument that God's *absolutely distinguishing characteristic* – namely His absolute unity or oneness – is nothing other than *his inability to be distinguished*. There is a sense in which God is simultaneously distinct and indistinct with respect to His creation and in which the more distinct He is from Man, the more indistinct He is from Man, and vice versa. This argument enables Eckhart to square the circle between the positive and negative discourses on God by making it possible for him to argue that God transcends His creation precisely *because* He is immanent to it.

Negative theology does not take place within a historical vacuum, as the example of Eckhart shows, and a key theme in this book will be the social, political and institutional contexts in which the *via negativa* was born and to which it in turn gave rise. It is hardly surprising that the place of negative theology within the institutions of the medieval and the Renaissance church was frequently an uncomfortable one. Its suspicion of every philosophical or theological attempt to gain knowledge and understanding of

God sits uneasily alongside the prevailing Aristotelianism of Scholastic theology in the medieval period. Its insistence that God is not life, being, eternity, divinity or even goodness historically provoked – most famously in the case of Eckhart though he is by no means the only example – allegations of heresy and even atheism. More generally, the emergence of Renaissance mystics such as St John of the Cross and St Teresa of Avila – though their body of work is not exactly coterminous with the *via negativa* – created a tension between an apparently interior, experiential way of negation and the hierarchically organized ecclesiastical structures of the Church (see Chapter 2 for Certeau's account of the crisis of mysticism in the Renaissance period). Michel de Certeau, Michel Foucault, Grace Jantzen and a host of other critics of Christian negative theology and mysticism have interpreted the *via negativa* in political terms as either a means of socio-political subversion or even as an ideological agent of the philosophical status quo (see Chapter 4 for Foucault's account of negative theology as contributing to a repressive Christian technology of the self). The fraught relationship between negative theology and the institutions of the Church produced both an institutional embrace of negative theologians on the part of the Church in an attempt to bind them more tightly to the liturgy, the sacraments and ecclesiastical life and an institutional retreat from the Church on the part of negative theologians to positions outside the established theological and patriarchal order (see Chapter 5 for Kristeva's account of the feminine sacred in Christian mysticism).

Modernity and postmodernity

Negative theology's position in modernity and beyond is, if anything, even more difficult to identify. It is debatable whether there is even such a thing as 'negative theology' from modernity onwards in the sense of a distinct Christian Neoplatonic tradition that has been inherited from antiquity. It seems more cautious – in the absence of any more rigorous vocabulary at this stage – to join Ilse Bulhof and Laurens ten Kate in speaking of nothing more than 'hints' or 'echoes' of the *via negativa* in the philosophical and theological projects of modernity and postmodernity (Bulhof and ten Kate 2000: 1–57).

Immanuel Kant's critical philosophy is famously hostile to religious mysticism (Kant 1998a) but recent criticism has detected a number of parallels between his work and the negative theology of the Dionysian tradition. Kant reproduces in secularized form the negative theological fissure between the kataphatic and the apophatic with his distinction between the phenomenal and the noumenal. Kant's famous argument that God's existence cannot be proved by pure reason but must be assumed as a regulative idea of morality has also been described by Don Cupitt as an *epistemological* rather than an *ontological* form of negative theology whereby the question of God's *existence* rather than His *essence* is posited as unknowable (Cupitt 1982: 56–67).

Søren Kierkegaard is, by contrast, an absolutely pivotal figure in the relationship between premodern and postmodern concepts of negation or apophasis. He stresses the disjuncture between human reason and any thought of the divine with his insistence on God as the wholly other whose revelation can only be articulated in a broken language of irony, paradox and fragmentation (Kierkegaard 1985). Kierkegaard's thought has been shown by critics such as David Law to pursue negative theology to its logical limits with its concept of Christian experience as an absolute surrender of all positive or negative forms of knowledge that prostrates itself, in fear and trembling, before God (Law 1994: 221). From this perspective, Kierkegaard's thought represents an important forerunner to the Heideggerian overcoming of ontotheology.

Martin Heidegger's fundamental ontology is avowedly a philosophical rather than a theological project but a number of critics (Carlson 1998) have drawn parallels between Dionysius's mystical theology and Heidegger's account of *Dasein*'s finite being towards death. Heidegger's later critique of ontotheology has also been seen as a philosophical continuation of the negative theological project of protecting the transcendence of God from human conceptions of Him (Kearney 1980; Sikka 1997; Westphal 2001). Heideggerian fundamental ontology criticizes Aristotle's metaphysics for seeking to complete its science of general being (ontology) by positing God as the highest being (theology) so that the deity comes into philosophy only insofar as it confirms philosophy's own view of itself (ontotheology). For Heidegger, the thought of Being revives the famous Pascalian opposition between the God of metaphysical philosophy and theology who is merely the transcendental anchor for certain Aristotelian concepts and the God of Christian faith and revelation: 'Man can neither pray nor sacrifice to this God. Before the *causa sui*, man can neither fall to his knees in awe, nor can he play music and dance before this God' (Heidegger 1969: 72). (See Chapter 5 for a fuller account and critique of Heidegger's critique of ontotheology.)

Negative theology's position in postmodernity – now, here, today – remains very much to be decided. It has already been observed that negative theology has made a dramatic entry into continental philosophy in the past 20 years or so with the appearance of explicitly apophatic themes in the work of philosophers such as Derrida and others. Its rapid and unpredictable rise has prompted a wholesale reassessment of the assumed secularism of such canonical thinkers as Derrida, Deleuze, Foucault or Irigaray together with a re-appraisal of hitherto more marginal figures like Certeau, Henry and Marion whose work has clear theological dimensions. The 'theological turn' in contemporary continental philosophy is now so complete that, as I suggested in the Introduction, it is no longer thought ridiculous to speak of the 'faith', the 'religion' or even the 'prayers and tears' of thinkers who often were or are confessed atheists. This phenomenon clearly requires a more rigorous means of accounting for it than is available under the standard rubrics of secularization or, more recently, re-enchantment, and this is one of the things the present study attempts to provide. My argument will explore the impact of the *via negativa* on contemporary French philosophy at length in the chapters that follow but let me raise three very basic and provisional questions about the relationship between the premodern and the postmodern to sketch the territory.

First, continental philosophy's defining interest in thinking or exploring an absolute alterity that is unthinkable or unpresentable to consciousness as such almost immediately brings it into dialogue with the *via negativa*. 'Western philosophy is in essence the attempt to domesticate Otherness', Rodolphe Gasché argues, 'since what we understand by thought is nothing but such a project' (1986: 101). Continental philosophy, by contrast, frequently defines itself as the attempt to establish a non-violent relationship with an absolute alterity that shatters our horizons of expectation and exceeds our attempts to understand it. Lévinas famously argues how ethics begins with the face of an other (*l'Autre*) who exceeds 'the idea of the other in me' (1969: 50); Foucault defends the alterity of madness against its domestication by Enlightenment rationalism as merely the other side of reason (Foucault 1961); Derrida criticizes Lévinas and Foucault for positing a purely heterological absolute other and ignoring the way in which it is inevitably absorbed into, and violated by, language (Derrida 1978c: 79–154). The precise relationship between the 'holy other' of negative theology and the 'wholly other' of post-Heideggerian philosophy has been one of the most contentious questions in continental thought since the publication of Dominique Janicaud's polemical *Le tournant théologique dans le phénoménologie française* (1991) at least and it is another recurring theme in the present study. Might it be possible, then, to forge a rapprochement between negative theology's attempt to posit an infinitely transcendent God and philosophy's dream of a non-violent relationship with an absolute alterity or does the *via negativa* inevitably belong to the philosophical tradition of domesticating otherness that continental philosophy sets itself against?

Second, continental philosophy's interest in what cannot be conceptualized as such often leads it to adopt a kind of *via negativa* that resembles negative theology almost to the point of being indistinguishable from it. It is certainly a striking coincidence that philosophers like Derrida, Foucault and others have acknowledged certain stylistic, structural and thematic parallels between their work and that of negative theologians like Pseudo-Dionysius even if they are at pains to deny any larger philosophical convergence. Derrida consistently denies deconstruction is a form of method, analysis, critique, a Kantian idea, a negative theology, X, Y or Z (Derrida 1991: 269–76); Foucault defines his archaeology of knowledge in negative terms insisting ultimately that his historical archive is not an object of knowledge (Foucault 1972: 130–1) whereas Lyotard insists on judgements without pre-determined criteria (Lyotard 1985) and re-writes the event via the Kantian concept of the sublime (Lyotard 1994). The impact of Christian negative theology on the work of particular continental thinkers has been the subject of important studies by Harold Coward, Toby Foshay, John. D. Caputo and Hent de Vries – all of whom focus predominantly or exclusively on Derrida – but the larger impact of the *via negativa* on the continental scene more generally remains to be seen (Coward and Foshay 1992; Caputo 1997: 1–69; de Vries 1999). Is continental thought – to take only the most clichéd possibilities or alternatives – a philosophical *continuation* and *extension* of negative theology's critique of language, identity and ontology or is it a *rejection* or *reaction* against a negative theological tradition that, for all its subversiveness, remains deeply indebted to the metaphysical and ontotheological tradition from which it departs?

Finally, to cast the net more widely, continental philosophy's interest in an absolute alterity that can only be conceptualized in negative terms raises the question of the ethical, social and political relationship between it and the *via negativa*. John D. Caputo speaks of continental philosophy as a generalized apophaticism or negativity that extends negative theology into the fields of ethical, anthropological and political thought:

> So to the *theologica negativa*, one could add a *anthropologia negativa*, an *ethica negativa*, *politica negativa*, where of the humanity, or the ethics, or the politics, or the democracy to come we cannot say a thing, except that they want to twist free from the regimes of presence, from the historically restricted concepts of humanity, ethics and democracy under which we presently labour. Humanity, ethics, politics – or whatever, *n'importe* – could belong to a general apophatics.
> (Caputo 1997: 56)

It is certainly possible to envisage a social or anthropological comparison between the mystical concept of the self as riven, wounded or annihilated by its desire for a consummation that transcends its understanding and the post-Heideggerian critique of the individual or autonomous subject that has dominated philosophical thinking from Cartesian rationality to Sartrean existentialism. Michel de Certeau writes of the mystical theology of St Teresa of Avila: ' "I is an other" [Je est un autre] – that is the secret told by the mystic long before the poetic experience of Rimbaud, Rilke or Nietzsche' (Certeau 1986: 96). Perhaps this premodern concept of the subject being grounded in a divine other anticipates the postmodern concept of the subject as split or divided by textual, psychoanalytic or historico-political alterities. Foucault, for example, situates the transcendental Cartesian subject as the historical effect of certain historico-political discourses or *epistemes* (Foucault 1991); Derrida and Nancy re-locate the subject within a network of infinitely extending spatio-temporal textual differences (Derrida 1976; Nancy 1991) whereas Cixous, Kristeva and Irigaray criticize the positioning of the female subject within phallogocentric hierarchies and insist that 'she' actually resists singular definition or nomination (Cixous 1981: 245–64; Kristeva 1982; Irigaray 1985). Do the ostensibly very different critiques of the Enlightenment subject offered by negative theology and continental thought overlap with each other? More generally, we need to consider the ethico-political relationship between negative theology and the generalized apophatics of continental philosophy. The political implications of negative theology – both within and without the institutions of the Christian Church and State – are explored by a number of thinkers in this book, most notably Michel Foucault and Jacques Derrida. For Foucault, negative theology remains – despite all the repression and persecutions inflicted upon its proponents in the medieval Church – an ideological instrument of oppression and subjectification that reduces the subject to a state of silence, sacrifice and obedience (see Chapter 4 for Foucault's critique of negative theology). Jacques Derrida is also critical of the uses to which negative theology has been put by ecclesiastical and political institutions but he is adamant that the *via negativa* gives rise to more than one mode of politics (see Chapter 6 for Derrida's account of the politics of the *via negativa*). To what extent, then, is the meaning of negative theology determined by the theological and political institutions of Church and State or can it be separated from its own institutional history and considered more generally?

What, to conclude this section, exactly *is* negative theology then? It is, appropriately enough, easier to say what is not. It is clear from the preceding discussion that there are a number of basic difficulties with the term itself that call into question the possibility of any singular definition. To begin with, it is highly questionable whether the long and rich tradition of negativity in theology ever adds up to a self-conscious theological mode called 'negative theology'. Pseudo-Dionysius, the theologian with whom it is still chiefly associated, actually uses the term only once in *The Mystical Theology*, and even then only in the plural form of negative *theologies*. Bernard of Clairvaux, Bonaventure and Thomas Aquinas regularly use negative or apophatic strategies in the medieval period but – as Aimé Solignac has pointed out – none of them ever actually talked about 'negative theology' at all (Solignac 1990: 513). Furthermore, negative theology's sheer historical reach – from Neoplatonism to postmodernism or from Damascius to Derrida – also begs the question of whether we are justified in using the term as if it always meant the same thing. Plotinus's negative theology is manifestly not identical to Pseudo-Dionysius's – for all the undoubted continuities between them – any more than Pseudo-Dionysius's negative theology is identical to Thomas Aquinas's, and so on. Negative theology, then, cannot be understood as 'theological' in any specific philosophical or doctrinal sense of the term if we want to apply it to all these thinkers but perhaps only in its broadest Greek definition as the thought of an ultimate ground which is variously named as the One (Plotinus) God (Pseudo-Dionysius) or even the Godhead beyond God (Eckhart). Faced with these problems, contemporary critics of negative theology have been forced to adopt a range of various approaches from outright rejection of the term to blithe acceptance of its flaws. Jean-Luc Marion is most uncompromising of all in his conviction that there is simply no such thing as negative theology in the sense of a singular, self-conscious and systematic philosophical or theological tradition (Marion 2002b: 130). Raoul Mortley, Denys Turner and the editors of the most recent collection of essays on the subject, Ilse Bulhof and Laurens ten Kate, continue to use the term while holding it, so to speak, at arm's length and expressing a more or less open scepticism about its viability (Mortley 1986: 13; Turner 1995: 2; Bulhof and ten Kate 2000: 1–57). So 'negative theology' still lingers on in current theological and philosophical discourse more than 2,000 years after its birth rather like 'Being' in the later Heidegger: *sous rature*, cancelled but legible, mentioned but not used, swathed in prophylactic scare-quotes. If there seems to be no question of continuing to use the term as if nothing was wrong, nor any likelihood of getting rid of it in favour of some notionally more accurate one, then what are the alternatives? Perhaps the sheer *impossibility* of affirming precisely what negative theology is might – in classic negative theological style – be the basis for a superior insight into its meaning. Negative theology's defining characteristic, Raoul Mortley argues, might be its transgressive or hyperbolic tendency to exceed any theological or philosophical context in which it finds itself: '[i]t covers the whole question of how it is that thought jumps beyond itself to other levels of being and experience: like an electric current, thought can jump out from that which conducts it along its path, making connections that are beyond it' (Mortley 1986: 13). Jacques Derrida goes so far as to suggest that any definition of negative theology can at best be a *via negativa* of the *via negativa* – a statement of what it *is not* – because negative theology is definitively suspicious of every concept of received identity including its own. The idea of negative theology as less a stable historical or theological tradition, and more a mode of transgression which consists of breaking with the contexts from which it arises, is one that we will explore at length in the remainder of this book. This concept of the *via negativa* as a mode of 'paradoxical hyperbole' – whose identity consists in its own self-difference – is articulated most clearly in Derrida's essay 'Sauf le nom' to which we will now turn. In Derrida's deconstruction, we encounter our first and most important engagement between negative theology and modern French philosophy.

Derrida and deconstruction

I want to begin my reading of Derrida with a brief description of deconstruction. It is impossible to define deconstruction as such but, of course, this is not quite the same as saying it does not exist. Deconstruction, Derrida repeatedly tells us, is *not,* nothing, impossible, not a method, not a critique, not a Kantian Idea of Reason, not a form of negative theology and so on to infinity. Derrida is reluctant to reduce deconstruction to a predetermined set of ideas that can then be applied in a given set of circumstances because to do so would be to militate against everything that is at stake in it. If we have a theory of something before we encounter it, then we are not keeping an open mind about the thing itself but merely carrying out a predetermined course of action in the manner of a computer running a programme or a bureaucrat carrying out an order. To think we already know what something is, is to avoid thinking about it at all – Derrida repeatedly insists – whereas to give oneself up to the thing itself, and let it think us, is the basis for any thinking worthy of the name. In Derrida's account, as we will now see, deconstruction is not an attempt to enclose the other within the circle of the same but is precisely this 'openness towards the other' (Kearney 1984: 124).

Deconstruction as a methodology

Jacques Derrida's work follows no pre-set theory or method, then, but in its earlier forms at least it habitually takes a number of recognizable forms. He famously argues that the Western philosophical tradition is what – *pace* Heidegger – he calls a metaphysics of presence (Derrida 1976: 12). Derrida suggests that presence takes various forms such as presence of thought or consciousness, present being of the subject, presence as substance, essence or existence, the temporal presence of the present moment, and so on. Western philosophy reveals its dependence upon the value of presence in different ways but its most consistent form is to oppose and hierarchize philosophical values by identifying a 'superior' value with presence and an 'inferior' value with the negation, mediation or complication of that presence. Speech is privileged over writing, the ideal over the material, the intelligible over the sensible, the transcendental over the empirical, the masculine over the feminine, content or meaning over form or style, and so on *ad infinitum.* The phenomenon that has become known as 'deconstruction' is not so much something Derrida *does to* the metaphysics of presence from outside, so to speak, so much as something that Derrida *reveals about* the internal construction of Western metaphysics. This 'deconstruction' brings Derrida into dialogue with almost every major figure in the Western philosophical tradition from Plato to Husserl together with a range of figures from literature, linguistics, anthropology and other disciplines such as Joyce, Saussure and Foucault.

Derrida generally targets two separate groups or categories of thinker in his early readings of the metaphysical tradition. He offers a series of readings of *philosophy* from Plato to Husserl, on the one hand, and the *human sciences* including figures like the linguist Saussure and the anthropologist Lévi-Strauss, on the other. It is possible to detect a consistent line of argumentation within these often bewilderingly different texts. On the one hand, Derrida is concerned to show that transcendental philosophy involves an unwarranted assumption of superiority over the empirical: Plato, Kant and Husserl remain indebted to the realm of the empirical, material and contingent even when they claim to transcend it. On the other hand, Derrida is at pains to demonstrate that this does not mean that the transcendental philosophical tradition can simply be dispensed with in favour of empiricism and that some complicity with it is unavoidable even or especially when we think we have avoided it: Saussure, Lévi-Strauss and Foucault are unable to reduce philosophy to empirical or material questions of language, history or power because they, like the rest of us, cannot help but use the terms the tradition supplies us with. Derrida's bigger purpose here is to question the classic binary oppositions between the transcendental and the empirical that defines Western thought from Plato to the present day. First, Derrida argues that these oppositions are characteristically presented as natural, objective or scientific by the philosophies that are responsible for erecting them but that they are actually the result of a series of contingent decisions that are anything but neutral. Second, and more importantly, Derrida demonstrates that such oppositions can be seen to depend upon a certain point of undecidability between them that precedes their appearance as oppositions or alternatives. The binary differences that constitute Western metaphysics are shown to be preceded by a third position that belongs to neither and that allows those differences to appear as oppositional. This unthought space between the transcendental and the empirical is the aporia that – however impossibly – deconstruction attempts to think.

Writing

Derrida's first and most famous articulation of this 'third position' which is neither inside nor outside philosophy occurs in the context of *writing*. It is the historic opposition between speech and writing that provides him with his initial entry point into the problematic constitution of Western metaphysics. He begins by arguing that the classic Platonic distinction between speech as the pure expression of a present intention and writing as the inferior materialization or mediation of that intention (which leaves it open to distortion, misinterpretation or simple destruction) dominates both philosophy and the human sciences from the *Phaedrus* to the present day. His argument is that any attempt to valorize speech over writing from the perspective of the transcendental or the empirical represents a contingent decision that does a violence to a certain defining undecidability within the opposition itself. On the one hand, for example, Husserl's phenomenology argues that we need to bracket off the historical contingency and facticity (*Verkörperung*) of the written word if we want to use it to preserve the identity of an ideal object, but Derrida shows that no such separation is possible and that the identity of even the most ideal idealities, like geometry, depend upon the very materiality of writing that Husserl wants to reject (Derrida 1973). On the other hand, for instance, Saussure's linguistics relegate writing to merely the signifier of a phonic signifier but – given that he elsewhere argues that *all* signifiers exist in an arbitrary and differential relationship with *other* signifiers – then Derrida insists that by his own logic it would surely be more accurate to call *language itself* by the name of writing (Derrida 1976). Derrida uses this deconstruction of the metaphysical speech/writing opposition in order to bring into view a third position behind the first two which cannot be conceptualized as such – because it is the force that brings all concepts whatsoever into operation – but for which he offers various strategic nicknames drawn from the immediate context of the discussion at hand like '*arche*-writing', '*différance*' or, in his recent works on negative theology, '*khōra*' (Derrida 1995a).

First, Derrida argues that I can only express myself because language is a system of differences without positive terms whereby every signifier does not refer to a transcendental signified but merely to other signifiers. Derrida here draws on and radicalizes Saussure's still-too phonocentric concept of the arbitrary and differential nature of the relationship between signifiers. Second, I cannot choose the language I use to express myself or the concepts it offers me because language is something I inherit passively, that I cannot help but embrace even if I wish to reject it, and that I must repeat more or less faithfully whether I want to or not. Derrida's concept of language as an affirmation, an act of saying 'yes', or a promise that I am committed to from the very moment I open my mouth, is (as we will see in Chapter 2 on Certeau) a recurring theme in his work (Derrida 1989a). Third, Derrida maintains that I am only able to use language to express myself on the basis that my written or spoken expressions can at the same time be repeated quite independently of me or my animating intention in a series of potentially infinite new contexts. If language is capable of operating independently of my intention, Derrida insists that this is not simply an empirical accident or chance that befalls me from outside but rather something that is built into language from the start as a condition of its possibility. My intended meaning is permanently and constitutively stratified across a range of potentially infinite past, present and future contexts and thus subject to a necessary undecidability. Fourth, Derrida generalizes this line of argument to encompass not simply language but the *entirety of the perceptual field* so that reality as we experience it has the characteristic of a language or text. The famous or notorious claim that 'there is nothing outside the text' (Derrida 1976: 157–8) is not some formalist attempt to reduce the world to a work of literature nor to redefine it as some vast Borgesian universal library but rather to say that reality as we perceive it has the structure of language, writing or textuality in the sense described by Derrida above. There is an important sense in which the identity of every subject or object depends not on any intrinsic quality within the thing itself but – like language – upon its *difference* from a potentially infinite series of other subject or objects. This difference is both the driving force that produces all identity whatsoever and – according to a double logic for which Derrida is famous – that which ensures that no identity is ever complete or self-sufficient in itself. Finally, and more generally, Derrida is at pains to argue that he is not seeking to 'deconstruct' the metaphysics of presence after the fact – as if it were somehow pure and self-identical before he got his grubby paws on it – but to demonstrate that metaphysics is already 'in' deconstruction in the sense that the foundational instability named by deconstruction is the only possible ground upon which it can operate in the first place. We need to see that the metaphysics of presence exists – like the statue of Ozymandias in Shelley's famous poem – in a state of permanent deconstruction poised somewhere between collapse and completion. For Derrida, then, deconstruction is neither the attempt to get beyond metaphysics once and for all nor to repeat it faithfully *ad infinitum* – neither position is actually possible – but rather to *repeat it otherwise* in such a way as to allow the hidden but essential instability upon which it depends to – at least partially – emerge.

Ethics, politics and theology

What, then, are the larger implications of deconstruction? It is well known, of course, that Derrida and his work have historically prompted polemical critiques from supporters and detractors alike, describing it as everything from a radical form of relativism or nihilism (Rorty 1984; Milbank 1997) on one extreme, to a suspiciously conservative neo-idealism or transcendentalism on the other (Habermas 1981; Eagleton 1990). If deconstruction was in many ways the chief victim of the 'theory wars' of the late 1970s and 1980s – assailed both by enemy and friendly fire – it was paradoxically only in the so-called post-theoretical 1990s that the attempt to draw out its implications for ethics (Critchley 1992), politics (Bennington 1994; Beardsworth 1996) and religion (Hart 1989; Caputo 1997; de Vries 1999) began in earnest. Let me briefly highlight some key themes.

For starters, it is extremely important to be clear about what Derrida is and is not claiming here. Derrida is not *valorizing* some nominally metaphysics-free zone called deconstruction as 'good' and *condemning* metaphysics as 'evil', of course, but *describing* the constitutive instability that is 'metaphysics in deconstruction'. He never suggests *anywhere* in his texts – despite numerous claims to the contrary – that writing, difference and absence are somehow 'better' than speech, identity and presence because the whole point of such quasi-concepts as '*arche*-writing' is to make clear that no such simple choice or distinction is possible. If deconstruction demonstrates that 'the structure of the [metaphysical] machine, or the springs, are not so tight, so that you can just try to dislocate [them]' (Salusinszky 1987: 20), it is striking that Derrida gives no clear direction about what the precise calibration of that machine should be in any given set of circumstances. Does, then, the absence of any uncompromised ethical or political injunction within deconstruction necessarily commit it to a relativist, quietist or nihilist position with all the understandable accusations of defeatism, irresponsibility or self-contradiction such a stance appears to involve?

Deconstruction insists that the existence of a point of aporia or undecidability within metaphysics does not paralyse decision-making because – on the contrary – it is precisely what makes an ethical or political decision or judgement possible. It is because we cannot determine the relationship between the transcendental and the empirical in any natural, impartial or scientific fashion that an ethical or political *decision* of sorts is called for. Far from destroying the possibility of decision-making, the very absence of a pre-existing reality that we can innocently describe or appeal to as the basis for our judgements is exactly what makes a decision concerning it necessary and inevitable. Derrida goes on to argue that every decision qua decision necessarily involves an element of contingency, arbitrariness or violence because it is taken in the absence of any ground for decision-making. If a contingent decision cannot be avoided, then, the question arises of exactly what kind of decision should be taken and Derrida contrasts the metaphysical decision which seeks to pass itself as 'real', 'natural' or 'scientific' with what he variously calls the 'mad decision', the 'impossible decision' or the 'decision without criteria' (Derrida 1990: 24). The impossible decision is the only decision worthy of the name because it alone does not seek to subsume the case to be decided under a set of given rules or a preconceived concept of justice or reality but rather seeks to do justice to that case as an absolute singularity that requires and defines its own singular criteria. There is a sense in which the 'impossible' decision – the decision taken in an instant of madness where no pre-existing criteria apply and where no decision seems possible and no outcome can be predicted – is the only decision that attempts to let the other itself speak. This decision is neither just nor unjust in itself – what existing body of law or thought could judge it to be so? – but a decision that acknowledges its own violence, contingency and openness to an infinite series of possible further decisions. For Derrida, the impossible decision is the decision of *lesser* rather than *greater* violence because it is the only decision that admits its own prescriptive force rather than seeking to bury it under some suspect appeal to the propriety of a metaphysical value.

Finally, and perhaps most importantly, however, deconstruction's location of a point of undecidability within metaphysics that calls for decision is also an affirmation of the infinite possibility of the *future*. It is Derrida's argument, we have seen, that all thought necessarily produces an irreducible residue or remainder that exceeds it. Its decisions are always *more* or *less* violent, contingent or groundless, and so they are always open to the possibility of what T.S. Eliot's Prufrock calls future 'decisions and revisions which a minute will reverse' (Eliot 1963: lines 47–8). Deconstruction, then, maintains that the possibility of all current thought and action is – whether it knows it or not – constituted by an openness to an infinite and essentially unknowable future. If all thought is defined by its relation to an absolute future, then the question again arises of exactly what relationship that should be, and again Derrida contrasts metaphysical thought that seeks to predetermine the future as a teleological goal to be progressively attained like perpetual peace (Kant), the absolute Idea (Hegel) or even consensus (Habermas) with deconstructionist thought that maintains the future's essential unpredictability and discontinuity. The future described by Derrida is arriving constantly, here and now in the sense that it forms the unavoidable condition for all present thought and action whatsoever but at the same time it will never become absolutely present as such because no one thought or action could ever completely predict or realize it. This affirmation of a radical future is both the condition of all ethical and political thought worthy of the name in the sense that it is what spurs them into action in the first place and the reason why all such action will be essentially infinite in the sense that it will never conclude in the attainment of any pre-conceived teleological end or goal. For Derrida, this affirmation of an absolute future that shatters every existing horizon of thought is figured in various forms throughout his career such as the 'monstrous' ('Structure, Sign and Play in the Discourse of the Human Sciences', 1978f), the 'promise' ('How to Avoid Speaking: Denegations', 1989a) and more recently, the' messianic', the 'democracy-to-come' and the 'arrival of the other as justice' (*Specters of Marx*, 1994). We will return to every aspect of deconstruction at length in the chapters to come – from its critique of metaphysics to its affirmation of a radical future – but we can now hopefully see why it is such a difficult, not to say impossible, subject to define. In summary, deconstruction is something whose meaning remains to be decided in – and by – the future and this is why we will never be able to say exactly what it is.

Derrida and negative theology

I now want to focus in more detail on Derrida's reading of negative theology. Derrida's interest in the *via negativa* is long-standing. He mentions it repeatedly if somewhat briefly in key early texts like 'Violence and Metaphysics' ([1964] 1978c), 'From Restricted to General Economy: A Hegelianism without Reserve' ([1967] 1978d) and 'Différance' ([1967] 1982c) before returning to it in more detail in comparatively more recent texts like 'How to Avoid Speaking: Denegations' ([1987] 1989a) and 'Sauf le nom: (Post-Scriptum)' (1995a). If his earlier treatment of the subject is somewhat cursory and critical in character, Derrida's later texts go on to explore negative theology in remarkably patient, grateful and affirmative terms for someone who, in his own somewhat ambiguous words, rightly passes for an atheist. The relationship between deconstruction and negative theology has been pondered by many critics over the years and, as we have seen, deconstruction has been criticized and congratulated for being everything from a closet negative theology to a mode of atheism or nihilism. In what follows, I want to suggest that deconstruction's relationship to Christian mysticism should be construed as neither a critique nor an apologia but as a potentially more complex attempt to *repeat negative theology differently*, or as Derrida puts it, to 'save the name' of the *via negativa*.

'Différance'

First, Jacques Derrida makes a number of incidental references to negative theology in his work of the late 1960s which have since been much documented. It is here, then, that we need to start. Derrida only mentions negative theology briefly in the context of other discussions but, even so, it is possible to detect a consistent line of argument that persists in his work to the present day. He tackles the subject of the *via negativa* most fully and symptomatically in the following passage from his seminal essay 'Différance':

> So much so that the detours, locutions, and syntax in which I will have to take recourse will resemble those of negative theology, occasionally even to the point of being indistinguishable from negative theology. Already we have had to delineate that *différance is not*, does not exist, is not a present-being *(on)*, in any form; and we will be led to delineate also everything *that* it *is not*, that is *everything*; and consequently that it has neither existence or essence. It derives from no category of being, whether present or absent. And yet those aspects of *différance* which are thereby delineated are not theological, not even in the order of the most negative of negative theologies, which as one knows are always concerned with disengaging a superessentiality beyond the finite categories of essence and existence, that is, of presence, and always hastening to recall that God is refused the predicate of existence, only in order to acknowledge his superior, inconceivable, and ineffable mode of being.
>
> (Derrida 1982c: 6)

Derrida's reading of negative theology in 'Différance' will be considered in detail from various perspectives in the remainder of this book but let me make a number of provisional points about it now. To begin with, it is clear that his main aim here is simply to insist that deconstruction is *not* a form of negative theology. *Différance* exceeds all concepts whatsoever as the condition for their operation, Derrida argues, and this status led one contributor to the discussion following the first oral presentation of Derrida's essay to compare it to the God of negative theology (Derrida 1988b: 84).[1] But Derrida explicitly rebuts this charge in the published version of the essay quoted above and in doing so he advances an important critique of the *via negativa* which will resonate throughout his future work on the subject. Negative theology remains a mode of theology even in its most radically apophatic forms, Derrida contends, and so it cannot be negative all the way down. If negative theology claims that God is beyond being, it does not do so in order to deny that He is a being in any sense but to affirm ever more hyperbolically the pre-eminent nature of His being. We can now see why Derrida goes to such pains to argue that – for all their undoubted syntactic similarities – deconstruction and negative theology should not be mistaken for one another. The reason why we cannot address *différance* is not because it hyper-ontologically transcends all language as God does but because, as we have seen, it is nothing more pre-eminent than the system of differences and deferrals in which all language is originarily enmeshed. There is a sense in which negative theology remains committed to the metaphysical dream of an 'ineffable transcendence of an infinite existence' (Derrida 1978a: 146) whereas *différance* is beholden to no being, present or absent, essential or superessential. This means that not only is *différance* not a mode of negative theology – but insofar as negative theology can be said to belong to the metaphysics of presence – negative theology is itself contingent upon *différance*. Now Derrida's early critique of negative theology clearly leaves a lot of questions unanswered – Which negative theologians does he have in mind here? To what extent is it possible to generalize about negative theology in this way? Does the obvious fact that deconstruction is not negative theology preclude any larger philosophical co-habitation between the two? – but his opening gambit at least seems to be clear. For Derrida, deconstruction is *not* a form of negative theology because negative theology is *already* in a state of deconstruction.

'How to Avoid Speaking: Denegations'

Second, Derrida expands this somewhat cursory reading of the relationship between deconstruction and negative theology 20 years after 'Différance' in the text 'How to Avoid Speaking: Denegations' (1989a): 'I knew that I wished to speak of the "trace" in its relationship to what one calls, sometimes erroneously, "negative theology"' (Derrida 1989a: 3). It is important to see 'How to Avoid Speaking' in the context of a number of remarks by Derrida in various publications acknowledging a sense of 'unfinished business' as far as negative theology is concerned. He certainly does not retract his early reading of the *via negativa* but he confesses a certain dissatisfaction with his monolithic reading of all negative theology as merely 'ontotheology to be deconstructed'(Derrida 1982b).[2] Derrida begins 'How to Avoid Speaking' by repeating his earlier position that deconstruction is not negative theology because negative theology remains committed to establishing an ontotheological hyperessentiality:

> First of all, *in the measure* to which this belongs to the predicative or judicative space of discourse, to its strictly propositional form, and privileges not only the indestructible unity of the word but also the authority of the name – such axioms as a 'deconstruction' must start by reconsidering (which I have tried to do since the first part of *Of Grammatology*). Next, in the measure to which 'negative theology' seems to reserve, beyond all positive predication, beyond all negation, even beyond Being, some hyperessentiality, a being beyond Being.
> (Derrida 1989a: 7–8)

Derrida goes on to argue, however, that – such essential differences notwithstanding – negative theology is a more complex and less monolithic phenomenon than his earlier remarks on the subject imply. The monolithic term negative theology has become 'negative theology' (Derrida 1989a: 3); the singular historical or theological project of the *via negativa* is now seen as radically pluralized (Derrida 1989a: 3); there is no longer any question of restricting it to certain exemplary figures or texts like Pseudo-Dionysius (Derrida 1989a: 3) because negative theology cannot, for essential reasons, be attributed to any figure or tradition *as such* (Derrida 1989a: 3–4). This leads Derrida to see negative theology not so much as 'ontotheology to be deconstructed' but something to be repeated differently so as to allow its hidden instabilities and potentials of meaning to emerge: 'Perhaps there is within it, hidden, restless, diverse, and itself heterogeneous, a voluminous and nebulous multiplicity of potentials to which the single expression "negative theology" yet remains inadequate' (Derrida 1989a: 12).

Derrida proceeds to examine this 'voluminous and nebulous multiplicity of potentials' from antiquity to modernity. It is not my intention to rehearse the arguments of this essay in detail here because they will recur in different forms in the chapters that follow, but let me again make a few provisional points. Derrida argues, first and foremost, that the negative theological attempt to not speak of God is always contaminated by what we have seen he calls the pre-originary 'promise' of language that has already quasi-mechanically committed us to speaking about the ineffable even if it is merely to say nothing at all:

> Thus, at the moment when the question 'How to avoid speaking?' arises, it is already too late. There was no longer any question of not speaking. Language has started without us, in us and before us. This is

what theology calls God, and it is necessary, it will have been necessary, to speak.

(Derrida 1989a: 29)

Derrida's essay goes on to exemplify this point by examining three different modes of negativity that are respectively named the 'Greek' (Plato's *Timaeus*); the 'Christian' (Pseudo-Dionysius's *The Divine Names* and *Mystical Theology*) and the 'neither Greek nor Christian' (Heidegger's critique of ontotheology). Plato posits a radically anonymous and indeterminate space called the *khōra* where the demiurge cuts images of the intelligible forms; Dionysius praises God as absolutely *hyperousios*, beyond or without being, whereas Heidegger imagines one day writing a theology in which the word 'being' will not appear. First, Derrida maintains that negative theology from Plato to the present day *cannot help speaking* of that which it claims is essentially unspeakable because it remains originarily committed to what he calls the 'promise' of language. Platonic philosophy re-appropriates the radical anonymity of the *khōra* into ontological or analogical figures such as the maternal womb, space or receptacle; Dionysian theology predicates God as Father and Trinity while at the same time praising Him as absolutely beyond all Being; Heideggerian ontology insists that the revelation of God can only appear against the revelation or flashing of Being. Second, Derrida insists that what negative theology calls 'God' is *nothing other* than this essential openness or incompleteness of language which has always already started and will never be absolutely finished. If negative theology is a response to the absolute transcendence of God, it is first and foremost a response to the infinitude of a language whose transcendental signified will never absolutely arrive. Finally, and perhaps most importantly, negative theology can be repeated outside of its original or animating intention so that the distinction between the spoken and the unspeakable, the philosophical and the non-philosophical, the theological and the non-theological remains open to decision. The reason why negative theology is ultimately impossible to attribute to any singular figure, corpus or tradition such as Neoplatonism or Christianity as such is because it remains – for essential, that is, a priori reasons – open to the possibility of repetition outside its nominally original place or context. There is a sense in which negative theology's defining feature is 'to jump out from that which conducts it along its path, making connections that are beyond it' – as Raoul Mortley puts it – but this transgressive or hyperbolic mode is not due to historical or political forces but because it is originarily inscribed within language. This increasingly leads Derrida away from a simple or monolithic reading of negative theology as 'ontotheology to be deconstructed' and towards a rehabilitation of the *via negativa* as an irruptive, transgressive and radically pluralized phenomenon strangely akin to deconstruction itself. So, upon Derrida's reading, then, 'negative theology' increasingly becomes a name worth saving.

'Sauf le nom (Post-Scriptum)'

Finally, then, I would like to turn to Derrida's longest meditation on negative theology to date, namely, the remarkable dialogue or polylogue 'Sauf le nom (Post-Scriptum)' ([1993] 1995a). I will again do no more here than briefly indicate some of the key themes in this text because we will be returning to it at length in almost every chapter that follows. It is clear from the outset that 'Sauf le nom' represents Derrida's single most patient, grateful and affirmative reflection on negative theology so far. Derrida no longer sees negative theology as 'ontotheology to be deconstructed' ('Différance') or even as an inevitable and almost tragic articulation of the ineffable ('How to Avoid Speaking') but as an affirmative experience analogous to that of deconstruction:

> This thought seems strangely familiar to the experience of what is called deconstruction. Far from being a methodical technique, a possible or necessary procedure, unrolling the law of a programme and applying rules, that is, unfolding possibilities, deconstruction has often been described as the very experience of the (impossible) possibility of the impossible, of the most impossible.
> (Derrida 1995a: 43)

Derrida's argument is that negative theology recalls deconstruction because it is the desire for an experience that is absolutely heterogeneous to the order of being. Negative theology seeks something beyond the language, traditions and socio-political institutions that house it. First, negative theology belongs to a Graeco-Christian heritage or institutional order but it continually exceeds its original socio-political context (Derrida 1995a: 36). Second, negative theology is a language but it is simultaneously something that calls into question propositional, theoretical and constative language (Derrida 1995a: 48, 54). Third, and perhaps most pertinently for us, negative theology is a theological discourse on the transcendence of God but it applies to believers and non-believers alike and what it says about God applies equally to every other (Derrida 1995a: 69, 74). For Derrida, to summarize, the *via negativa*'s distinctive feature is its capacity to exceed or transgress the order of being from the inside and it is this that brings it close to deconstruction. Why, though, is this the case?

Derrida's argument is that negative theology's meaning is radically indeterminable and remains to be *decided*. He assembles a number of related arguments to sustain his case. First, he argues that negative theology is once again an event that takes place *within* the promise of language. Negative theology speaks of a God of whom nothing whatsoever can be said except His name [sauf son nom] (Derrida 1995a: 55). But what negative theology calls 'God' is at the same time the radical infinitude and anonymity of a language that has always already started and will never be completed: '"God" "is" the name of this bottomless collapse, of this endless desertification of language' (Derrida 1995a: 55–6).

Second, he insists that negative theology functions as a discourse of what he calls 'paradoxical hyperbole' (Derrida 1995a: 63) whose mission is to continually exceed or surrender any determined object it comes across. If negative theology appears to speak in a Neoplatonic sense of some hyperessential being beyond being (*hyperousios*), it hyperbolically exceeds even that ontological excess to achieve a serene indifference or *Gelassenheit* regarding its object:

> Now the hyperbolic movements in the Platonic, Plotinian, or Neoplatonic style will not only precipitate beyond being, or God insofar as he is (the supreme being [étant]), but beyond God even as name, as naming, named, or nameable, insofar as reference is made there to some thing.
>
> (Derrida 1995a: 65)

Third, Derrida argues throughout 'Sauf le nom' that negative theology's mode of operation is not singular or monolithic but is radically plural or multiple. Perhaps the expression 'negative theology' always designates a point of chiasmus or crossroads between two or more lines – Neoplatonic and Christian, theological and non-theological, and so forth – rather than a single point of origin. Most importantly, perhaps, negative theology's plurality of origin gives rise to (at least) two voices competing under its name:

> These two powers are, *on the one hand*, that of a radical critique, of a hyper-critique after which nothing more seems assured, neither philosophy nor theology, nor science, nor good sense, nor the least *doxa*, and *on the other hand*, conversely, as we are settled beyond all discussion, the authority of that sententious voice that produces or reproduces mechanically its verdicts with the tone of the most dogmatic assurance.
>
> (Derrida 1995a: 66–7)

Finally, and more generally, Derrida again argues that negative theology is a priori open to the possibility of repetition or, as he puts it here, translation, outside its linguistic, historical and political contexts. The *via negativa* cannot be restricted to theological figures or texts like Pseudo-Dionysius and Angelus Silesius any more than it can be excluded from the work of atheological figures or texts like Heidegger or Wittgenstein. There is a sense in which this negative theological discourse on the otherness of God can be generalized into a discourse on the otherness of every other: 'one should say of no matter what or no matter whom what one says of God or some other thing: the thought of whomever concerning whomever or whatever, it doesn't matter [n'importe]' (Derrida 1995a: 73). This leads Derrida to conclude that negative theology is ultimately suspended between a very Christian desire for kenosis, asceticism and the 'desert of God' and a more radical desire for indeterminacy, anonymity and what Derrida calls the 'desert in the desert' of *khōra*:

> Is this place created by God? Is it part of the play? Or else is it God himself? Or even what precedes, in order to make them possible, both God and his Play? In other words it remains to be known if this non-sensible (invisible and inaudible) place is opened by God, by the name of God (which would again be some other thing, perhaps) or if it is 'older' than the time of creation, than time itself, than history, narrative, word, etc. It remains to be known (beyond knowing) if the place is opened by appeal (response, the event that calls for the response, revelation, history, etc.), or if it remains impassively foreign, like *Khōra*, to everything that takes its place and replaces itself and plays within this place, including what is named God.
> (Derrida 1995a: 75–6)

For Derrida, then, negative theology – or what goes by or under that name – increasingly assumes a generalized role within thought that exceeds its specific historical, theological and philosophical boundaries. Now 'Sauf le nom' represents the culmination of Derrida's work on negative theology but – on first reading at any rate – it raises more questions than it answers. What form does his salvation or rehabilitation of negative theology take? Who precisely does negative theology need to be saved from or saved for? Why, finally, does he allocate negative theology such a central place in contemporary thought, politics and culture? In the concluding section of this chapter, I want to suggest that Derrida canvasses for a reading of negative theology as essential to any thought, ethics and politics worthy of the name.

Save the name?

I want to conclude this chapter, then, by evaluating Derrida's reading of negative theology in a little more detail. Derrida's reading has polarized critics of many different persuasions. It has been seen by Christian theologians as a secular appropriation or distortion of negative theology which bears no relation to the original theological phenomenon whatsoever and by atheists or secularists as a quasi-religious rehabilitation and generalization of the *via negativa* in a secular modernity that has long since rejected it. It has also sharply divided Derrida critics into those who applaud the theological turn in deconstruction as an act of affirmation or valorization (Hart 1989; Caputo 1997) and those who criticize the comparatively recent adoption of a quasi-religious vocabulary of promise, *khōra* and negative theology as a disavowal or retreat (Beardsworth 1996). The argument of this chapter so far has been that Derrida's reading is not a *critique* of negative theology – which somehow expresses a preference for 'more' or 'less' negative theology – but a highly characteristic *demonstration* about the *via negativa*. There is an important sense in which Derrida is neither distorting negative theology beyond all recognition or repeating it faithfully *ad infinitum* but revealing that negative theology is *itself* not simply negative theological all the way down. This is the basis for Derrida's reading of negative theology as something that hyperbolically exceeds the distinction between the Christian and the non-Christian, the theological and the non-theological, the sacred and the secular, and so on. In this final section, I want to consider some possible critical responses to Derrida's reading in more detail before concluding with my own view of what 'saving the name' of negative theology might mean in the context of contemporary French philosophy.

Theological objections

First, however, I think it is appropriate to register a very basic concern about whether Derrida's critique of negative theology is historically or theologically valid in the first place. It goes without saying that Derrida never offers a definitive or comprehensive reading of negative theology as such, so the question arises of whether he is justified in making such apparently large claims about it. He does not refer specifically to the work of any negative theologian in 'Différance' although elsewhere in his early work he cites Meister Eckhart as evidence that the negative way always remains committed to the establishment of a superior being beyond being: 'when I say God is not being, is superior to being, I do not with that deny him [*sic*] being: I dignify and exalt it in him' (Derrida 1978a: 337n). But before we take this claim as clinching proof of negative theology's commitment to metaphysics we should remember that Eckhart's corpus comprises a number of apophatic strategies or approaches – none of which takes precedence over the others – and so we could ask how justified Derrida is in isolating one statement from the mass and according it a privileged status as the definitive meaning of his text. If no one would deny that there is a strong element of metaphysics or ontotheology in Eckhart, his concept of God as *esse simplictus* or *absolutum* does not so much suggest that God occupies merely a *superior* form of being to creation as an absolutely *transcendent* form which bears no relation to the being of creation whatsoever and can be predicated of Him alone. Derrida offers a much fuller reading of Pseudo-Dionysius in 'How to Avoid Speaking: Denegations' but, as we will see in Chapter 3, questions have been raised about the legitimacy of his treatment of the '*hyperousios*' or hyperessential gesture in Dionysius's texts. Following the appearance of Derrida's essay, numerous critics – including most notably Kevin Hart and Jean-Luc Marion – have charged him with neglecting what we have seen to be a third gesture or way which bypasses the kataphatic and apophatic routes. More dubiously still, Derrida himself admits that the reading of Angelus Silesius in 'Sauf le nom' is far from exemplary, is deeply selective (he is working from extracts) and dependent upon nothing more than an 'autobiographical chance' (he wrote the essay while nursing his dying mother who was slowly losing the power to name) (Derrida 1995a: 85). Finally, we would have to consider the old question of whether Derrida's consistent use of the term 'negative theology' – particularly in his early work – is justified in gathering together the remarkably diverse corpuses of Plotinus, Proclus, Damascius, Pseudo-Dionysius, Aquinas *et al.* under one umbrella. Does Derrida's attempt to 'save the name' of negative theology do violence to the differences between and within the thought of those thinkers whose work goes under the dubious title of the *via negativa*?

In his defence, Derrida has never actually *claimed* to offer a definitive or comprehensive reading of the work of any negative theologian or of the *via negativa* more generally. He frequently admits to a sense of personal unease and even professional incompetence in his writings on negative theology and has been known to profess bewilderment that anyone should be interested in the views of a non-Christian, non-theologian and non-believer on this Christian theological tradition. His reading does not simply acknowledge that he *personally* is in no position to offer a totalizing perspective on the subject, however, because on a more general level he is concerned to show that *no such perspective* on the *via negativa* is actually possible. If Derrida's reading of negative theology has any one abiding theme at all, it is that the *via negativa* is not a homogenous entity but a pluralized chorus of competing voices or desires. Derrida's texts on the subject are, as he himself makes clear in an exchange with Jean-Luc Marion, marked throughout by a self-conscious plurality, selectivity and performativity that mean they could never be mistaken for transparent descriptions of some prior 'real':

> Marion constantly refers to what I said about negative theology as if I had a thesis, one thesis, phrased in one form through a single voice – concerning the metaphysics of presence, the distinction between position and negation and so on. Now I think that if time permitted I could show that my texts on this subject are written texts, by which I mean they are not a thesis on a theme.
>
> (Caputo 1999: 43)

For Derrida, 'negative theology' does not name a singular event, corpus or tradition so much as identify a problematic. The reading of negative theology advanced in 'Sauf le nom' does not seek to resolve the *historical* or *institutional* problems attendant upon defining negative theology – its theological plurality, its apparent indistinguishability from atheism or nihilism, its chosen or imposed marginalization with ecclesiastical orders – but rather to situate them within a much larger *philosophical* problematic of a generalized crisis of identity. There is an important sense in which the indeterminate nature of negative theology might not merely be indicative of its own historical, theological or philosophical bastardization but of the inability of these categories to be identical with themselves: 'this theology launches or carries negativity as the principle of auto-destruction in the heart of each thesis' (Derrida 1995a: 67). This crisis of identity of which negative theology represents a privileged example cannot be resolved as such but – as we will see – only *decided* in such a way that does the least possible violence to it.

Deconstructive theologies

Second, Derrida's precise – and entirely accurate – claim that deconstruction is *not* a form of negative theology raises the larger and more interesting question of the relationship between the epistemological truth-claims of the two discourses. It remains to be seen whether the truth-claims of deconstruction and negative theology are mutually complementary or exclusive. It goes without saying that the relationship between deconstruction and theology more generally has been the subject of an exhaustive debate over the years and my aim here is to do more than indicate some of the basic historical trends. Gayatri Chakravorty Spivak first packaged Derrida for the anglophone world in her famous or notorious 'Translator's Introduction' to *Of Grammatology* (1976) as a successor to such late Enlightenment secular philosophers as Marx, Nietzsche and Freud (Derrida 1976: ix–lxxxvii). But Kevin Hart, John D. Caputo and other critics challenged the prevailing secular reception of Derrida by advancing a theological revisionary reading of his work in the late 1980s and 1990s. Kevin Hart arguably inaugurated the 'theological turn' in Derrida studies with the recognition that deconstruction revives Heidegger's distinction between the God of metaphysics or ontotheology (who operates as the Aristotelian anchor for philosophical concepts of being and essence) and the God of faith or revelation (who remains essentially irreducible to human knowledge) (Hart 1989: 71–104). John D. Caputo offered the most commanding reading of Derrida's 'religion' to date in a study which argues that deconstruction has the structure of a generalized 'religion without religion' or 'messianism without messianism' that exceeds the dogmatic certitude of every determined religion or messianism:

> Deconstruction regularly, rhythmically repeats this religiousness, *sans* the concrete, historical religions; it repeats nondogmatically the religious structure of experience, the category of the religious. It repeats

the passion for the messianic promise and messianic expectation, *sans* the concrete messianisms of the positive religions that wage endless war and spill the blood of the other, and that, anointing themselves God's chosen people, are consummately dangerous to everyone who is not so chosen.

(Caputo 1997: xxi)

If Hart, Caputo and other critics have undoubtedly made a decisive intervention into Derrida studies, the concept of a 'deconstructionist theology' remains a controversial one for a number of reasons at the time of writing. For starters, John Milbank, Catherine Pickstock and the neo-Thomist Radical Orthodoxy movement have advanced a serious critique of deconstructionist theology as part of their more general assault upon the so-called nihilism of postmodernity. Milbank *et al.* argue that Derrida's supposed affirmation of an infinite and absolute difference leads to a transcendentally univocal situation in which all differences are equally different and so finally undifferentiated from each other (Milbank 1997: 61).[3] More generally, and certainly less polemically, Derrida's apparent distinction between the determined messianisms of the religions of the book and the generalized messianism of deconstruction in texts like *Specters of Marx* ([1993] 1994) remains unsatisfactory on a number of counts to supporters and detractors alike. The distinction between the determined and the general religion or messianism seems to bring Derrida uncomfortably close to a set of traditional – and highly deconstructible – Kantian distinctions between fact and essence, form and content or particular and universal. There is a sense in which Derrida is faced with an unpalatable choice between subscribing to a very problematic Kantian concept of a universal messianic on the one hand (which, given everything he has said about the transcendental in 'Différance', would seem unsustainable) or conceding that deconstruction is nothing more than just another particular messianism on the other (which, given everything he has said about the violence of the religions of the book, would seem unacceptable). To what extent does deconstruction itself remain nothing more than a determined messianism and – if this is the case – where does this leave its critique of the dogmatic violence inherent in Christianity, Judaism and Islam?

Derrida's work is once again the victim of a – more or less – understandable misreading here, I think. It is certainly clear, to begin with, that Radical Orthodoxy's critique of what it claims to be an infinite privileging of difference that collapses into indifference is based on a deeply partial and selective account of what is going on in deconstruction. Milbank, Pickstock *et al.* concentrate exclusively on Derrida's discussions of the infinite, the undecidable and the unconditional and simply ignore the discussions of the finite, the decision and the conditional that go hand in hand with them in every text from *Speech and Phenomena* ([1967] 1973) onwards.

Derrida does affirm the existence of a certain undecidability as the condition of all thought and action whatsoever but, as we have seen, he is adamant that we *cannot* simply remain within that undecidability but *must* take a contingent decision regarding it that has an ethical dimension inasmuch as it always results in a greater or lesser violence. But Derrida's distinction between general and determined messianisms does seem vulnerable to criticism, I think, not least on the grounds that it appears to fly in the face of his own professed distrust of binary oppositions. If this is the case, however, it might still be possible to manufacture a Derridaean response to the criticism that deconstruction is either an empty Kantian universal or one more determined messianism that has no greater or lesser truth-value than any other by questioning the very distinction between the general and the determined. The logic of deconstruction would insist that there are no absolutely determined messianisms because every religion of the book needs to open itself to the possibility of repetition in contexts outside its own choosing in order to be itself in the first place and – by the same token – there can be no completely general messianism either because every messianism still contains the traces of its historical context and there is no possibility of escaping context and historical contingency *per se*. Finally, to respond to the specific allegation that deconstruction is itself nothing more than a determined messianism, it is still important to draw a distinction between 'messianisms of greater violence' such as the religions of the book – which seek to define their politics as nothing more than a description of a prior real – and what we might term 'messianisms of lesser violence' like deconstruction – which admit the violent contingency of their own decision-making by avoiding appeals to metaphysical values of any sort and leave themselves open to future decisions. For Derrida, as we shall see in Chapter 3, the essential instability of the distinction between determined and general messianism is something that is brought to light very well by the *via negativa*.

Saving the name

Finally, and to conclude this chapter, I want to return to the concept of 'saving the name' of negative theology with which we began. It should be clear from the preceding discussion that Derrida's 'Sauf le nom' is neither an implausible crusade to Christianize the world nor to dispense with the name of God altogether but to repeat that name differently. 'Sauf le nom' is an attempt to bring out the plurality, the multiple voices at work behind and within the deceptively singular name and restricted tradition of negative theology. Negative theology is not an *appellation contrôlée* reserved for Christian Neoplatonist cellars only, as Derrida amusingly puts it, but a name that is capable of translation and exportation throughout the world into Christian and non-Christian, theological and non-theological markets. The essay makes clear that the multiplicity of negative theology is

Derrida and 'saving the name' 41

a priori infinite but in the particular context of the time and place he is writing – in the aftermath of what we must now learn to call the 'first' Gulf War – Derrida indicates a number of finite forms that the salvation of negative theology might take. This act of salvation takes – as is so often the case with Derrida – two forms that might respectively be named the 'conditional' and the 'unconditional'. Let me briefly indicate some of the lines of his argument.

On the one hand, Derrida makes clear that negative theology today is strongly committed – who could deny it? – to the Neoplatonic Judaeo-Christian tradition of salvation. It speaks in a tone of the most dogmatic assurance to a chosen people of a salvation to come in a promised land. It thus gives rise, he argues, to a disturbing ecclesiastical and ultimately even a secular politics of Christian hegemony: 'uprooting and expansion of Christianity, in Europe and outside of Europe, at the very moment when vocations, some statistics tell us, seem on the wane there' (Derrida 1995a: 78). Its recondite theological tradition of silence, solitude and secrecy can still be traced within the – apparently very different – geo-political tradition of the polis, the nation–state and the super-state. The marriage of theology and politics comes to a head in the 1990s, Derrida argues, with the rise of Christian fundamentalism, the increasingly blurred division between Church and State, Pope John Paul II's call for a new Holy Alliance in the aftermath of the Cold War and perhaps most disturbingly of all, the crusading rhetoric of the Allies during the 1991 Gulf War: '[i]n the course of the so-called Gulf War, the allied western democracies often kept up a Christian discourse while speaking of international law' (Derrida 1995a: 78). There is a filial connection between the premodern crusades of Christendom and the postmodern *Pax Americana* of widening democracy, free trade and international law. This argument seems all the more compelling following the 2003 Gulf War when a Christian US President and a British Prime Minister abandoned the pretext of international law altogether in order to wage what – before his advisors got him under control – President Bush did indeed call a 'crusade' against Islamic fundamentalism and secular Middle Eastern dictatorships. Now what interests Derrida here is the decisions, the determinations and the hierarchizations that have gradually turned what was once 'a memory, an institution, a history, a discipline' (Derrida 1995a: 54) into a situation where – with apologies to George Orwell – highly civilized human beings are flying overhead trying to kill Iraqis as I sit writing this at my word processor (Orwell 1968: 56).[4] In the Gulf War(s), the rich and very diverse corpus of negative theology was honed into a so-called 'smart' bomb aimed at Baghdad.

This is the point at which someone who is a self-confessed man of the Left, an Enlightenment man, not to mention a man who describes his childhood self as 'a little black and very Arab Jew' (Derrida 1993: 58b) begins to think that negative theology needs saving from itself. Derrida's respect for the resources and traditions of the *via negativa* convinces him that it should not be dispensed with altogether, however, but that it should be saved from the particular history and tradition to which it has given rise. Negative theology needs to be rescued from the decision-makers who have determined its current politico-theological fate: from Christian ontotheology, from those neo-conservative examples of repetition in alterity John Paul II and George W. Bush, from the more or less disguised hegemonies of the USA, the UN and NATO. There are other resources within negative theology which its historic Graeco-Christian filiation has left untapped, other voices which are as yet unheard.

On the other hand, then, Derrida sees 'saving the name' of negative theology as a question of rescuing it *from* its increasingly ossified politico-theological context and preserving it *for* other contexts, other forms of politics, other theologies yet to be written. Negative theology's fate is not sealed forever. 'Smart' bombs, as every Iraqi civilian knows, don't always hit their targets. It is important to not simply accept the decisions, determinations and traditions that have adhered to negative theology as given but to seek to rehabilitate aspects of the *via negativa* that have been marginalized or repressed:

> How would what still comes to us under the domestic, European, Greek, and Christian term of negative theology, of negative way, of apophatic discourse, be the chance of an incomparable translatability in principle without limit? Not of a universal tongue, of an ecumenism or of some consensus, but of a tongue to come that can be shared more than ever?
>
> (Derrida 1995a: 47)

Derrida seeks to listen to negative theology's *other* voice, then, the voice that questions every certitude including its own, that refuses to remain content within any theological, institutional or political doctrine or body and surrenders itself to an unknowable object. Derrida's text imagines that the second voice of negative theology exceeds the hegemonic, ecumenical and crusading rhetoric of Pope John Paul II in favour of something that could certainly be called more universal, more democratic and more fraternal even if it never totally coincides with the Graeco-Christian definitions of those terms either. For Derrida, this voice saves negative theology from being a Judaeo-Christian discourse that surrenders itself solely to the otherness of the Christian God – as important and unavoidable as that still is – and gives it the chance to be a discourse that surrenders *even that act of surrender* to an otherness that is essentially indeterminable:

> Unless I interpret it too freely, this *via negativa* does not only constitute a *movement* or a *moment* of deprivation, an asceticism or a provi-

sional kenosis. The deprivation should remain at work (thus give up the work) for the (loved) other to remain the other. The other is God or no matter whom, more precisely, no matter what singularity, as soon as any other is totally other [tout autre est tout autre].

(Derrida 1995a: 74)

The second form of negative theology does not foreclose the alterity of the other by identifying it exclusively with the God of Christian negative theology but maintains a serene indifference towards its object and lets the other be (see Chapter 6 for further discussion of this indifference as a form of hospitality). This hyperbolic act of *Gelassenheit* translates the *via negativa* from a discourse addressed with dogmatic certitude to the Christian community into a discourse addressed to the 'no-matter-whom' which drives a wedge between the distinction between being and knowing, between creator and created and between the human and the animal (Derrida 1995a: 85–8).

What, then, does Derrida ultimately mean when he proposes to 'save the name' of negative theology? I think it is clear that Derrida is not seeking to resolve or determine the identity of negative theology but to *save it from* determination. It is impossible to choose between the competing desires or voices within it because they are not simple oppositions or alternatives but two sides of the same system in its constitutive state of deconstruction. It is never suggested anywhere in the text that talking about consensus, the universal, and internationalism is likely to produce a 'better' outcome than talking about Christianity, ecumenicism and Eurocentricism. Far from advocating one position over the other, indeed, Derrida is at pains to stress that it is just as hegemonic to valorize such concepts as the 'world' as it is 'Europe'. If it is impossible to choose one form of negative theology over the other, then what is required is a *decision* on which does the least possible violence to that undecidability. Derrida goes on to argue in the conclusion of 'Sauf le nom' (which will be explored in more detail in Chapter 6) that negative theology might even be a privileged name for what he has elsewhere called the only responsible form of political decision-making whatsoever. Derrida's contention is that what passes under the name of 'negative theology' might provide the basis for a politics of decision-making that addresses *both* the conditional *and* the unconditional demands of justice (Derrida 1992a; 1995b; 1997b among many other texts). The radically ambiguous status of negative theology – both conditional and unconditional, faithful and irruptive, repetitive and hyperbolic, contingent and transgressive at the same time – offers a different concept of politics to pragmatic or idealist norms of the political. There is a sense in which the *via negativa* might represent the chance of a politics that does justice both to the pragmatic, judicial conditions in which politics must always take place and the moment of infinitude or unconditionality that every politics must have if it is not to merely accede to the prudential demands of the moment or apply some pre-existing rule. This last and most important attempt to save the name of negative theology completes its transformation under Derrida's hands from a theological tradition to be embraced or rejected at will to a logic that is absolutely central to every form of responsible thought and action whatsoever:

> – Would you go as far as to say that today there is a 'politics' and a 'law' of negative theology? A juridico-political lesson to be drawn from the possibility of this theology?
> – No, not to be drawn, not to be deduced as from a program, from premises or axioms. But there would no more be any 'politics', 'law', or 'morals' *without* this possibility, the very possibility that obliges us from now on to place these words between quotation marks.
>
> (Derrida 1995a: 81)

Conclusion

Jacques Derrida's reading of negative theology, to conclude, repeats the *via negativa* differently in such a way that its meaning remains to be – more or less violently – *decided*. It is impossible to describe it as if it were some pre-existing historical, theological or philosophical phenomenon because its defining characteristic is hyperbole. It is impossible to say where it begins or ends because it is central to any thought or action that claims to do more than simply apply or carry out a pre-set body of rules or criteria. It cannot be identified with any one theological tradition any more than it can be divorced from any secular philosophical tradition because it exceeds the distinction between the theological and the secular. Plato, Pseudo-Dionysius and Silesius cannot ever be completely negative theological because negative theology necessarily exceeds its Graeco-Christian filiation and – by the same token – Wittgenstein, Heidegger and even Derrida cannot escape contamination by negative theology for the same reason that negative theology necessarily goes beyond its Christian name:

> – Then you wouldn't say that the *Cherubinic Wanderer* comes under negative theology.
> – No, certainly not in any sure, pure, and integral fashion, although the *Cherubinic Wanderer* owes much to it. But I would no more say that of any text. Conversely, I trust no text that is not in some way contaminated with negative theology, and even among those texts that apparently do not have, want, or believe they have any relation with theology in general. Negative theology is everywhere, but it is never by itself.
>
> (Derrida 1995a: 68–9)

Negative theology is everywhere, but it is never by itself. If Derrida's thesis is now clear, the task of the remainder of this book is to put it to the test and explore the various ways in which negative theology impacts upon modern French philosophy from Certeau to Kristeva. The remainder of this book will argue that negative theology remains central to the work of each of these thinkers whether or not they claim any special interest or investment in it. There is an important sense in which all the thinkers in this book – whether Christian or non-Christian, theologian or philosopher, believer or atheist – remain indebted to the *via negativa* albeit often in unpredictable ways. This study will trace the decisions that each of these thinkers takes in relation to the *via negativa* in their work but – more importantly – it will demonstrate how these decisions qua decisions can never ultimately determine or resolve the relationships they seek to decide. In the remainder of this book, then, I want to show how Derrida 'saves the name' of negative theology in modern French philosophy.

Part II
Theologies

This Part examines the role of negative theology in the work of the theologian, historian and cultural theorist Michel de Certeau and the theologian and phenomenologist Jean-Luc Marion. It argues that Certeau and Marion seek, in their distinctive ways, to negotiate a concept of negative theology in postmodernity that is immune to deconstruction because it already takes as given the deconstructive critique of the metaphysics of presence. The argument goes on to show that Certeau and Marion's analysis retains the traces of an orthodox reading of negative theology, however, that seeks to restrict the hyperbolic status of the *via negativa*. This Part concludes by arguing that Certeau and Marion's readings of negative theology cannot exhaust the possibilities of the *via negativa* because it remains a priori open to heterodox interpretations. In this Part, saving the name of negative theology involves saving it from Christian theology and opening it up to a theological future that is radically unpredictable.

2 Certeau's 'Yes, in a foreign land'

Michel de Certeau's complex body of work can perhaps best be introduced by one brief, enigmatic speech act: '[y]es, in a foreign land' [Oui, à l'étranger] (Derrida 1988a: 118).[1] It is an act that affirms the other, the stranger, the foreigner. It is repeated again and again – but each time differently – from his earlier works on Christian theology to his later texts on everyday life. It can be heard in the texts of all the different, seemingly conflicting Certeaus that are gathered together under his signature: the life-long Jesuit, the theologian, the historian, the Lacanian psychoanalyst, the cultural theorist, the philosopher of walking, shopping and cooking, and so on. The significance of this strange affirmation is – or so I want to argue here – that it is an expression of belief without criteria. This ambiguous act of belief – which we can provisionally define here as belief in the absence of any independent authority for belief whatsoever – goes to the heart of Certeau's engagement with negative theology and Christian mysticism. If we want to understand the role of the *via negativa* in Certeau's work, we need to begin by answering three basic questions about this mode of belief. What exactly is Certeau saying 'yes' to? Is it – to take only the most clichéd and extreme examples – the biblical cry in the wilderness of the life-long Jesuit or the 'death of God' elegy of the Lacanian agnostic? Do we have to choose between these different positions or alternatives or can we establish some common ground between them? In this chapter, I want to argue that Certeau's 'yes, in a foreign land' is an act of belief in a *terra incognita* that ultimately exceeds the distinction between the theological and the non-theological.

Michel de Certeau

I would like to begin with a brief overview of Certeau's work but, for reasons that will become clear, this is easier said than done. Michel de Certeau's body of work is difficult to define according to any normal criteria. It seems to belong to many disciplines and at the same time to none. It often takes the form of a plurality of micro-stories that do not coalesce into an overarching grand narrative. It is characterized by a highly performative, 'written' *modus loquendi* that refuses to be gathered together into a corpus under the signature of a proper name. More generally, it reads, as Certeau himself admits, like a calculated evasion of the academic policeman's customary question 'Who are you?'. Certeau's answer to that question is typically revealing: 'Michel is "Who is like El?" – who is like the unnameable, God? This word says the opposite of the proper' (Certeau 2000a: 242). To write about 'Michel de Certeau', then, is to be confronted by the unanswerable question 'Who is like El?'. The attempt to categorize his work inevitably confirms the disappearance of his proper name but this inevitability should definitely not be the occasion for pathos. For Certeau, the 'empty tomb' of the text – and the reference to the resurrection here is entirely deliberate – is not tragedy but comedy, not an end but a beginning, not a work of mourning but something that gives us the chance of a future. If there is any consistent theme in Certeau's theology, it is that the absence of the other is the originary event that permits, makes room, renders possible, and reappears incessantly in the massive truth of its disappearance. In this sense, I do not think Certeau would want us to see the 'empty tomb' of his work as an absence or a dearth so much as a space in which to begin that work anew and so that is what we will attempt to do.

Michel de Certeau was born in 1926. He entered the Society of Jesus after completing his degrees in 1950 and was ordained a priest in 1956. His study took a theological turn with the completion of a doctorate on Jean Favre at the Sorbonne in 1960 and the publication of numerous articles in Catholic journals throughout the 1960s and 1970s (Certeau 1987a). It is these early theological writings – many of which are still relatively unknown and untranslated – that will be the main subject of this chapter. But Certeau's work increasingly began to range across disciplinary boundaries as his career progressed, encompassing history, social theory, ethnography and anthropology and – as a founder member of Lacan's *Ecole freudienne* in 1964 – psychoanalysis. Following the 'events' of May 1968 – which Certeau, like so many of his contemporaries, saw as a seismic rupture in French culture – his work turned more explicitly towards social, political and cultural analysis with the publication of *The Capture of Speech* ([1968] 1997b). During the early 1970s, Certeau was given a grant by the French Ministry of Culture to fund a long-term research project into cultural developments. The first fruits of his research led to his best-known and biggest-selling text *The Practice of Everyday Life* ([1980] 1984) which we will also consider in detail later on. This was followed by, among other texts, the first part of a major study of Renaissance mysticism entitled *The Mystic Fable* ([1982] 1992). For Certeau, it seems the next major project was going to be a study of the anthropology of belief but this was sadly left uncompleted by his untimely death in early 1986.

Certeau provisionally christened his work-in-progress 'heterology' (Certeau 1986).[2] Heterology is, of course, the name for the philosophical discourse on otherness or alterity. It is a label that – in the absence of anything more original – has been retrospectively applied to Certeau's work as a whole without generating much in the way of insight. It is, to put it bluntly, blindingly obvious that a concern with otherness – whether theological, philosophical or both – characterizes Certeau's work from his earliest work on mysticism to his latest texts on contemporary culture and society. He was deeply interested in the way in which others – whether they be Renaissance mystics or modern consumers – carve out a niche for themselves within the order of the same but this in itself does not get us very far. His fascination with alterity raises the inevitable question of what the exact theological or philosophical status of that alterity is. What – to put the question as crudely as possible – is the relationship between the otherness of God described in a relatively early text like 'How is Christianity Thinkable Today?' ([1971] 1997a) and the blank, anonymous alterity of the haunting late essay 'Extase blanche' (1987b)?

Certeau's critics give no clear answers. It is still difficult to separate the facts of Certeau's life and work from a scholarly field that has been more than usually dominated by clubby, hagio-biographical anecdotes about 'the Michel I knew', odd or unwarranted editorial policies, and the politics of academic publishing and debate (Buchanan 2000: 2–10). He has been variously styled as everything from a lifelong Christian to a radical sceptic or agnostic (Geffré 1991; Ahearne 1995: 5; Bauerschmidt 1996: 1–26; Ward 1999: 156; Buchanan 2000: 2; Dosse 2002). His passage from Jesuit theologian to doyen of cultural studies has been critically narrativized as everything from a tragic dark night of the soul to a heroic entry into the brave new world of postmodern, late-capitalist chic. My contention is that the decision to Christianize or secularize Certeau represents just that – a decision – that always does a greater or lesser violence to his work. The following discussion is less interested in settling the debate one way or the other – as if that were possible – than in re-evaluating the terms of the discussion as a whole. This is not an attempt to sit on the fence – still less to canvass for some spurious happy medium between the two basic positions – but to register a dissatisfaction with a debate that often seems to be informed by assumptions and positions that Certeau's texts notably question or complicate. There seems to me to be little point in pursuing the question of whether Certeau was *personally* a Christian for instance – as if he himself had nothing to say on the subject – when his texts never cease to explore the meaning of what it is *to be* Christian. We might also wonder what Certeau himself would have made of a debate that is too often driven by unacknowledged agendas which have nothing to do with his work and which seeks to recruit him to causes that he was often at pains to criticize. For me, there is no better example of what can happen when – to borrow his own definition of a strategy – 'a place ... can be circumscribed as *proper* (*propre*) and thus serve as the basis for generating relations with an exterior distinct from it (competitors, adversaries, "clientèles", "targets", or "objects" of research' (Certeau 1984: xix) than the professional academic claiming Certeau is this, says that, belongs to the other. In an essay on Foucault, Certeau himself described this kind of critical demand for proof of identity as the very antithesis of thought and if this is true then – *pace* Heidegger – perhaps we have not yet started to think about him and his work (Certeau 1986: 193–8).

Michel de Certeau's work badly needs to be thought otherwise, then, and I want to begin this almost unthinkably large and difficult project here. I will start by putting to one side biographical anecdotes and assumptions and exclusively considering Certeau's texts and concepts. It is my contention that Certeau's own personal Christian faith – or lack of it – simply cannot be understood except against the background of his life-long explorations of what it means to believe in God and in fact to believe in anything whatsoever. Following this analysis, we will try to critically interrogate the relationship between the various opposing positions that animate Certeau studies: theology and heterology, mysticism and cultural studies, belief in God and belief *per se*. The only thinking that could hope to do justice to Certeau, I would argue, is one that does not succumb to the rival biographical simplifications that plague readings of his career – where he either stops being a Christian sometime post-1968 (Ahearne 1995: 2) or he remains one until and in some cases even *beyond* his death (Ward 1999: 156) – but which seeks to establish the common ground or basis from which these readings appear as oppositions or alternatives. This common ground or point of origin – which displaces and reconfigures the opposition between the theological and the secular – appears in Certeau's work on mysticism and negative theology under the figure of that strange 'yes, in a foreign land'. In the next section, I want to trace the contours of this ambiguous act of belief in Certeau's little-known Christian theology.

Certeau on Christianity

I want to begin by looking at some of Certeau's early essays on Christian theology from 'How is Christianity Thinkable Today?' ([1971] 1997a) onwards. Certeau's abiding concern in these essays is, as their titles reveal, Christianity's articulation within its current historical situation. His work is characterized by a wide range of influences from nineteenth-century sociology (Weber, Troeltsch) through contemporary Christian theology (Rahner) to psychoanalytic theory (Lacan). It is prompted by what he saw as the ever-increasing difficulty of negotiating a distinctive Christian *topos* or praxis in a modernity that leaves little or no room for it. The solution to this problem that suggests itself to Certeau is a – very risky – re-conceptualization of Christianity in quasi-psychoanalytic terms. There is an apparent turn in Certeau's theology from a discourse on the otherness of God towards a discourse on the otherness of every other that antici-pates the secular discourses on alterity advanced in later work like *The*

Practice of Everyday Life. This recruitment of heterology to the cause of theology seems designed to guarantee the future of Christian practice in modernity but – or so I want to argue – it increasingly encroaches upon and imperils the existence of the distinctive theology Certeau wants to achieve. In other words, Certeau's theology becomes increasingly difficult to distinguish from his heterology and, as we will see, the only means of telling them apart seems to be a belief that they are different.

'How is Christianity Thinkable Today?'

Michel de Certeau begins his essay 'How is Christianity Thinkable Today?' ([1971] 1997a) by affirming that Jesus Christ's life and death is the historical event that inaugurates Christianity. He quickly moves away from such modestly orthodox beginnings. It could half-seriously be said that Certeau's big idea is to read Christian theology as a Freudian family romance – some 30 years before the Lacanian heterodoxies of Žižek. Christ, Certeau asserts, does not found Christianity by His presence but by His absence. He dies in order to give birth to the Christian faith and his disappearance permits the appearance of what follows Him. He is an absent cause, a cut or rupture whose presence can only be registered in His impact or effects. Certeau's belief is that the Christian experience is motivated by *both* the desire to be faithful to the absent Christ *and* the necessity of being different from Him because He is no longer there. The desire to repeat the moment that originates it goes hand in hand with the necessity of erasing that originary moment because it is unrepeatable as such. This leads Certeau to make the Lacanian leap that characterizes all his work on Christianity. Christianity can only repeat Christ *by* differing from Him: '[t]his fidelity itself is not of an objective kind. It is linked with *the absence of the object* or of the particular past which inaugurated it' (Certeau 1997a: 145). For Certeau, then, Christianity is not a timeless *content* that has been handed down from Christ but an increasingly diverse set of *forms* that seek to reveal Him by His very absence.

Certeau expands on this thesis in the remainder of the essay. He lays particular stress on the role of Christian plurality as the means of revealing Christ's disappearance. Christ's kenosis or desertification is made manifest in the communitarian structure of Christianity language : 'the "kenosis" of presence gives rise to a plural, communitarian language' (Certeau 1997a: 147). Christian communities manifest their singular origin in the act of becoming differentiated from it. Christianity is not Christian because it perpetuates the unchanging fact of Christ's incarnation but because it repeats His enabling act of difference or disappearance. If Christ can be said to 'make room' for Christianity by differing from it, so Christianity repeats His founding act of difference by making room for other possible ways to think itself. Christianity is, then, to be understood as the repetition of the form of Christ's original departure in a range of new contexts (Certeau 1997a: 147). More generally, Christian authorities like Scripture, tradition, the councils and the Pope are also constituted by this founding lack of Christ. The disappearance of the Christ event now means that no one authority can be the central, defining or absolute authority. There is an important sense in which Christian authority lies in an irreducible plurality of authorities where each individual authority recognizes its dependence upon the others: '[t]he plural is the manifestation of the Christian meaning' (Certeau 1997a: 148). This pluralization of authority not only has implications for authorities *within* Christianity – like the canon of Scriptures – but for the authorities *without* it as well. For Certeau, in other words, Christ is *necessarily different* from Christianity and so this means that there is no reason why He cannot be found in the non-Christian as well.

Certeau's essay concludes by returning to the guiding question of how Christianity is to be thought in the contemporary moment. It is Certeau's argument that Christianity must always recognize its current historical position but that it can only move forward by *transgressing* that position. It could be argued – to anticipate by a few years the terms of *The Practice of Everyday Life* – that Christianity is in a constant tension between establishing strategic places and breaking out of them to create tactical spaces. Christian faith is not simply a determinate content or doctrine that must be *said* but an almost content-free praxis that must be *done*: '[i]t is not a consequence of a knowledge, but a beginning and a risk' (Certeau 1997a: 152). If Christianity has a praxis, it does not simply consist in the application of existing laws and teaching but once again in a logic of *departure* in order to make room for new laws, new teachings. The best example of this kind of praxis is Christ Himself who, Certeau argues, repeats the Old Testament differently in the New Testament and makes room for a new configuration of the relationship between them. This new relationship subscribes neither to the logic of the either/or (which violently affirms one truth at the expense of the other) nor the both/and (which accomplishes some equally dubious synthesis) but to the logic of a double negation that opens a third hypothesis without determining it: '[i]t opens a future but without fixing that future' (Certeau 1997a: 154). In Certeau's conclusion, he offers a stirring justification of his key concept that Christianity is the repetition in alterity of Christ's original act of departure: 'it is impossible to be Christian without a common risk, without the creation of a new divergence in relation to our past and to our present, without being alive' (Certeau 1997a: 155).

Finally, then, Michel de Certeau's answer to the demand of thinking Christianity today is that Christians must repeat Christ's founding act of thinking God otherwise. It is obviously an original and daring idea but before carrying on we need to put one or two questions on notice about it. It goes without saying that Certeau's definition of Christianity is theologically heterodox – with friends like these, who needs Žižek or Richard

Dawkins? – but even within the restricted context of his own argument it is a tantalizingly sketchy concept. He is perhaps understandably better at saying what Christianity is not – a doctrinal creed, an institutional authority, a quasi-Hegelian mode of dialectic – than what it is. He has to tread a very fine line between defining Christianity so much that it ossifies into the kind of identity he hates and defining it so little than it dissolves into the ether. His concept of Christianity as the repetition in alterity of Christ's absence seems to be a means of guaranteeing this balance but – to put it more crudely than he deserves – he seems more interested in the alterity than the repetition. Certeau runs the risk of emptying Christianity of all doctrinal content or institutional status in order to suffuse it with a quasi-Lacanian logic of difference over which it has no rights of privileged access, let alone ownership. But this raises a crucial question about the relationship between the theological and the secular that we will have to come back to again and again in this chapter. The definition of Christianity as nothing more or less than the repetition in alterity of the Christ event raises the question of how we can identify different repetitions as Christian or not. There are no obvious means in Certeau's argument of distinguishing between practices that are *differently Christian* on the one hand and practices that are just *different from Christianity* on the other. These problems do not seem to bother Certeau who oddly keeps using the term 'Christianity' in an unproblematic way to describe events separated in time by thousands of years as if it were exactly the kind of stable, self-identical and trans-historical phenomenon his argument insists it cannot be. This kind of criticism is neither a demand for a more 'traditional' concept of Christianity nor for a more modern or 'relevant' Christianity but simply an answer to the question of what Certeau means by Christianity *per se*. For Certeau, then, repetition in alterity is less a tragic fate where Christians are consigned to an ever-increasing alienation from Christ and more an affirmative opportunity for Christians to renew their faith, but at the same time his argument deprives us of the means to tell these two different situations apart.

'The Weakness of Believing' and other essays

Certeau continues his exploration of Christianity in its current historical situation in the essays 'Lieux de transit' (1987c), 'La misère de la théologie' (1987d) and most prominently 'The Weakness of Believing: From the Body to Writing, a Christian Transit' ([1974] 2000c). He displays an increasing scepticism about finding a distinctive niche for Christianity within modernity even though revealingly he never gives up on the task. He refines almost to the point of non-existence the already highly attenuated way of articulating Christianity advanced in 'How is Christianity Thinkable Today?' Christianity's claim to be a received truth, embodied in an identifiable institution and governed by a body of authorities is still rejected by Certeau but now he seems to find it harder and harder to identify it as even the content-free Christian community he imagined in the earlier essay. The distinctive role of Christianity as a practice of heterology or alterity is increasingly overtaken by modern secular discourses like politics, history and psychoanalysis which have begun to usurp what he once apparently believed was Christianity's distinctive role as the practice of the necessarily other: '[i]f *the relation to the other* remains, today as yesterday, essential to the constitution of the individual or collective subject, this other is no longer God' (Certeau 1987a: 244). This means that the question of how to think Christianity in an increasingly non-Christian society emerges with greater urgency in Certeau's writing throughout the 1970s but, despite everything, and sometimes against the drift of his whole argument, he still wants to affirm the possibility of thinking, speaking and being in a distinctively Christian way. In 'La misère de la théologie', for example, he writes: 'I do not know what religion will become tomorrow, but I firmly believe in the urgency of this modest and radical theology' (Certeau 1987d: 262).

Certeau gives what is arguably his last and most detailed attempt to articulate a distinctive Christian theology in the essay 'The Weakness of Believing' (2000c). He characteristically begins by positing and rejecting three possible strategies for rehabilitating Christian values. He floats the idea that Christians could try to compensate for their loss of authority (1) by reasserting doctrine with greater force and didacticism; (2) by identifying themselves with recognizable secular sites of authority such as the working class, or the poor, or anti-war movements instead which could – in their very foreignness – become indicative of the defining alienation of the Christian experience; or (3) by seeking to carve out a distinctive niche within those discourses by effecting certain ethical checks and balances upon them such as opposing abortion, contraception or, today, globalization. He rejects each of these different approaches, however, on the grounds that (1) Christians would be seeking to return to some non-existent ecclesiastic community; (2) that they would be allowing themselves to be defined by a socio-political vocabulary of class or gender divisions that is alien to them (Certeau 2000a: 224); and (3) that there is nothing *essentially* Christian about taking a so-called 'pro-life' line on abortion or campaigning for Third World debt relief. Certeau argues that the only distinctive contemporary mode of Christian experience remains his own distinctive heterological concept of Christianity as the repetition of Christ's inaugural absence. Certeau's contention is that it is simply missing the point to look for a proper or distinctive Christian place in the past, present or future because Christian community – or 'belief' as he revealingly prefers to call it here – is called into being from an absent place and its response is to reproduce that no-place infinitely. For Certeau, then, Christianity is less and less the reiteration of a timeless truth or content and more and more the performance of an empty praxis of departure.

Certeau's definition of Christianity is now familiar but again it raises as many questions as it answers. He is clearly defining Christianity as a form of heterology but he still does not answer the question of how we can identify it as such. It is not clear how we can recognize that defining difference without betraying it, let alone how we can tell the difference between it and non-Christian forms of alterity. Certeau himself alerts us to the danger that defining Christianity as a departure for 'Nowhere' always risks turning into just another kind of arrival at 'Somewhere':

> The temptation of the 'spiritual' is to constitute the act of difference as a site, to transform the conversion into an establishment, to replace the 'poem' which states the hyperbole with the strength to make history or to be the truth which takes history's place, or, lastly, as in evangelical transfiguration (a metaphoric movement), to take the 'vision' as a 'tent' and the word as a new land.
> (Certeau 2000a: 236)

To promote one's difference from every place is to risk turning difference itself into the most privileged place of all. The point Certeau is making is that the Christian tactic of departure has a tendency to become reified into the traditional establishment of places. There is a salutary warning to a certain tendency in Certeau studies here – and perhaps cultural studies more generally – that seeks to valorize or objectivize heterology by turning the departure from places into a privileged 'no-place' or to promote difference as the moral or ethical watchword of liberal good conscience (Bennington 1999: 103–23).[3] This claim might also contain a warning to Michel de Certeau himself, however, that his attempt to baptize the practice of difference as definitively Christian also risks transforming the conversion into an establishment, so to speak, the poem into history, the word into a new land. In Certeau's 'The Weakness of Believing', as we have seen, Christianity is a form of transit or wandering into foreign territory but once again the question arises of how he can know this Abrahamic journey to the other is Christian without turning it into an Odyssean return to the same.

Certeau and Christian belief

Certeau attempts to articulate a new concept of Christianity for the contemporary period, then, but the problem with his account is that it removes so many of the properties by which Christianity has historically been recognized and replaces them with ones over which it has no obvious jurisdiction or monopoly. Christianity is neither an institution, a set of doctrines or creeds but nothing more or less than a praxis of departure, a journey towards a foreign land with no guarantee that it can ever actually arrive. The problem is that Certeau continues to *use* the term

'Christianity' as if its meaning were still self-evident, however, and so the question inevitably arises of how he can justify doing so. This is not something that Certeau himself is unaware of, I think, but being aware of it is not the same as solving it and many of the solutions he advances are either unsatisfactory or undeveloped. There is a passing attempt to borrow the Heideggerian formula of the 'not-without' (*nicht ohne*) to suggest that contemporary Christianity exists in a kind of negative relation with its traditional sites of authority, for instance, but a negative authorization is still an authorization and this sits uneasily alongside his claim that doctrine and institutions no longer have any authority whatsoever (Certeau 1997a: 146). In my view, however, Certeau's single most interesting definition of Christianity is as a particular mode of *belief*.

Certeau floats the idea that Christianity constitutes a distinct modality of belief in a very brief discussion towards the end of 'The Weakness of Believing'. He briefly cites an anecdote about the nineteenth-century French mystic Thérèse de Lisieux before going on to link it with Derrida's deconstruction of the Cartesian transcendental subject in 'Cogito and the History of Madness' (Derrida 1978e):

> It is a will which cuts across possibilities, which are only its symptoms. Fundamentally, *to be a believer is to want to be a believer*. Thérèse de Lisieux, attempting, at the end of her life, to account for her faith, declared herself a Christian because she 'wanted to believe', a term which she emphasized as essential. A word akin to that of Derrida on Descartes: 'To be Cartesian, ... is to want to be Cartesian ...'.
> (Certeau 2000a: 231)

It is possible to raise a number of questions about Certeau's definition of belief – which, as is so often the case in his published work, is floated without ever being fully explained or justified – that we can return to later in this chapter. It is first clear that Certeau is at pains to distinguish the will to be a Christian from the voluntary decision of a believer to give assent to a given set of Christian beliefs because he says it is closer to pre-subjective states such as desire or the dream-state, and as we know, he has no time for doctrinal definitions of faith. The question thus arises of who or what does authorize it as the will to be Christian rather than anything else – if not existing doctrine or institutions – and the answer would seem to be that it is paradoxically self-authorizing. This would appear to be the logical conclusion of Certeau's argument – and one which his citation of Derrida on the performativity of Cartesian subjectivity endorses – but it is one that his argument surprisingly seems to shy away from in the above case perhaps on the grounds that it would necessitate a more radical dispersal of Christian identity than even he is willing to contemplate. There is no other obvious reason why he settles on the somewhat orthodox and uncontroversial figure of a French Catholic saint as his Christian believer of choice – whose religious identity already carries with it a doctrinal and institutional seal of approval – but we might get a better idea of the radical trajectory of this argument if we instead imagine a heterodox character like a cultist or zealot claiming that 'to be Christian is to want to be Christian' without being able to take issue with him. If to be Christian is simply *to want to be Christian*, there is no means of distinguishing between the Christianity of the believer and the fanatic, the faithful and the charlatan, St Thérèse de L'Enfant-Jesus and David Koresh or Ian Paisley. Now Paisley's Free Presbyterian Church certainly represented *one* way of thinking Christianity in the early 1970s but not one that Certeau – who was all too aware of the blood relations between religion, nationalism and politics from his travels to Brazil and the USA[4] – would have been very willing to embrace, I believe. What, then, are the implications of Certeau's reading of Christian belief for his understanding of Christian identity more generally? Why doesn't the definition of Christian belief supplied here put in an appearance elsewhere in his work? Does the concept of Christian belief as essentially groundless necessarily lead it to a form of relativism or subjectivism or might it be an opportunity to reinvent faith in the absence of a metaphysical ground? In Certeau's later work on culture (Certeau 1984: 177–205), he attempts to supply a more extensive anthropology of belief *per se* – what belief is, what makes believers believe and whether belief is itself still believable – and we will come back to this at the end of the chapter.

Michel de Certeau's attempt to re-define Christianity in postmodernity is thus a failure in my book, to conclude, but this does not mean that it does not raise original and interesting questions. It has been interpreted by theological critics as everything from a nihilistic surrender to secular modernity to a postmodern apologia for Christianity a generation before the polemics of Radical Orthodoxy. Certeau himself has been stereotyped as both a nihilist or secularist who wants to reduce Christianity to nothing, or a Jesuit missionary who wishes to elevate it to almost everything. Certeau's theological project could generate three different lines of enquiry or response, I think, and I would like to close this section by briefly setting them out here.

First, I think Certeau's basic diagnosis of Christianity's place in modernity needs examination before anything else. Frederick Christian Bauerschmidt argues that Certeau's attempt to defend Christianity against the threat of modernity concedes too much ground to its secular opponents and presumes far too quickly that there are *no* places left that can be defined as Christian. Bauerschmidt argues that Certeau's unduly pessimistic outlook leads him to underestimate Christian communities – he gives the example of the Pennsylvania Amish – who do not accept the values of modernity but continue to thrive within it (Bauerschmidt 1996: 20–1). My feeling is that there certainly is a tinge of 'death of God' defeatism in Certeau's position that – in the context of his constant

60   *Theologies*

emphasis on the endlessly plural and creative nature of everyday life – seems uncharacteristically categorical and totalizing. If Certeau's definition of Christianity as the desire *to be* Christian is accepted, then there are still plenty of Christians out there even if not all of them – Ulster Orangemen, the US Christian Right – are as sympathetic as the Amish. So is Certeau's basic diagnosis of the crisis facing Christianity in modernity, and his proposed solution to it, legitimate, or is he, in effect, throwing the baby out with the bathwater?

Second, Certeau's relationship to orthodox Catholic theology is another fertile area for study. Graham Ward, for instance, sees in Certeau's re-conceptualization of Christianity the possibility of a genuinely postmodern theology (Ward 1999: 156). Ward argues that Certeau's theology still manages to project a distinctively Christian voice in the wilderness of collapsing meta-narratives, the irreducible mediation of language, and so on. Ward's note of caution is that Certeau's postmodern theology takes him to the far shores of Catholic orthodoxy (Certeau 2000a: 9) and it is certainly possible to wonder whether it is more postmodernist than theological. Certeau presents a concept of Christianity as an empty, identity-less praxis that guarantees it a spectral future of sorts but deprives it of distinctive content or meaning. Certeau's *kenosis* or emptying of Christianity from a set of doctrinal contents into a formal structure of alterity anticipates what Derrida calls the attempt to develop a 'religion without religion' (in which the Blanchotesque 'without' signifies both continuity and separation) but it is prone to the same objections of a recidivist Kantianism. Christianity's supposedly distinctive role as the 'constant marking of an alterity within established positions' is so nebulous that it increasingly becomes indistinguishable from the tactics of everyday life as set out in Certeau's later work. So it could reasonably be argued that Certeau's theological project rejects a specific if increasingly marginalized definition of Christianity in favour of one that is in many ways central to the experience of modern life but voided of everything that makes it meaningfully Christian. If Certeau does not feel able to offer an orthodox future for Christianity, then the onus on him is to provide a heterodox one that remains recognizably Christian, but to what extent does he manage to do this?

Finally, however, I want to concentrate on the question of Certeau's understanding of belief. It is hopefully clear from what I have argued up till now that Certeau's definition of Christianity is deeply problematic and thus it is no surprise to learn that he gave up writing theology in the conventional sense altogether from the mid-1970s onwards. His historic task of thinking Christianity today falls between a Christian past that is increasingly disappearing into nothingness and a Christian future that is emptied of all meaning. Certeau is undoubtedly aware of this dilemma because every criticism we have made of his theology is already voiced implicitly or explicitly within his own texts but until the mid-1970s at least he still wanted to affirm the possibility of thinking, speaking and acting in a Christian way. So ultimately, I have argued, he telescopes all possible historical and theological definitions into one fascinating but perilously ambiguous act: '[f]ondamentalement, *être croyant, c'est vouloir être croyant*'. The sole justification for continuing to think Christianity today is the individual's act of belief in or desire to be Christian. This act of belief without criteria – a profession of faith in the absolute absence of any prior idea of creed, doctrine, institution or community – is alone what makes Christianity possible today. But this inevitably raises the question of exactly what *kind* of Christianity it makes possible and it is undoubtedly a rough beast that is slouching towards Bethlehem to be born. If the single defining characteristic of being a Christian is *to want to be* a Christian (Certeau 2000a: 226), then it becomes impossible to distinguish a priori between, say, the Christianity of St John the Evangelist and that of the Reverend Jerry Falwell, the televangelist. Now I think we can safely assume that this kind of relativism would have been an utterly appalling prospect for Certeau – who elsewhere can be heard bemoaning the fact that people are nowadays more likely to believe in television adverts than God (Certeau 1984: 177–89) – and this may be why he chooses as his example the altogether more reassuring figure of Thérèse de Lisieux. Perhaps Certeau's unwillingness to follow through the logical conclusion of his argument here indicates that there are some Abrahamic journeys even he is not prepared to take. Is he really willing to accept that this belief is all we have? How can he be so sure that the desire to be Christian is actually a Christian desire? What exactly (to go back to where we started) are we affirming when we say 'yes, in a foreign land?' In the remainder of this chapter, I want to explore the radically unpredictable nature and meaning of this affirmation in Derrida's critique of Certeau's reading of Christian mysticism.

Derrida and 'A Number of Yes'

I want to consider Derrida's reading of Certeau in some detail. Derrida's essay 'A Number of Yes (*Nombre de Oui*)' ([1987] 1988a), which appeared shortly after Certeau's death, explores Certeau's reading of Christian mysticism in the seventeenth century. It is important to understand the essay in the context of Derrida and Certeau's roughly contemporaneous work on performative speech acts (Derrida 1988c; Certeau 1992). Its aim is to compare Derrida's concept of a pre-originary 'yes', promise or affirmation to a language that precedes us, that we cannot control and that can be repeated independently of us with Certeau's concept of an originary postulate, 'yes' or will that exceeds all subjects and objects in Renaissance mysticism. The essay compares Derrida's concept of language as capable of repetition outside the animating intention of the subject with Certeau's crucial theory of Christianity (and, in this case, Christian mysticism) as the repetition in difference of Christ. There is a sense in which 'A Number of Yes' is about nothing other than the relationship between fidelity and difference, beginning and separation, openings and cuts, or as Derrida puts it, the paradox of saying '[y]es, in a foreign land' (Derrida 1988a: 118). This essay is both a faithful tribute of gratitude to Certeau's concept of Christianity and an equally faithful and grateful statement of difference from that concept. In provisional terms, I want to propose that Derrida and Certeau are united by a common commitment to say 'yes, in a foreign land' but the crucial difference between them concerns exactly how foreign that 'yes' should be.

Certeau and the Mystical 'Yes'

Jacques Derrida's 'A Number of Yes' focuses on the first volume of Michel de Certeau's final major text *The Mystic Fable* ([1982] 1992). Michel de Certeau uses this text to explore the programmes and discourses that conditioned Christian life in the sixteenth and seventeenth centuries and the means which subjects used to evade or exploit those discourses. It concerns itself with the major themes that condition his work from his earliest texts onwards, namely, the endless dialogue between tradition and innovation, fidelity and difference, and so on. Certeau situates his analysis against a historical backdrop that informs so much of his other work, namely, the transition from one form of understanding the relationship between writing and speech to another (Certeau 1984). Certeau argues that, in the early modern period, Holy Scripture was ceasing to be understood as the transparent message of a divine speaker and this resulted in a fragmentation and disintegration of the concept of Christendom. The breakdown in a common Christian scripture resulted in a proliferation of compartmentalized forms of political and rational writings. This proliferation of secular writings created a crisis for Christians not unrelated to the one they face in modernity, namely, the absence or alienation of what makes them themselves.

Michel de Certeau seeks to address this linguistic, political and theological crisis in *The Mystic Fable*. He analyses how Christian mystics managed to develop a space for themselves within the discursive place of increasingly secularized Renaissance scriptural economies. He brilliantly argues that Christian mysticism *invents* a site to speak from which is outside the authority of their society and which enables them to mark their difference from the language they have to speak and the objects to which that language refers. Christian mysticism can no longer presuppose a transparent relationship between God and language in modernity, Certeau argues, so it has to produce its own conditions of possibility. Certeau contends that Christian mysticism is brought into being by a originary act or event that he calls the *volo* or the act of saying 'I want'. Certeau's argument is that mystical speech can only be spoken by those who 'want' to utter it, and heard only by those who 'want' to hear it, but this *volo* is very different from any ordinary subjective desire or will. If the *volo* retains the formal appearance of subjective desire, it is an absolute and unconditional commitment to God that is foreign to all subjects and objects. The desire for God obliterates the desire for a particular object with the longing for nothing and everything: 'I want nothing, I want everything, I want only God' (Certeau 1992: 168). There is an important sense in which the *volo* also rules out any attachment to a willing subject:

> [t]he will is stabilized (in affirmation and negation) only if it is attached to a particular object ('I want' or 'I do not want' *that*) and, consequently, if there is a distinction between a particular subject ('I') and a particular object ('that').
> (Certeau 1992: 169)

This renunciation of the object and the subject leaves only the dislocated act of wanting itself. For Certeau, this act of the *volo* is repeated in a different tradition of Christian mysticism by the act of saying 'yes' and, as we will see, it is this 'yes' that will particularly interest Derrida.

Certeau goes on to offer his single most rich and detailed analysis of what I have called the 'yes, in a foreign land' or expression of belief without criteria in 'The Weakness of Believing' (2000c). It occurs in a long and remarkable passage on the history of the 'yes' that I would like to quote in full:

> In a more discrete but insistent tradition, the 'performance' of the subject is also taken to be marked by the 'yes', a 'yes' as absolute as the *volo*, without objects, without goals ... Its model is in the surprising statement of Saint Paul about Christ: 'In Him there has only been Yes [*nai*]'. This paradox of a 'yes' without limit in the compass of a singular (Jesus) outlines a contradictory and placeless theory of the (Christic) Subject. An infinite 'yes' pierces the field of separations and distinctions practiced by the entire Hebraic epistemology. This 'yes' is repeated later. The same historical lapsus (the same forgetting) recurs. In the seventeenth century, Angelus Silesius went even further. He identified the written expression of the Separated (*Jah*, or *Jahvê*) with the limitlessness of the 'yes' (*Ja*). In the very place of the sole proper Name (a Name that distances all beings), he installs disappropriation (by a consent to all). The same phoneme (*Ja*) brings together separation and openness, the *No-Name* of the Other and the *Yes* of volition, absolute separation and infinite acceptance.
>
> *Gott spricht nur immer Ja.*
> God always says only Yes [or: I am].
>
> There is identity between Christ's 'yes' and the 'I am' (the Other) of the burning bush. The Separated is reversed, becoming the

exclusion of exclusion. Such is the cipher of the mystic subject. The 'yes', a figure of 'abandonment' or 'detachment', is, ultimately, 'interiority'. In that land, a whole population of intentions cries out on all sides 'yes, yes', like Silesius's God. Is that space divine or Nietzschean? The speaking word [*Wort*], originator of this place [*Ort*], participates in the 'essence' which, according to Evagrius, 'has no opposite'.

(Certeau 1992: 174–5)

Certeau's complex argumentation would take a book in itself to unpack properly but let me make a few quick points about it. His argument about the history of the 'yes' needs, I think, to be understood in the context of his understanding of Christianity as the repetition in alterity in Christ. First, Certeau says that the 'yes' embodies in a single phoneme the dialectic of fidelity and difference, tradition and innovation, continuity and rupture that defines the Christian experience. If the 'yes' has a model, it is the Pauline Christ who is both a historical distinct singularity and the site of a limitless and infinitely repeatable affirmation that can never be identified with a subject or an object. Second, then, Certeau is arguing that Christian mysticism is faithful not so much by seeking to slavishly follow Christ's original teaching but in repeating his act of limitless affirmation in new contexts. Christian mysticism repeats Christ's infinite 'yes' by creating new ways of enacting Christian practice, new places to speak from, new modes of utterance that echo Christ's own transformation of the Old Testament. Finally, Certeau presents Angelus Silesius's mystical affirmation as an example of how the 'yes' manages not simply to strike a balance between faithfulness and transgression but apparently even to overcome this distinction altogether. The Silesian 'Yes' of *kenosis* and abandonment manages – by an Aristotelian feat of double negation – to exclude its act of exclusion and to somehow return to the interiority from which it was expelled. For Certeau, then, Christian mysticism's affirmation performs the impossible task of simultaneous repetition and alterity that characterizes the Christian experience *par excellence*.

Certeau's dazzling erudition and argumentation almost defy criticism but it does not seem to me that the analysis of the mystic 'yes' entirely overcomes the problems we have already encountered in his account of Christianity. It may well be true that Christian mysticism is the articulation of a limitless 'yes' but it is still extremely difficult in the above passage to see where Certeau would draw the line between affirming Christianity *differently* and affirming something that is just *different* from Christianity. His consistent objective of articulating a distinctive *Christian* identity again seems to come into conflict with a logic of alterity that would seem to preclude any identification as such. If the mystic postulate is foreign to all subjects and objects, then what gives Certeau the right to identify it *as* mystical in the first place? *The Mystic Fable* seems to betray a certain doubt or anxiety about this problem when Certeau briefly ponders whether the mystic 'yes' is divine or Nietzschean. There is certainly no obvious reason why he should be moved to ask such a question – and to clearly feel that it has an answer – when he has already said that the 'yes' precedes the labour of making exactly this kind of distinction. This kind of issue again reveals Certeau's determination to baptize the 'yes' as Christian – despite the fact that the general drift of all his arguments tends to remove the criteria by which he can do so – and tends to suggest the hidden presence of an unargued and even dogmatic process of decision-making within his texts. For Certeau, then, the foreign land of the yes is firmly – if somewhat vulnerably – annexed as a 'mystic postulate' and it is at this point of utmost vulnerability that Derrida chooses to intervene in the debate.

Derrida's critique of Certeau

Derrida wants to explore Certeau's concept of the mystical 'yes' from the perspective of his own concept of a pre-originary promise or affirmation that precedes all subjective intention and has to be repeated in an infinite series of new contexts. He wants to pursue a logic or trajectory at work in Certeau's concept of the mystical postulate that exceeds the philosophical or theological decisions Certeau himself takes regarding it. He is keen not to turn his reading into a crude critique or point-scoring exercise but rather to demonstrate that there are resources with Certeau's own analysis that Certeau himself does not take account of. Derrida's concern is that Certeau is too willing to situate the 'yes' within a transcendental or ontological framework where a determinate subject affirms a determinate object. The difference between Certeau and Derrida's account of the promise or affirmation that precedes all language is that Certeau wants to trace the 'yes' back to an ontology whereas Derrida argues that ontology is itself an effect or symptom of the 'yes'. There is a sense in which Certeau's text *forecloses* the heterodox nature of the 'yes' by prematurely turning it into a transcendental or ontological postulate whereas Derrida's text wants to *open up* the heterogeneity of that affirmation by arguing that it exceeds or complicates all identity whatsoever. This leads Derrida's text to show that Certeau circumvents the drift of his entire argument by identifying the foreignness of the 'yes' as an exclusively mystical property, and it is exactly this foreignness that Derrida wants to restore to Certeau's account. In Derrida's account, Certeau's 'yes, in a foreign land' is not quite foreign enough.

Derrida's reading of Certeau takes the form of four questions that I would briefly like to recapitulate here. First, Derrida asks, what is the significance of the fact that Certeau's 'yes' is repeatable? He notes that Certeau talks about two different repetitions of the 'yes' by Christ and Angelus Silesius ('This "yes" is repeated later') but he does not explain the relationship between them. He raises the issue of whether it is necessary to supplement Certeau's account with an analysis of the common root of these different repetitions.

66 *Theologies*

Second, Derrida asks whether it is necessary to choose, as Certeau apparently does, between a 'divine' and a 'Nietzschean' analysis of the 'yes'. It is again important to consider whether there is a common root of the divine and the Nietzschean that underlies their status as oppositions or alternatives. Third, Derrida asks whether – given the fact that Certeau says there is an identity between the Christly 'yes' and the 'yes' of the burning bush – this means that the 'yes' also exceeds the distinction between the Christian and the Judaic. If so, then this again begs the question of whether there might be some more 'ancient' third possibility that underlies Certeau's particular analysis.

So Derrida begins, then, to repeat Certeau's account of mystic speech acts independently of Certeau himself by showing how it exceeds the transcendental and ontological assumptions in which he encases it. Derrida's text goes on to argue that Certeau is wrong to claim that the 'yes' simply *precedes* language as a transcendental origin or presence in the way that God precedes the world because this affirmation can only be properly understood as *both* inside *and* outside language. The 'yes' is prior to language in the sense that it is the pre-subjective promise that we must all make in order to speak at all but – as a promise or obligation – it is also what brings language itself into being. There is a sense in which the originary 'yes' *before* language of which Certeau speaks necessarily obligates its own repetition *after* language as well. This *quasi*-originary 'yes' cannot be the subject of a transcendental or ontological analysis of the type practised by Certeau because, as we will see, its ground or origin is already doubled or divided at root.

Fourth, Derrida asks whether the proximity of the *volo* mean that Certeau's 'yes' remains tied to an account of the subjective will. It is Derrida's – possibly unjustified[5] – concern that Certeau is seeking to reduce the 'yes' to the property of a transcendental subject saying 'I want'. Derrida, however, raises the question of whether it is possible to detach Certeau's account of the 'yes' from an account of the *volo* which, in his view, remains indebted to a metaphysical tradition of thinking being in terms of the will of the subject that stretches from Descartes to Hegel. If this is the case, Derrida's answer is that Certeau's account of the 'yes' raises the paradoxical question of who or what comes after the subject of modernity: 'it would then become a matter of experience without experience, of description without description: there would be no determinable presence, no object, no possible theme' (Derrida 1988a: 130). The 'yes' precedes not only ontology, but subjectivity and everything that rationalist philosophy associates with it: subjectness, objectness, the *cogito*, the rationality principle, calculability and so on. This means that Certeau's 'yes' ultimately promises something which exceeds the order of the rational, programmable or calculable, '[t]he yes gives or promises *just that*, it gives it with the promise: the incalculable itself' (Derrida 1988a: 130). In the remainder of 'A Number of Yes', Derrida restores this element of the incalculable to Certeau's still too rationalist account of the 'yes'.

Derrida's 'Yes, yes' in a foreign land

Derrida begins to set out his own *quasi*-transcendental account of the 'yes' in the final pages of 'A Number of Yes'. It is Derrida's argument that Certeau's transcendental and ontological 'yes' is actually conditioned by a promise of repeatability that compromises the notion of a pure or simple origin, ground or structure. Its radically plural status exceeds any ontological or egological concept of being or the self as ground and opens itself up to the order of the incalculable. Derrida advances a number of arguments to support his claim that Certeau's 'yes' ultimately exceeds the transcendental and ontological methodology in which he envelops it.

First, Derrida argues that the originary 'yes' is necessarily a response whether it be to history, context or language (Derrida 1988a: 132). It is not the affirmation of a self-identical *cogito* but a quasi-Lévinasian originary response where the subject is brought into being as originarily responsible to the other.

Second, he maintains that the 'yes' has the structure of a promise or engagement that necessarily contains the seed of a future affirmation within it (Derrida 1988a: 132). The 'first' yes is actually second, then, whereas the 'second' yes already resides *in potentia* in the first. There is no question that this promise of repetition is something that accidentally or empirically befalls the first 'yes' either. If the concept of a promise necessarily implies some future fulfilment – regardless of whether it *actually* arrives or not – then by the same token the first yes structurally demands its fulfilment in the second 'yes'. This promise to repeat itself is the *structural* condition of there being a first 'yes' at all, then, rather than merely an *empirical* by-product of it.

Third, Derrida turns to the nature of this repetition itself in a long and complex piece of argumentation. He argues that the possibility of repetition not only makes the first 'yes' possible but *menaces* it with the threat that it could become something mechanical, something that is done so automatically that it operates quite independently of the affirmation it is nominally repeating. Just as there is no chance of separating the first 'yes' and its repetition, so there is no possibility of choosing between the 'good' repetition and the supposedly 'bad' one by consigning the latter to the realm of empirical accident. The demand for fidelity, sincerity and re-presentation of the origin goes hand in hand with forgetting, difference, supplementation at origin. This radical inability to distinguish between fidelity and forgetting, sincerity and automaticity is, Derrida concludes, the condition of all memory, fidelity and responsibility:

> Promise of memory, memory of promise in a place of eventness which precedes all presence, all being, all psychology of the *psyche*, as well as

all morality. But memory itself must forget in order to fulfill what is, since the *yes*, its mission. Promised simultaneously with the 'first', the 'second' *yes* must come as an absolute renewal, again absolutely, once again absolutely inaugural and 'free', failing which it could only be a natural, psychological or logical consequence. It must act as if the 'first' were forgotten, far enough past to require a new, initial *yes*. This forgetting is not *psychological* or accidental, it is structural, the very condition of fidelity, of both the possibility and impossibility of a signature; it is the divisibility against which a signature extends. Voluntarily and involuntarily [*sic*], the non-will of the unconditional will, the second first *yes* splits from the first *yes* (which was already double), it *cuts itself off* from the other so as to be that which it must be, 'first', unique, uniquely unique, opening *in its turn, in vicem, vice versa*, in its day, each time the first time (*vices, vez, volta, fois, Mal,* etc.). Thanks, if this may be said, to the menace of forgetting, the memory of the promise, the promise itself can take its first step, that is to say the second. A *yes* always *renders thanks* to this danger – and is it not here that, as Michel de Certeau says, the same *yes* 'repeats itself again' in 'the time same lapsus of history (the same forgetting)' and that 'the same phoneme (Ja) makes the cut and the opening coincide'?

(Derrida 1988a: 132–3)

Finally, Derrida gathers together the various threads of his argument about the 'yes, yes' in the conclusion of 'A Number of Yes'. It is now possible to state quite explicitly the challenge of Derrida's concept of the 'yes' to Certeau. Derrida, we have seen, posits a concept of the 'yes' as an originary promise or commitment to speak that is taken before we ever open our mouths. He argues that the subject is originarily committed to a language it did not create, does not control, and that it must repeat whether it wants to or not. If repetition is unavoidable, then the question arises of what form that repetition must take and Derrida's argument is that the condition of fidelity, sincerity, the repetition in good faith is inseparable from the menace of forgetting, mechanical or automatic repetition, the repetition in bad faith. Derrida's characteristic argument is that the absence of any criteria for distinguishing between the 'good' and 'bad' repetition does not paralyse memory, fidelity or responsibility but is rather their very condition. The only way of faithfully repeating the originary force of the first 'yes', Derrida argues, is by being absolutely different from what you are repeating. There is a sense in which the second 'yes' is compelled to repeat the absolutely inaugural gesture of the first, in other words, but it can only be 'once again absolutely inaugural and "free"' if it forgets the existence of the first 'yes'. This second 'yes' can only hope to be faithful to the original inaugural force of the original if it no longer knows what it is repeating, whether it is repeating it successfully or not, or what its repetition will bring into being. Now we can begin to see the radical nature of the challenge that Derrida's reading of the 'yes' as affirming an absolute future poses to Certeau's deeply vulnerable attempts to trace this affirmation back to a proper name and a historical event. For Derrida, to summarize, Certeau's 'yes' contains within it an affirmation of incalculability that exceeds the distinction between the subject and the object, the Christian and the Judaic and even the theological and the non-theological. In this sense, Derrida's 'yes, yes' is truly a 'yes, in a foreign land'.

Jacques Derrida's analysis of Certeau is, to conclude, a deeply affirmative one that supplies possible answers to many of the questions we have raised about Certeau's work. I would argue that Derrida's text is more faithful to the radical demand of Certeau's analysis than Certeau sometimes is himself. It refuses to foreclose its commitment to alterity by identifying it as theological in advance. It also helps to answer the question of why Certeau has such difficulties sustaining his early theological positions and why I think he ultimately has to resort to extra-textual means to support them. It is the absolute singularity of the 'yes' that helps us explain, in other words, why Certeau is unable to make good his definition of Christianity, why he is ultimately unable to negotiate a distinctive space for Christianity in the seventeenth century or the twentieth, and why his determinedly Christian 'yes, in a foreign land' is always shadowed by an older yes that is as foreign to all theologies as it is to all atheisms. More positively, however, I want to argue that Derrida's analysis not only explains some important tensions in Certeau's text but also points the way towards rehabilitating his basically untested concept of Christian belief. If Certeau begins to develop a concept of Christianity as the *volo* to be Christian, he is unwilling to face the fact that this leaves the identity of Christianity in an essentially indeterminable state and so fixes the outcome of his own argument in advance by identifying it with Christian orthodoxy. The 'yes, yes, in a foreign land' described by Derrida here cannot by definition know in advance whether it is Christian or not – whether, as Certeau would put it, it belongs to Jahweh or Nietzsche – without betraying its basic affirmation of alterity. This radical undecidability has serious implications for Certeau's theological project but – far from bringing it to a close – my feeling is that it actually constitutes an opportunity to re-invent it as less an extreme form of relativism or subjectivism than an affirmation of singularity. In Derrida's analysis, Certeau's 'yes, in a foreign land' affirms a theologically unpredictable future but it *is* a future nonetheless, and I want to close this chapter by imagining what it might look like in the context of Certeau's promised but never completed anthropology of belief.

Beyond belief?

I would like to conclude, then, by looking at Certeau's famous analysis of belief in the chapter 'Believing and Making People Believe' in *The Practice of Everyday Life* (1984). It is necessary to preface a discussion of this essay with a brief analysis of *The Practice of Everyday Life* itself. The text remains Certeau's most famous and influential piece of work – to the extent where it exercises an excessive influence upon the reception of his œuvre as a whole – and remains a controversial subject of debate today. There is no doubt that Certeau's text plays a fascinating, and still ambiguous role, within cultural anthropology of the period but my interest here is with how we might read it in future. This section will argue that Certeau's early and basically untested concept of theological 'belief without criteria' might, if sharpened through dialogue with Derrida, offer a means of rehabilitating his increasingly pessimistic analyses of a secular modernity in which belief has become literally unbelievable. In my view, Certeau's concept of belief not only has the resources to reinvent his analysis of contemporary secular belief systems but of Christian faith as well.

The Practice of Everyday Life

Michel de Certeau defines his project in *The Practice of Everyday Life* quite explicitly as 'part of a continuing investigation of the ways in which users – commonly assumed to be passive and guided by established rules [*discipline*] – operate' (1984: xi). It is thus only the first fruits of a never completed work-in-progress and this fact has to be borne in mind in any attempts to describe or evaluate it. It is a work that is clearly influenced by predecessors like Propp, Lévi-Strauss and Foucault but – as Ian Buchanan (2000) has recently made abundantly clear – Certeau seeks to negotiate an individual space for himself within the structuralist hegemony that dominated social anthropology or historical archaeology at the time. He analyses acts of deviance and subversion within everyday culture rather than the ethnic cultures of Lévi-Strauss or the sub-cultures of resistance anatomized by Foucault in his histories of madness, illness and sexuality. His definition of the subject as a 'user' working within, and selecting from, established practices shows that Certeau subscribes neither to the Cartesian notion of a transcendental subject nor the structuralist idea of an all-determining discursive grid of subjectivity. He criticizes the humanist tradition because he believes that the subject is conditioned by discourse but typically he also criticizes the structuralist tendency to play down the significance of the individual event. The subject may exist within a structure of pre-determined statements, in other words, but this does not explain why any particular subject should produce any particular statement at any particular moment (Certeau 1984: 20). This leads Certeau to negotiate a highly imaginative concept of everyday living as neither free agency nor conditioned subjectivity but as a site of resistance or evasion *within* the dominant system. For Certeau, the cultural logic of everyday life is to be found neither in the subject nor the grid or structure of subjectivity but in the acts, practices or transactions that are exchanged between the two. In other words, Certeau is interested in developing a concept of cultural logic as a kind of pre-determined set, catalogue or inventory of practices from which users choose those that best suit them and in doing so attain a degree of individualization or customization in their lives (Certeau 1984: xi–xxiv).

'The Scriptural Economy'

Certeau aims, then, to demonstrate and articulate the existence of a cultural logic or set of rules that underpins everyday life. His work consists of two basic lines of enquiry: a set of quasi-poetic essays on particular but potentially exemplary everyday cultural practices (walking, reading, taking the train), on the one hand, and a set of theoretical hypotheses developed in relation to structuralists (Foucault, Bourdieu), anthropologists (Propp, Lévi-Strauss) and linguistic philosophers (Wittgenstein and Austin), on the other. Certeau develops a new and very provisional vocabulary to articulate the underpinnings of the ordinary which has gone on to enter the armoury of cultural studies: strategies and tactics (Certeau 1984: xix), places and spaces (Certeau 1984: 117), scriptural economies, the recited society, and so on. Certeau's discussion of strategies and tactics, for example, represents his most explicit if by no means complete theorization of the ways in which subjects manage to negotiate individual places for themselves within monolithic cultures through apparently minor acts of deviance carried out in the interstices or blind spots of panoptic gazes (Certeau 1984: 37). The chapter entitled 'The Scriptural Economy' maps the larger shift in the early modern period from oral culture to print culture, from Christendom to secular enlightenment, from a society which is, as it were, spoken by God towards one which is enunciated by the universal, enlightened subject of modernity, against which the rest of the book is situated. There is an important sense in which the entirety of Certeau's work from his earliest Christian theology to the later work on culture is a response to the progressive loss of God's voice and the critical question it poses: '[w]ho is going to speak? And to whom?' (Certeau 1984: 138). This earlier oral economy can never be made present again – modernity is predicated on its disappearance – but Certeau's answer is that different linguistic communities have been able to make manifest its absence by becoming active makers or producers of languages that are less decipherable systems of signs than material, instrumental means of achieving power (Certeau 1984: 131–53). For Certeau, as we have already seen, Christian mysticism – with its constant attention to what exceeds language – constitutes a privileged example of the attempt to surreptitiously 'speak' or enunciate within a culture of writing: 'orality insinuates itself, like one of the threads of which it is composed, into the network – an endless tapestry – of a scriptural economy' (Certeau 1984: 132). In its concluding section, *The Practice of Everyday Life* turns to the subject of belief and asks how subjects might manipulate the abuses of credibility in contemporary culture to their own advantage.

'Believing and Making People Believe'

Certeau's argument in 'Believing and Making People Believe', which concludes *The Practice of Everyday Life*, is that belief is itself no longer believable. It once attached itself to totalizing belief systems like religion and politics but today it either fritters itself away in media, advertising and the consumer industries or it has exhausted itself entirely. It is Certeau's despondent conclusion that, to borrow a nice line from Ian Buchanan, people are now more likely to believe in the miraculous power of a new kitchen cleanser than the redemptive power of God (Buchanan 2000: 95). He argues that this dismal state of affairs is basically the result of what – pre-empting by a few years the work of Jean-François Lyotard – is clearly the collapse in the believability of grand narratives like, first, Christianity and, later on, Marxism (Lyotard 1979a: xxiv). Certeau's argument is that Christianity compromised its own credibility following the break-up of ecclesiastical power in the late Middle Ages by retreating from the political sphere into the spiritual. Christianity's increasing privatization and individualization vacated vast spaces of public power and authority which subsequently attached themselves to the political (Certeau 1984: 182). Politics, Certeau contends, appropriated religious credibility to validate its secular project in various ways but he focuses particularly on the way in which nineteenth- and twentieth-century left-wing movements transported the religious desire for paradise into utopianism (Certeau 1984: 182). Marxism's explosion as a credible political alternative to liberal capitalism in the twentieth century has, however, resulted in a further dispersion of belief in the post-ideological, technocratic *polis* of the late twentieth and twenty-first centuries. Contemporary politics, advertising, information technology and so forth consist of increasingly desperate attempts to legitimate the body politic by re-capturing the credibility that used to attach itself so readily to religious and political belief systems. For Certeau, it would have been no surprise to find political parties like New Labour using opinion polls and focus groups to keep up the pretence that it is governing by a clear political will or mandate, conglomerates like Shell Oil drawing upon ethico-theological values to describe the economic relationship between the producer and the consumer as a familial bond, and Coca-Cola tapping into the theological vocabulary of transcendence to suggest that consuming their product will transform your life.

Now Certeau's famous name for the culture that endlessly fabricates the real is the *société récitée* or recited society: 'it is defined by *stories* [*récits*] (the fables of our advertising and information media), by *citations* of stories, and by the interminable *recitation* of stories' (Certeau 1984: 186). It consists of an infinite multiplicity of media, advertising and political narratives that define the field of subjectivity so completely that they turn seeing into believing and appearance into reality. It works not because people are so gullible that they will believe everything they see or read – in fact, they know perfectly well it is all nonsense – but because a residue of belief survives even that act of refutation (Certeau 1984: 188). The recited society makes people believe not by producing some inherently believable object but by making them believe that *other* people of expertise and authority believe (Certeau 1984: 189). This means that belief in the recited society exists in a kind of infinitely deferred credit economy where A believes because they think B does, B believes because they think C does, and so on forever. For Certeau, the abyssal nature of this system is clearly deeply depressing and – in the context of the overall argument of *The Practice of Everyday Life* – the question necessarily arises as to whether there is any way in which its victims might be able to take advantage of it for their own tactical ends:

> [I]t is right to enquire about the capacities it offers to change 'belief' into 'mistrust', into 'suspicion', indeed into 'denuniciation', as well as into the opportunity for citizens to manipulate politically what serves as a circular and objectless credibility for political life itself.
> (Certeau 1984: 189)

We are not told the results of this enquiry – if any such enquiry ever existed – as the essay ends at this point. In his proposed anthropology of belief, Certeau perhaps might have gone on to give us some idea about how we could re-invent the possibility of the political – and it is revealing that now he does not even mention the religious – but sadly he was never able to do so.

Certeau after deconstruction

What, then, are we to make of *The Practice of Everyday Life* today? It goes without saying that Certeau was unable to complete his work but this does not mean we cannot imagine some alternative futures for it. Certeau has been interpreted as everything from a utopian dreamer to a cynical defeatist, a cultural quietist to a political revolutionary and a postmodern butterfly to a dialectical structuralist in the 20 years since his text first appeared in English (Fiske 1988; Frow 1990; Bauerschmidt 1996; Ward 1999; Buchanan 2000) and the debate is still ongoing. The intention of this chapter has been to imagine a 'Certeau after deconstruction' and in what follows I want to consider what form this future might take. There is a deconstructive trajectory in Certeau's thought that he himself did not always personally follow, perhaps because it would necessitate a more radical plurality of religious and cultural identity than even he was willing to contemplate, but which is open to readers of his work to pursue. This Derridaean supplement to Certeau could never be an adequate substitute for Certeau himself, of course, but hopefully it will remain faithful to a certain spirit in his work. Let me raise three basic questions that point the way towards such a reading.

Structuralism

First, I think it is important to consider whether Certeau's methodology in *The Practice of Everyday Life* works on its own terms. It is undoubtedly true that Certeau's text represents a significant advance on the kind of structuralist sociology or anthropology of the period but whether the cultural logic beginning to be elaborated in this text entirely escapes the possibility of deconstruction is a matter of debate. Certeau certainly tries to distance himself from contemporary versions of structuralism by making some unsubtle but, for me, wholly legitimate criticisms of Propp, Lévi-Strauss, Foucault and Bourdieu. Structuralism is variously described as a-historical, de-contextualizing, self-fulfilling, too interested in the productions of the powerful, and far too willing to reduce the plurality and originality of existence to the status of a laboratory experiment or computer program (Certeau 1984: 15–28, 45–61). But Certeau's criticisms make it all the more surprising that – at this stage at least – they seem to add up to not much more than a neo-structuralist corrective to existing models rather than a genuine attempt to work through to a post-structuralist position. Certeau's preliminary reading of Foucault, for example, seems to assume the basic validity of his analysis of structures of surveillance and discipline and only takes it to task for not supplying an account of how those structures can also be exploited or manipulated by the dominated (Certeau 1984: xiv). More pointedly, Certeau's objection to Propp's structuralist account of proverbs, for example, is not that it is self-exempting because (as Derrida would presumably argue) it assumes a position above and beyond all structure, but that its cultural analysis is too monolithic and needs to be supplemented with an (apparently equally structured) account of the specific uses to which cultural practices are put by individual users (Certeau 1984: 21). The cultural criticism he is canvassing for seems to assume the basic structuralist position that normative frameworks for cultural practice *per se* exist and can be articulated and all he wants to do is to ring-fence the limited freedom for subjects to customize or personalize usage within those basic norms. This focus on arts of making or doing is never formalized or taxonomized in *The Practice of Everyday Life* as such but, as we shall see in a moment, the repeated emphasis on the applicability of formal categories like rhetoric and speech act theory suggests that this may have been the direction in which Certeau's work was heading. To what extent, though, does Certeau's neo-structuralist methodology impede his – totally admirable – aim to articulate the plurality of the everyday?

Phonocentrism

Second, I also want to consider whether Certeau's historical account of the scriptural economy in which cultural practices take place might not also require supplementation. His analysis of the scriptural economy in *The Practice of Everyday Life* is a self-conscious attempt to write what we might, far more grandly than the modest Certeau, call a 'phonology after deconstruction'. He is all too aware of the charges of phonocentrism, logocentrism and so forth that could be levelled at his rather neat historical schema and is evidently determined to avoid the fate that befalls, say, Lévi-Strauss in *Of Grammatology*. He even name-checks Derrida and stresses that the opposition between orality and writing implies no prelapsarian unity or teleological reconciliation (Certeau 1984: 133). But Certeau goes on to replace the metaphysical account of the relationship between writing and speech with one that seemingly owes more to Foucault than Derrida: 'These "unities" (e.g. writing and orality) are the result of reciprocal distinctions within successive and interconnected historical configurations. For this reason, they cannot be isolated from these historical determinations or raised to the status of general categories' (Certeau 1984: 133).

Certeau's recent defenders have gone as far as to argue that this historicization of the purity of orality means that his concept of the voice is somehow undeconstructible or that it has already deconstructed itself (Ward 1999: 153) but my feeling is that this kind of judgement may be slightly too generous. The fact is that while Certeau does insist on the originary mediation of speech, he is still a long way from Derrida's more radical insistence that the death of the context of the original *vouloir-dire* is the a priori condition of writing in essays like 'Signature Event Context' (1982d). There is an Austinian confidence in the ideality of the speech act throughout Certeau's work that would have to be complicated by a reading of Derrida's 'Limited inc a b c . . .' (1988c). This ultimately means that there is a residual Cartesianism in Certeau whereby the human subject still retains a level of autonomy from and control over the scriptural economies that define it – even if it is simply the negative freedom of marking its difference from them – which contrasts with the inescapably linguistic inscription of the Derridaean subject: 'I would say that it is in the relation to the "yes" or to the *Zusage* presupposed in every question that one must seek a new (post-deconstructive) determination of the responsibility of the "subject"'(Derrida 1995c: 268). To what extent, we might again ask, does Certeau's analysis of orality contain phonocentric or logocentric assumptions which fly in the face of his professed study of alterity? Might it be possible to detach Certeau's objectives from a methodology which today seems far too totalizing and monolithic?

Belief

Third, I want to pursue this line of enquiry in a little more detail by returning to Certeau's uncompleted anthropology of belief. It is important to establish whether Certeau's account of why we have lost belief and where we should go from here works on its own terms or whether it, too, stands in need of supplementation. He presents his readers with what is almost a kind of fable of belief. He mythologizes believing as the fall from an edenic plenitude of limitless belief into the realm of unlikeness of objectless credit: '[l]ittle by little, belief became polluted, like the air and the water' (Certeau 1984: 179). His prelapsarian mythology of belief – and the temporality of past innocence, present fallenness and (possible) future redemption it inevitably carries with it – inevitably raises the question of whether this is the only way of narrativizing this situation. Certeau has been accused of indulging both a 'certain romanticism' as far as the medieval church is concerned (Ward 1999: 155) and an unnecessary pessimism about the break-up of Christendom from the early modern period onwards (Bauerschmidt 1996). Certeau's methodology produces, I would argue, a self-fulfillingly totalizing and linear narrative of rise, decline and fall. Is there – as there often seems to be – something structurally inevitable about the eclipse of the Church's authority in Certeau's account that exceeds his simple historical analysis of an ecclesiastical retreat? For Certeau, the apparently optimistic idea of everyday people making do in myriad infinite ways is drenched in a tragic world-view worthy of such cultural pessimists as Alasdair MacIntyre and George Steiner. The problem is that Certeau almost seems to take it as a given that the inability of metanarratives to command belief in an object is tragic but we could argue that a roughly analogous situation is seen in ecstatic terms by Jean Baudrillard and in ethical ones by Jean-François Lyotard. There is again a nostalgia for the kind of totalizing presence offered by grand narratives in Certeau which contrasts markedly with Lyotard's definition of the postmodern condition as the war on totality. This is not to say that Certeau is not entitled to his opinion about modernity or postmodernity but merely to make it clear that it is *just* an opinion and not one that we necessarily have to share. If I were to play the role of devil's advocate here, I would again want to ask Certeau exactly what is so *wrong* with the concept of objectless credibility? Is the continuing belief in something which cannot be made present necessarily a form of injustice or could it be the basis for a different concept of justice based on what Lyotard calls 'the unpresentable' (Lyotard 1984: 81)? Now Certeau's problematic analysis of the past and present is carried over into his tentative and obviously very incomplete futurology which, as we have already seen, holds out the prospect of possible redemption from the tragedy of the recited society without telling us how that redemption is to be achieved:

> [I]t is right to enquire about the capacities it offers to change 'belief' into 'mistrust', into 'suspicion', indeed into 'denunciation', as well as into the opportunity for citizens to manipulate politically what serves as a circular and objectless credibility for political life itself.
> (Certeau 1984: 189)

Is a hermeneutics of suspicion the only way in which we as citizens can rehabilitate what he calls the objectless credibility of political belief? And is that why Certeau no longer even mentions the possibility of redeeming *religious* belief? Is it the case that the religious is now literally *beyond* belief?

Jacques Derrida helps us to imagine a possible future for Certeau's work beyond Michel de Certeau himself. It has been my contention in this chapter that deconstruction could usefully supplement (in both senses of Derrida's key term) the fable of belief set out by Certeau here. It works by pursuing the radical nature of Certeau's affirmation of alterity straight through its particular philosophical and theological contexts. Derrida shares with Certeau a fascination with the story of the fall, for example, but he is perhaps more willing to think that fable outside its Christian perimeters: '"usurpation" has always already begun' he famously writes in *Of Grammatology* (Derrida 1976: 27–73). Certeau tends to see the mobility of belief as a historical fall from plenitude into mediation but, in the absence of any more extensive analysis, it might prove interesting to complicate that with Derrida's suggestion that there is a structural fall built into plenitude from the beginning. Derrida's account would be one way of accounting for the curious sense in Certeau's account of Christianity, that, so to speak, the barbarians are always already inside the gate. If the possibility of mobility is built into belief at the start, then we do not need to share Certeau's analysis of modernity as a kind of tragic reversal of fortune into objectless credibility either. The same kind of system that Certeau bemoans here – where receipt is permanently deferred in an economy of credit – is described in very different terms by Derrida as the a priori possibility of the gift in *Given Time* (1992a). This situation is seen as a kind of pathetic lack or absence in Certeau but, as Derrida abundantly shows in 'A Number of Yes', there is every possibility of seeing the impossibility of presence in affirmative terms as faithfulness, responsibility or justice.[6] For Certeau, the recited society is an injustice that has to be overturned by a hermeneutics of suspicion but from a Derridaean perspective we might see it as the scene for a new belief in justice as what he calls 'the impossible' (Derrida 1992a: 24).

Derrida might enable us to re-invent Certeau's concept of belief as less a form of extreme relativism or subjectivism, then, and more as an affirmation of that which is unpresentable as such. It is important to summarize the argument so far before taking this final step. Michel de Certeau developed a concept of Christianity as the desire to believe, in the total absence of any legitimating authority for belief in his early work. Certeau was unwilling to make the final break between belief and authority, however, because he only applied his concept of belief to cases that still carried vestiges of doctrinal or institutional authority anyway when it could just as easily be used to legitimate the actions of any charlatan or fanatic who wants to call himself 'Christian'. Certeau's theology still wanted to baptize this logic of departure as a self-defining act of Christian *belief* despite the fact that, as we have seen, everything in his argument militates against the possibility of such a pre-determined act of identification. The first attempt to articulate an anthropology of belief is an advance on his theology because it gives up on the possibility that Christianity could offer any kind of authority nowadays but it is apparently no more willing to accept that belief without criteria might be possible. This blind spot can be seen in the essay 'Believing and Making People Believe' where Certeau argues that the collapse of credible authorities like Christianity and Marxism is precisely what brings about the contemporary crisis in belief (Certeau 1984: 178). If we follow Certeau's original logic further than he was willing to, however, it becomes possible to see that the practice of belief is in no way contingent upon the existence of criteria or authority for belief and that there is not necessarily a crisis here at all.

Derrida's work has famously followed Lévinas and Lyotard in developing a concept of ethical or political responsibility in the radical absence of any determining criteria (Derrida 1990) and I want to suggest that this might point the way towards a rehabilitation of Certeau's original position on belief. He argues that the 'impossible decision' is the only decision worthy of the name for several reasons. First, it is the only decision that seeks to do justice to the absolute singularity of the event at hand. Second, it does not seek to subsume that event under a set of given rules, a preconceived concept of justice or the pragmatic exigencies of the moment. Third, it is an attempt to invent the criteria according to which that event will be judged – or better still to let the event determine its own criteria for judgement – none of which, however, exonerates 'me' of responsibility. Fourth, its judgement is neither just nor unjust – according to what existing rule could it be so judged? – but violent, contingent, provisional and prone to future judgements. The impossibility of relying on any authority for decision-making is not the end but the beginning of the story – in Derrida's account – precisely because that absence of authority is what gives us decisions to make. This logic is present in Certeau's early work on the theology of Christian belief without criteria – remember how he makes reference to Derrida's famous remark about the performative excess or madness of the Cartesian decision – and I would like to conclude by considering how it might have contributed to his anthropology of belief and believing more generally.

So Derrida's concept of the impossible decision enables us to argue that one way of completing Certeau's anthropology of belief might be to say that the impossibility of belief *itself* contains the means of making belief possible again. It is my contention that the collapse of credible authority does not have to lead to the objectless credibility of the recited society or to the hermeneutics of suspicion seemingly favoured by Certeau but rather to his own fundamentally untested concept of belief without criteria. It could be argued that Certeau's recited society deconstructs authority in the same way that contemporary technology deconstructs ontology in Derrida's *Specters of Marx* (Derrida 1994: 169). Certeau himself certainly understood that the absence of an object was certainly no obstacle to the experience of it from his reading of Merleau-Ponty: 'it might even be the case ... that we find in [experience] a movement towards that which cannot possibly be presented to us in the original and whose irremediable absence could therefore count as one of our originary experiences' (Merleau-Ponty 1964: 211). The tragedy of the recited society – a disassociation of belief from authority so fundamental that it makes it possible for us to believe in the existence of something that *never* appears to us as an object – is also its opportunity. There is an unarticulated sense in which the same logic that condemns subjects to continue believing in the miraculous cleaning powers of the latest washing powder – despite knowing that this object will never be presented to them – might give them the means to believe in what Lyotard calls the unpresentable, Derrida calls the arrival of the other as justice or Certeau's own much-patronized belief in the infinite inventiveness of the everyday. This politics of belief without criteria has the potential to transform the injustice of believing in an object that never appears into the belief in a justice which cannot be made absolutely present by any *récit,* citation or recitation because it is structurally to come.

Finally, I want to close this chapter by proposing that Derrida's concept of the impossible decision might also enable us to re-open Certeau's abandoned theological project. It is striking that Certeau does not even consider the possibility that religious believers could manipulate the objectless credibility of the recited society and here is another area where his analysis could usefully be supplemented. Certeau assumes too quickly for my liking that the absence of Christianity's historical authority makes Christian faith impossible but my response would be that this absence is actually an opportunity. Derrida has argued that deconstruction constitutes a kind of generalized faith or religion in a number of recent texts (Derrida 1994; 1995b; 1999a) and I think this analysis again clarifies Certeau's concept of belief without criteria. First, deconstruction has the structure of a faith because it is an affirmation of the arrival of the absolutely other. Second, it seeks – however impossibly – to absolutely suspend the horizon of expectation for the arrival of that other. Third, deconstruction is a generalized faith because it necessarily operates in the radical absence of any criteria for determining the status of that alterity:

> What would faith or devotion be when directed towards a God who would not be able to abandon me? Of whom I would be absolutely certain, assured of his concern? A God who could but give or give of himself to me? Who could not not choose me?
> (Derrida 1999a: 181)

The concept of Derrida's deconstruction as a kind of generalized faith that takes place in the radical absence of any criteria points the way towards a re-invention of Certeau's concept of belief without criteria. There is a sense in which Certeau's enigmatic claim in his early work that 'to be Christian is to be want to be Christian' does not have to reduce faith to a subjectivist free-for-all – as Certeau himself may have feared – but could point towards that moment of absolute incalculability that is 'the very condition of fidelity' (Derrida 1988a: 132). This is a perilously Kierkegaardian leap of faith – and anyone can understand why even so adventurous a thinker as Certeau would have been reluctant to stake Christianity's future upon it – but it does propose one possible response to his unanswered question 'How is Christianity Thinkable Today?'.

Conclusion

Michel de Certeau's 'yes, in a foreign land' brings into view a different concept of Christian belief and I would like to conclude with some loose and polemical speculations about what form that belief might take. It is a concept of belief that cannot know in advance whether it is sincerely meant or mechanically recited, orthodox or heterodox, Christian or non-Christian because it is determined by nothing other than what he calls the will or elsewhere the *volo* or 'I want' of the believer. It proposes a concept of faith that is not a constative description of, or assent to, a prior set of doctrinal or institutional authorities, in other words, so much as a performative invention that seeks to bring into existence the authorities according to which it will be judged or, to adapt Lyotard's famous definition of postmodernism, to ascertain not what *was* but *what will have been* Christianity. The concept of belief without criteria imagined here does not so much paralyse belief as transform it because, as Derrida famously argues, the absence of criteria is precisely what makes it belief as opposed to a more or less disguised form of knowledge. This concept of Christian belief has to risk the solace of good conscience, the consolations of beautiful but increasingly empty and fetishized rituals *and even ultimately the certainty that it is truly Christianity at all* if it is to have a future. For Certeau, it may be true that 'to be a Christian is to want to be a Christian' but it also seems to be the case that to be a Christian is also to never know for sure what it *is* to be a Christian, whether one actually *is* a Christian, whether one is ever being Christian *enough*. In Michel de Certeau's 'yes, in a foreign land', Christianity can still perhaps hear the echo of Nicolas Malebranche's uncanny promise in the *Dialogue on Metaphysics*: 'I will not take you to a foreign country; but I will perhaps teach you that you are a foreigner in your own country' (Malebranche 1992: 610).

3 Marion and 'a paradoxical writing of the word *without*'

Jean-Luc Marion's theology contains within it what could be called 'a paradoxical writing of the word *without* [sans]' (Derrida 1989a: 64n). It is possible to detect this strange preposition at various points in his increasingly influential theological discourse on the gift, the saturated phenomenon, the idol and the icon and most famously the concept of Gxd without Being. Its paradoxical status becomes most clear, however, in the context of Marion's increasingly well-known debate with Jacques Derrida about the work of the fifth-century Neoplatonist negative theologian Pseudo-Dionysius the Areopagite. The Derrida–Marion debate partially hinges, I want to suggest, upon their conflicting interpretations of a key concept in Dionysius's theology – '*hyperousios*' – that is variously translated into English as 'hyperessential', 'superessential', 'beyond being', and perhaps most ambiguously, 'without being'. This chapter will attempt to mediate between the conflicting interpretations of '*hyperousios*' advanced by Derrida and Marion by putting them in the context of Derrida's complex and aporetic uses of the word 'without' in his essays on Pseudo-Dionysius, Angelus Silesius and Maurice Blanchot. Finally, and more provisionally, I would also like to raise the possibility that Derrida and Marion's disagreement about this 'paradoxical writing of the word *without*' in negative theology has profoundly political implications. My guiding questions in considering Marion's reading of the *via negativa* will be as follows. What – if any – is the precise meaning of the '*hyperousios*' in Dionysius, Derrida and Marion? Does it remain within the category of metaphysics of presence or in some way go without it? To what extent is the Derrida–Marion debate indicative of the hyperbolic concept of negative theology we have begun to negotiate in this book? In this chapter, I would like to argue that this 'paradoxical writing of the word *without*' indicates an aporia 'within' the *via negativa* that has important implications for our understanding of its position in Marion's thought.

Pseudo-Dionysius and negative theology

I want to preface my discussion of Marion and Derrida with a brief overview of Pseudo-Dionysius the Areopagite's negative theology and, particularly, the Dionysian concept of the 'third way'. It is with the Dionysian concept of the third way that the Derrida–Marion debate begins and to get a purchase on that debate we need to get a preliminary idea of what Dionysius means by the term. The chapter will then go on to compare Derrida's argument that the third way remains within the orbit of predicative theology, ontotheology and the metaphysics of presence with Marion's argument that the third way somehow exceeds all predication as a mode of pragmatism that acknowledges the divine distance between God and man.

Pseudo-Dionysius gives a systematic account of the names of God in *The Divine Names*, *The Mystical Theology* and other texts. His theology is generally agreed to fall into three distinct phases and I would like to briefly recapitulate these here. First, Dionysius's theology takes a *kataphatic* form. Kataphatic theology is a product of the believer's desire to gain account of God by representing Him through a series of positive, human images that are perceived to be 'like' Him. Dionysius affirms, in strict hierarchical order, the Unity and Trinity (*The Theological Representations*), the conceptual names (*The Divine Names*) and the perceptible and multiple symbols of God via the Neoplatonic theory of emanation (*The Symbolic Theology*). Second, Dionysius's theology involves an *apophatic* dimension. The apophatic stresses the infinite transcendence of God from all human images of Him by attaching negative prefixes or suffixes to their positive images or by using a series of obviously incongruous images that are clearly 'unlike' Him (*The Celestial Hierarchies*). So Dionysius also works backwards, according to the Platonic concept of return, negating all the hierarchical names he has previously attributed to God before he arrives once again back at the Unity and the Trinity (*The Divine Names* and *The Mystical Theology*).

Dionysius and his theology beg the question of the precise relationship between the kataphatic and the apophatic ways. It is clear that the two forms of theology are equally necessary and it would be a mistake to prioritize one at the expense of the other. Kataphasis without apophasis would reduce God to human images of Him and thus risk idolatry. Apophasis without kataphasis would find nothing secure to say about God in the first place and would thus fall into agnosticism or atheism. So apophasis and kataphasis are mutually complementary theologies, in other words, and the relationship between them is commonly represented in dialectical or economic terms (Hart 1989). The kataphatic way provides the root affirmation of God without which apophasis could not take place, whereas the apophatic way corrects and refines kataphasis by checking that it *really* does refer to God and not just some human image of Him. There is a dialectical process of affirmation and negation or verification and falsification at work here that enables mystical theology to arrive at a more accurate image of God, as Dionysius himself signals when he adapts the famous Plotinian image of the sculptor to show how negations can be used to progressively elicit what God is by chipping away at everything that He is not (Pseudo-Dionysius 1980: 215). This dialectical relationship between kataphasis and apophasis would not seem to be the whole story, however, for there is a third form of theology in Dionysius's texts that supersedes the other two. Now this mysterious third form of theology has been given various names over the years including mystical theology, hyper-negation and negative (mystical) theology but for reasons of clarity I would like to follow Jean-Luc Marion here and simply call it 'the third way'.

Dionysius's theology involves a third dimension, then, that insists that God is subject to *neither* kataphatic *nor* apophatic theologies because He infinitely transcends both: '[t]hink not that affirmations and denials are opposed but rather that, long before, is that – which is beyond all position and denial – beyond privation' (*Mystical Theology*; Pseudo-Dionysius 1980: 212). It is important to make clear from the outset that the third way not only appears to transcend the kataphatic and apophatic ways but also the dialectical truth-game of affirmation and negation or verification and falsification that these two theologies play out. If kataphasis and apophasis share a common desire to speak the truth about God, then the theology that transcends them must also transcend the metaphysical truth-value to which they are committed. Dionysius would no longer appear to be attempting to say something true or false about God because the third way is not the slightest bit interested in the Aristotelian concept of truth as an adequation between judgement and reality. For Dionyius, the third way is no longer a predicative discourse which attempts to speak *of* God, but a more pragmatic use of language which attempts, however imperfectly, to speak *to* God. The third way offers praise to God because He is infinitely unknowable and incomprehensible: 'God is not known, not spoken, not named, not something among beings, and not known in something among beings' (Pseudo-Dionysius 1980: 178). There is a need to stress that when Dionysius talks about the incomprehensibility and unknowability of God here, he is not bemoaning a failure or absence of knowledge of God but a different way of knowing Him which he calls 'unknowing'. This 'unknowing' of God is certainly not the consequence of a *lack* of God but of a *fullness* or excess of Him that exceeds all conceptuality. In summary, Dionysius's third way represents a mode of theology that apparently bypasses the metaphysics of presence and in this way it offers the stage for the now quite well-known confrontation between Marion and Derrida.

Marion on Pseudo-Dionysius

I would like to continue, then, by examining Jean-Luc Marion's reading of negative theology and Pseudo-Dionysius in particular. Jean-Luc Marion has recently been described as the most important religious thinker in continental philosophy today (Caputo 2002: 8). It is first crucially important to put Marion's argument into the philosophical context of the debate between metaphysics and theology. The discussion will then go on to look at Marion's specific reading of Pseudo-Dionysius's negative theology as a *counter-metaphysical* theological discourse. This reading of negative theology as counter-metaphysical brings Marion into conflict with what we have already seen in Chapter 1 to be Derrida's reading of negative theology as metaphysics or ontotheology *par excellence*.

Marion and ontotheology

Jean-Luc Marion's theological project has been to interrogate the relationship between the God of the philosophers and the God of faith or revelation. He operates, in other words, within the Pascalian cleavage between the God who stands as the ground of Aristotelian ontology and the regulator of Kantian morality, the God whom Nietzsche famously declares is dead, on the one hand, and the God of scripture and revelation, the God of Moses, Abraham and Jacob, the God of love, on the other. Let me briefly sketch the background to his work.

Marion sees his career-long project as the attempt to liberate the God of faith or revelation from the concepts, or as he puts it, idols, of essence and existence imposed upon it by metaphysical theology and philosophy. He identifies Thomas Aquinas's famous definition of metaphysics as an example of this process in his essay 'Metaphysics and Phenomenology: A Summary for Theologians' (Marion 1997b: 279–97). Thomas Aquinas defines metaphysics as a project that 'simultaneously distinguishes the general being and the prime being, separate from matter' (Marion 1997b: 280). Aquinas's distinction between 'general being' and 'prime being' paves the way for a number of further developments in the history of metaphysics. First, it permits a sub-division to be made between *general* metaphysics (*metaphysica generalis*) and *special* metaphysics (*metaphysica specialis*). Second, the argument that these modes of being are 'separate from matter' means that abstract or immaterial qualities can be attributed to material things or seen as substances in themselves. Third, by observing 'general being', the abstract and immaterial qualities that constitute 'prime being' may be deduced. Fourth, this extrapolated concept of prime being must constitute the ground, cause or reason of being in general. Finally, and for our purposes most importantly, this prime being may ultimately be equated with God.

Marion's deeply controversial view – in his early work at least – is that scholastic theology represents a decisive moment in the idolization of the God of Christian faith and revelation. It is Marion's contention, in other words, that Aquinas's account of metaphysics exemplifies what Heidegger famously diagnoses under the catachretic name of ontotheology, namely, the Aristotelian project by which God is brought into philosophy as the highest being purely as a means to complete and legitimate its science of general being. Heidegger famously rejects what he sees as the ontotheological Thomist proofs of God as First Cause *et al.* as blasphemous and futile philosophical endeavours that inevitably lead to atheism because they are unable to absolutely verify themselves. Heidegger's fundamental ontology instead designates theology as an ontic science of faith whose object is not some supreme being but the fact of *Dasein*'s faith in the Crucified:

> I believe that Being can never be thought as the ground or essence of God, but that nevertheless the experience of God and of his manifestedness, to the extent that the latter can indeed meet man, flashes in the dimension of Being, which in no way signifies that Being might be regarded as a possible predicate for God.
>
> (Heidegger 1980: 60–1)

In Marion's theological work, he takes on – and ultimately seeks to surpass – the Heideggerian critique of ontotheology.

L'Idole et la distance

Marion enters the debate between metaphysics and theology in his book *L'Idole et la distance* (1977). He agrees with Heidegger that the problem with the God of ontotheology is that ontology is permitted to dictate the terms by which theology must exist. Marion's argument consists of a series of attempts to develop a non-ontotheological concept of God that is irreducibly distant from the question of Being (Marion 1977: 187). He moves from Heidegger's ontological difference through Lévinas's concept of 'distance-in-relation' and Derrida's *différance* to develop this concept of God's distance from Being in more depth. His argument briefly entertains the possibility that Derrida's *différance* might offer a more radical means of thinking God's distance than Heideggerian ontology or Lévinasian ethics before going on to dismiss the idea in emphatic terms:

> Thus *différance* seems to offer distance the traits which it claimed to conceptualize of itself: to go beyond the Being of beings, in not only inverting ontological difference, but marginalizing it in favour of an 'older' difference. But the indifferent levelling exercised by *différance* over the ontological difference does not only play against 'that other face of the nostalgia that I will call Heideggerian *hope*' for the proper word that suits Being; it attempts to undo as well what it already no longer conceives but as '*nostalgia* ... myth of the purely maternal or purely paternal language, of the lost fatherland of thought'. This means at the least that the paternal question, in the sense that the anterior distance is finally named the distance of the Father, is reduced to 'nostalgia' and, perhaps more banally, to the nostalgia for the proper, original and absolute language. In rejecting such a

nostalgia, has one finished with the paternal element of distance? Has one even approached it?

(Marion 1977: 286)

The tantalizing reference to *différance* as a possible means of thinking the distance of God from ontotheology – not to mention the decisive if rather hasty rejection of it for conflating too easily and predictably the distance of the Father and the nostalgia for a proper or original language – is highly significant in the context of *L'Idole et la distance*. This point raises the possibility that, contra Derrida's argument in his early essays on negative theology, the God of Christian theology does *indeed* exceed the metaphysics of presence as defined by Heidegger and Derrida. Now this point is very forcefully made in Marion's subsequent discussion of the Christian negative theologian Pseudo-Dionysius to which we will now turn. For Marion, Pseudo-Dionysius's mystical theology offers the possibility of a counter-metaphysical theology that corrects what he sees as an anti-theological blind spot in Derrida's argument.

Marion's crucial argumentative move here is that Pseudo-Dionysius represents an important precursor to, rather than a potential target of, Heidegger's critique of ontotheology. He focuses particularly on the language of praise in Dionysius's text. He contests the Thomist interpretation of Dionysius's text *The Divine Names* that reads it as predicating the existence, or *esse*, of God. First, Marion argues that the encomium, or celebratory discourse, which anticipates the opening prayer of *The Divine Names*, tends to 'substitute another verb for the speaking of predicative language ... to praise'. Marion contends that Dionysius's substitution of praise for predication is crucial to an understanding of his theology because it indicates the passage from a discourse that seeks to speak the truth about God to a discourse that 'is "neither true nor false" (Aristotle)' (Marion 1977: 232). Second, Marion's contention is that prayer is no longer a question of speaking *of* God, in other words, but of speaking *to* Him, praising Him, and so it exceeds the metaphysical and more specifically Aristotelian concept of truth as *adequatio*. Dionysius's emphasis on prayer rather than predication in this context begins to distance his discourse from the idolatry of ontotheological concepts of God as prime being. Finally, and more importantly, this process of distancing becomes all the more pronounced as we move into *The Divine Names* proper because Dionysius does not make predicative statements about God's essence but rather praises Him as the Good beyond being. For Marion, Dionysius's decision to *praise* God as the Good rather than to *predicate* Him as essence does not mean that goodness thereby becomes the proper name of God but rather that he acknowledges an unbridgeable difference between God and the idolatrous thought of being: '[p]raying, man acknowledges the unthinkable' (Marion 1977: 205).

So Marion's reading of Pseudo-Dionysius's negative theology reinstates the long-forgotten difference between metaphysics and theology. It is at this exact point that Marion also begins to come into conflict with Jacques Derrida's forcefully non-theological reading of *différance* in his early work. Marion's critique of Thomistic interpretations of Dionysius is not just an arcane historical dispute but a highly contemporary sally against what he elsewhere calls the 'bottomless chessboard' of deconstruction (Marion 1977: §18). Derrida's reading of negative theology, as we have already seen, insists that Pseudo-Dionysius, Meister Eckhart and other negative theologians deny the being of God only in order to better affirm the pre-eminent nature of His being. The critique of negative theology as metaphysics or ontotheology *par excellence* presented by Derrida would seem to be a devastating one *unless* it can be shown that the God of negative theology also somehow exceeds the ontotheological reduction of God to being. This is precisely what Jean-Luc Marion sets out to do when he counters Derrida's presumption in the essay 'Différance' that 'as one knows' negative theologies are always concerned to re-establish a hyperessentiality with the following strongly worded rejoinder in *L'Idole et la distance*:

> What does 'one knows' mean here? We have seen that, precisely, the so-called negative theology, in its depths, does not aim to re-establish a 'hyperessentiality' [*super-essentialité*], since it aims at neither predication, nor at Being; how, *a fortiori*, could there be a question of existence and essence in Dionysius, who speaks a sufficiently original Greek to see in it neither the idea nor the usage?
>
> (Marion 1977: 318n)

If Dionysius speaks of 'hyperessentiality' in his texts, it is not to re-establish God as a pre-eminent being, as Derrida claims, but to praise Him as absolutely beyond being. For Marion, Derrida is – as bizarre as it sounds – the last of the Thomists because his reading of negative theology as a mode of hyperessentialism assumes far too quickly that God can be subsumed under the sign of a general metaphysics of being. In *L'Idole et la distance*, then, Marion's theological delimitation of deconstruction from the vantage point of negative theology begins to take shape.

God without Being: Hors-Texte

Marion refines and expands his earlier critique of ontotheology in his most famous theological text *God without Being: Hors-Texte* ([1982] 1991). It widens Marion's critique of ontotheology to convict even Heidegger of the very idolatry his fundamental ontology supposedly denounces, namely, the reduction of God to the horizon of being. He criticizes a continuing prioritization of Being in Heidegger's account of theology that leads even the latter to see Being as the necessary backdrop or horizon against which alone God can appear. His contention is that Heidegger's concept of theology as an ontic 'science of faith' still represents an implicitly ontotheological move that makes theology dependent upon the more fundamental ontological project of philosophy which alone, it seems, is able to consider the question of Being. Marion also argues that Heidegger's concept of the Fourfold constitutes a surreptitious double 'idolatry' because it insists that the revelation of God ascends from, and depends on, the *prior* revelation of Being: '[t]his anteriority suffices to establish idolatry' (Marion 1991: 41). For Marion, God is neither the Thomist communal being nor the Heideggerian ontological Being but what he famously calls 'God *without* Being' (stress mine) or, in a further radicalization of, and riposte to, Heidegger, God *sous rature* or Gxd.

Marion's critique of ontotheology paves the way for an entirely new phenomenology of religion based upon a now famous distinction between the idol and the icon. He argues that humanity's attempts to envisage the divine tend to fall into two basic categories. First, he argues that the gazer may see objects as *idols* which are representative of the divine and make its invisibility visible to the naked eye, but Marion contends that the idolic gaze confuses the idol with the divine, the visible symbol with the invisible referent, and thus its encounter with the divine can proceed no further (Marion 1991: 1–16). Marion predictably identifies ontotheological attempts to identify God with being from Plato to Kant as examples of what he brilliantly calls the 'invisible mirror' of idolatry in which the gazer sees nothing other than themselves (Marion 1991: 11). Second, however, Marion claims that the gazer may see the divine as an *icon* which does not reduce the invisible to the visible but rather *saturates* the visible with the invisible divine (Marion 1991: 17–24). If the idol teaches the person who gazes upon it to rest content with the object itself, the icon invites him or her to proceed beyond what is visible into a contemplation of the invisible. The example Marion gives of the icon is Christ, who, in Paul's letter to the Colossians, is described as the visible icon of the invisible God (Colossians, 1:15). There is only one name of God that Marion thinks fits his notion of a non-idolatrous saturating givenness of invisibility and that name is Love or *Agape* (1 John 4:8). This is the only name of God that remains unthinkable by ontotheology because, Marion suggests, it posits God as a gift of unconditional love that requires neither the existence of an abode to accommodate it, nor a recipient to receive it, nor a condition to assure or confirm it (Marion 1991: 47). In this way, Marion's Gxd without being becomes the God of love.

Jean-Luc Marion's theology is ambitious and ground-breaking but it has inevitably raised a number of questions. First, his controversial critique of Aquinas and metaphysical theology, Heidegger and fundamental ontology and Derridean deconstruction as participating in the same process of ontotheologization has prompted criticisms.[1] Second, and more generally, Marion's phenomenology of Christianity in terms of iconology, invisibility and the saturated phenomenon has sparked an ongoing debate about the relationship between phenomenology and theology and particularly the highly ambiguous status of givenness or donation in his work from critics such as Janicaud, Derrida and others.[2] Finally, and perhaps most importantly from our perspective, however, Marion's critique has initiated a wide-ranging discussion of the metaphysical or non-metaphysical status of negative theology in Pseudo-Dionysius. The great benefit of Marion's work has been that it raises the possibility that the God of negative theology does not confirm the metaphysics of presence at all because it is what we have called a *counter-metaphysical* theology. This raises the question of whether negative theology can truly be seen as a target of deconstruction – as Derrida contends in Chapter 1 of this book – or whether it might more accurately be described as a theological form of deconstruction itself. In Derrida's response to Marion, he tackles this critique head on.

Derrida on Pseudo-Dionysius

I want to look at Jacques Derrida's response to Marion's critique in his essay 'How to Avoid Speaking: Denegations' ([1987] 1989a). Jacques Derrida begins his essay by promising to offer the rigorous, differentiated reading of negative theology that he had been promising and postponing since those earliest remarks back in the late 1960s: 'I knew that I wished to speak of the "trace" in its relationship to what one calls, sometimes erroneously, "negative theology"' (Derrida 1989a: 3).

Derrida argues, as we have already seen in Chapter 1, that negative theology remains originally committed to the 'trace' or 'promise' of language so that it cannot help speaking of the supposedly unspeakable. He analyses three different modes, tropes, or paradigms of negation in the essay which are respectively named Greek (Plato's discussion of the *khōra* in the *Timaeus*), Christian (Pseudo-Dionysius's negative theology in *The Divine Names*) and neither Greek nor Christian (Heidegger's distinction between theology and its ontotheological equivalent theology). In Derrida's discussion of Pseudo-Dionysius, which I want to focus on here, he argues that Dionysian theology remains within an explicitly Neoplatonic and hence metaphysical tradition and this brings him into explicit engagement and disagreement with Marion's counter-metaphysical reading of the *via negativa*.

'How to Avoid Speaking'

Derrida focuses, like Marion, on the prayer and encomium that precede Dionysius's *Mystical Theology*. He explicitly takes issue with Marion's claim that his own reading of negative theology is inaccurate because, as we have seen, Dionysius substitutes the language of pure praise for the language of predication. Marion's argument, to summarize, is that Dionysius is not saying something – predicatively – about God so much as saying something – performatively and pragmatically – to God. But Derrida counters that Pseudo-Dionysius's encomium still clearly, explicitly and predicatively directs his prayer not to some absolutely unknowable and transcendent alterity but to no-one other than the trinitarian Christian God. If Pseudo-Dionysius attempts to pray *to* God, in other words, Derrida insists that in his encomium he nevertheless cannot help saying something *of* God as well. Derrida's point is that, without the explicit attribution of Dionysius's prayer to the trinitarian God, it would be impossible to identify it as *Christian* as opposed to anything else:

> How can one deny that, in this movement of determination (which is no longer the pure address of the prayer to the other), the appointment of the *trinitary* and hyperessential God distinguishes Dionysius' *Christian* prayer from all other prayer? To reject this doubtless subtle distinction, inadmissible for Dionysius and perhaps for a Christian in general, is to deny the essential quality of prayer to every invocation that is not Christian. As Jean-Luc Marion correctly remarks, the encomium is 'neither true nor false, not even contradictory,' although it says something *about* the thearchy, about the Good and the analogy; and if its attributions or namings do not belong to the ordinary signification of truth, but rather to a hypertruth that is ruled by a hyperessentiality, in that it does not merge with the movement of prayer itself, which does not speak *of*, but *to*.
>
> (Derrida 1989a: 42)

The larger question for Derrida is whether Dionysius can succeed – as Marion claims he does – in addressing the totality of his discourse purely and non-predicatively towards the goodness of God. There is no doubt that Derrida's answer to this question would be 'no' because, as we have already seen in Chapter 2, the clinching point is that Dionysius's discourse remains originarily beholden to a promise to speak that he must oblige even if he wishes to break it. This originary affirmation or promise of language has always already been made before we open our mouths – it constitutes the possibility of all thought, language and subjectivity whatsoever – even or especially if we wish to remain silent:

> At the moment when the question 'how to avoid speaking?' is raised and articulates itself in all its modalities – whether in rhetorical or logical forms of saying, or in the simple fact of speaking – it is already, so to speak, *too late*. There is no longer any question of not speaking. Even if one speaks and says nothing, even if an apophatic discourse deprives itself of meaning or of an object, it takes place. That which committed or rendered it possible *has taken place*. The possible absence of a referent still beckons, if not towards the thing of which

one speaks (such is God, who is nothing because He takes place, *without* [*sans*] *place, beyond Being*), at least towards the other (other than Being) who calls or to whom this speech is addressed – even if it speaks only in order to speak, or to say nothing. This call of the other, having always already preceded the speech to which it has never been present a first time, announces itself in advance as a *recall*. Such a reference to the other will always have taken place. Prior to every proposition and even before all discourse in general – whether a promise, prayer, praise, celebration. The most negative discourse, even beyond all nihilisms and negative dialectics, preserves a trace of the other.

(Derrida 1989a: 27–8, square brackets mine)

Derrida's response to Marion would, then, place Dionysius's discourse on praise within the larger structure of the pre-originary promise or affirmation of a linguistic situation that we cannot choose or control but must simply inherit and more or less mechanically repeat. First, Derrida's argument is that Dionysius cannot help but speak predicatively of God's transcendence even if he merely wishes to praise Him or even to remain silent altogether because he remains committed to this pre-originary commitment to language. Second, Derrida argues that Dionysius's promise to speak not only belongs to an immemorial past – in the sense that it is the pre-condition of all discourse altogether – but it opens onto an immemorial future as well – because language never arrives at a transcendental signified and is capable of being repeated in a potentially infinite series of new contexts. For Derrida, Dionysius's attempt to address God in silence and secrecy must inevitably open itself to the possibility of repetition in non-silent, non-secret and – nothing excludes this a priori – even non-theological contexts (Derrida 1989a: 48). Finally, and perhaps most importantly, Dionysius's essential commitment to the trace of language is both the *condition* of his prayer in the first place – in the sense that there could be no prayer without it – and the *ruination* of any pure, unique prayer – because prayer will always be open to distortion and contamination:

> Perhaps there would be no prayer, no pure possibility of prayer, without what we glimpse as a menace or as a contamination: writing, the code, repetition, analogy or the – at least apparent – multiplicity of addresses, initiation. If there were a purely pure experience of prayer, would one need religion and affirmative or negative theologies? Would one need a supplement of prayer? But if there were no supplement, if quotation did not bend prayer, if prayer did not bend, if it did not submit to writing, would a theology be possible? Would a theology be possible?
>
> (Derrida 1989a: 62)

92   Theologies

Jacques Derrida's response to Marion reiterates his original critique but it also paves the way for a more complex and multi-faceted reading of negative theology. First, Derrida responds with great force to Marion's original objection that 'in its depths' negative theology did not aim to reestablish a hyperessentiality by pointing to the major role a discourse on hyperessentiality plays in Dionysius's texts:

> What does 'in its depths' mean here? What does it mean that 'negative theology', in its depths, does not aim to reestablish a 'hyperessentiality'? First of all, as Marion knows better than anyone else, it is difficult to consider accidental the reference to this hyperessentiality which plays a major, insistent, and *literal* role in so many texts by Dionysius – and by others, whom I will cite later.
>
> (Derrida 1989a: 64n)

Derrida's position is that Dionysius remains firmly and explicitly committed to the extension of ontology into theology via the concept of hyperessentiality – despite everything Marion says about praise, Gxd without Being and the gift of *Agape* – and to that extent his discourse is ontotheological and thus susceptible to deconstruction. If Marion were allowed a right of reply here, I think he would not contest the *presence* of the term 'hyperessentiality' in Dionysius's texts so much as Derrida's *interpretation* of it as connoting a supreme being beyond being, but we will come back to this point later on. Second, however, Derrida's position is that Dionysius's text – irrespective of the position of its author – is already in a state of deconstruction because it is originarily open to repetition in contexts outside its own choosing. For Derrida, Dionysius's discourse necessarily rather than contingently or accidentally confirms to what Marion calls idolatry because it cannot help speaking of that whereof it wants to remain silent:

> Thus, at the moment when the question 'How to avoid speaking?' arises, it is already too late. There was no longer any question of not speaking. Language has started without us, in us, and before us. This is what theology calls God, and it is necessary, it will have been necessary, to speak.
>
> (Derrida 1989a: 29)

Finally, and perhaps most intriguingly, however, Derrida goes on to imagine a new kind of discourse on negative theology that locates within it a multiplicity of voices both ontotheological and non-ontotheological:

> [I]t is necessary to elaborate an interpretive discourse as interesting and original as that of Marion, at the crossing, in the wake, sometimes beyond thoughts like those of Heidegger, Urs von Balthasar, Lévinas, and some others, to distinguish the 'depths' (the thinking of the gift,

of paternity, of distance, of celebration, etc.) from what in the so-called 'negative theology' still seems to be very concerned with hyper-essentiality.

(Derrida 1989a: 64n)

The essay thus concludes with yet another promise to speak of negative theology – or in this case negative theologies in the plural – that is at least partially fulfilled in the polylogue 'Sauf le nom (Post-Scriptum)' ([1993] 1995a). There is an increasingly obvious sense in Derrida's work that negative theology is a complex, differentiated or pluralized body of thought or work that oscillates between Christian and non-Christian, ontotheological and non-ontotheological, hyperessential and hyperbolic imperatives and this is why it is able to support such radically divergent discourses as that of Heidegger, Urs von Balthasar, Lévinas, Marion or Derrida himself. This demands an interpretive discourse that does not seek to reduce negative theology to a singular or monolithic identity but which opens itself to the plurality of contradictory voices that can be detected within it. In Derrida's reading of Jean-Luc Marion, we discover a new concept of negative theology as a 'a paradoxical writing of the word *without*'.

Derrida and Marion on the third way

I think the main differences between Derrida and Marion are now clear but I want to conclude this summary by briefly mentioning the most recent – if not, I hope, the last – contribution to it. The two philosophers were finally brought together in the same room for a roundtable discussion during a conference on God, the gift and postmodernism at Villanova University in 1997. This occasion afforded them the opportunity to explore the points of agreement and disagreement between their respective analyses of negative theology, pragmatic language, the gift, and so on. In general terms, it seems fair to say that both were more concerned to defend and expand upon their previously held positions, but the similarities and differences between them were certainly clarified and particularly on the question of the so-called third way in Dionysius's texts.

Marion delivered a paper entitled 'In the Name: How to Avoid Speaking of "Negative Theology"' (1999). It reiterates his belief that Derrida is wrong to argue that negative theology seeks to re-establish a hyper-essentiality. Pseudo-Dionysius is actually praising God in a way that goes beyond simple questions of truth or falsity, affirmation or negation:

> [i]t therefore does not contend face-to-face with the affirmative way, as in a duel where the last to enter the fray would be at once the victor over and the heir to the first; for both must in the end yield to a third way.

(Marion 1999: 24)

His name for this third way is 'denomination': the paradoxical process carefully traced in *L'Idole et la distance* and *God without Being* whereby God's radical distance from all names is exposed in the very act of naming Him (Marion 1999: 24–8). Dionysius's mode of negative theology is – again contra Derrida – written in a pragmatic, performative mode of discourse which is always speaking *to* rather than *of* God:

> It is no longer a matter of naming or attributing something to something, but of aiming in the direction of ..., of relating to ..., of comporting oneself towards ..., or reckoning with ... – in short of dealing with ... By invoking the unattainable as ... and inasmuch as ..., prayer definitively marks the transgression of the predicative, nominative, and therefore metaphysical sense of language.
>
> (Marion 1999: 30)

For Marion, Derrida's failure to acknowledge the counter-metaphysical status of negative theology conveniently misses the fact that the *via negativa* historically pre-empts and theologically usurps the exclusive role the latter claims for deconstruction: '[t]here is a powerful argument confirming that it is indeed the theologians themselves who have the most extreme speculative interest in freeing God from any and all inclusion in presence' (Marion 1999: 35).

Derrida responded to Marion's critique of his critique (of his critique ...). His remarks were given orally, briefly, in a foreign language, and in a context where he was clearly keen to emphasize the common ground between their positions but they are still worth noting. He did not re-visit the question of the predicative or performative status of prayer although it may be possible to re-construct a possible critical response based upon his earlier texts.[3] He also postponed the vast problematic of the gift in Marion's work to the last day of the conference when a formal debate between the two thinkers on this topic took place.[4] But Derrida did take time to re-emphasize the fact that his texts on negative theology do not suggest that all negative theology is metaphysical and that they do take account of what Marion calls the third way: '[t]he arguments that he opposed to me, notably around what he calls the third way and denomination, can be found in my own texts' (Caputo 1999: 42). The remainder of his brief response merely noted the extent to which he has taken into account the tripartite nature of Dionysius's remarks on beyond-beingness or hyperessentiality in his deconstruction of negative theology. For Derrida, it is clear that the third way remains within the promise or trace of language and this is perhaps one of the reasons why Derrida seemed less perturbed by Marion's claim that deconstruction had already been done and dusted by theologians fifteen hundred years ago than Marion seemed to think he should have been.[5]

What, to summarize, are the main points of difference in the

Derrida–Marion debate? Derrida himself writes that 'Marion's thought is both very close and extremely distant; others might say opposed' (Derrida 1989a: 65n). Marion responds that 'we agree to a large extent on many issues and nevertheless the questions remain open' (Caputo 1999: 47). It seems fair to say that the debate appears to revolve around four related questions. First, the negative or positive status of *hyperousios*. Second, the predicative or performative status of prayer. Third, and more generally, the theological or non-theological status of the gift and with it the relationship between phenomenology and theology. Finally, and for our purposes most pertinently, the metaphysical or non-metaphysical character of negative theology. The debate between them is important and ongoing and I will sketch some possible future areas for enquiry before concluding. This chapter, however, is only going to focus on Derrida and Marion's very specific disagreement about the meaning of the term '*hyperousios*' – signifying hyperessentiality, beyond being or without being – as a means of getting a purchase on the ambiguous status of negative theology within modern French thought. Can negative theology exceed, go beyond, or go *without* the categories of ontotheology, metaphysics, and even theology itself? In the following section, I want to examine this question in a slightly less provisional way by looking at the Derrida–Marion debate in a little more detail and, in particular, their disagreement about what Derrida calls 'a paradoxical writing of the word *without*' (Derrida 1989a: 64n).

Derrida and Marion on the '*hyperousios*'

I would like to continue, then, by focusing more precisely on Derrida and Marion's conflicting interpretations of Pseudo-Dionysius's use of the word '*hyperousios*' as 'without being'. It is generally accepted that in early texts like 'Différance' Derrida interprets the term in a positive sense, to mean, or at least in the context of, 'beyond' or 'more than' being. Marion does not, to my knowledge, offer any explicit translation of '*hyperousios*' in *L'Idole et la distance* or *God Without Being* but the whole thrust of his argument in those texts tends to assume a different and non-metaphysical understanding of the term: 'the so-called negative theology, in its depths, does not aim to re-establish a "hyperessentiality", since it aims at neither predication, nor at Being'. In my view, Derrida and Marion's different readings of '*hyperousios*' are not simply divergent interpretations but symptomatic of a larger problematic within negative theology.

Jacques Derrida is very consistent in his reading of '*hyperousios*' as a positive term meaning something like 'beyond being'. It could even be argued that his entire reading of negative theology as ontotheological in some sense *depends* upon the intepretation of '*hyperousios*' as signifying a 'superior, inconceivable, and ineffable mode of being' (Derrida 1982a: 6). If 'supereressentiality', as he translates the word in 'Différance', did not mean 'beyond being' and hence designate a supreme being, Derrida would be hard pressed to prove his argument that Pseudo-Dionysius's text remains within the orbit of being, ontotheology and the metaphysics of presence. The consistent argument of a text like 'How to Avoid Speaking: Denegations', for example, is that Marion has no grounds for suggesting that God is somehow without being when Dionysius explicitly and consistently says that He is beyond being: 'it is difficult to consider accidental the reference to this hyperessentiality that plays a major, insistent and *literal* role in so many texts by Dionysius'.

Jean-Luc Marion appears to interpret '*hyperousios*' in a negative sense to mean 'without being'. It was Kevin Hart, in his seminal book *The Trespass of the Sign* (1989), who first argued that Dionysius's '*hyperousios*' has a negative rather than a positive sense, and thus does not mean 'beyond being' at all but something closer to Lévinas's 'otherwise than being' or Marion's 'without being':

> It may be objected that even at the end of *The Mystical Theology* Pseudo-Dionysius makes positive statements about God; in Chapter 5, God is still the transcendent 'superessentiality' addressed in Chapter 2. And if this is so, we cannot rightly say that negative theology is a mode of deconstruction, since deconstruction is always directed against presence. While this objection is pressing when directed to Rolt's translation, it is beside the point when one returns to the actual text of Pseudo-Dionysius. The word Rolt translates by 'superessential' is *hyperousious* [sic]. The English word, when used to describe God, suggests that God is the highest being, that he exists yet in a way which transcends finite beings. The Greek word, however, makes no such claim; indeed, the prefix '*hyper*' has a negative rather than a positive force. To say that God is *hyperousious* [sic] is to deny that God is a being of any kind, even the highest or original being. As Jones remarks, Pseudo-Dionysius denies that God is a being and denies that God is be-ing (*on*). The divinity, he says, is 'beyond be-ing beyond-beingly before all' – or to borrow Lévinas's concise formulation – *otherwise than being*. Given this, Derrida is wrong to say that negative theology reserves a supreme being beyond the categories of being. Just as 'sign' must be crossed out in the deconstruction of metaphysics, so too must 'God' in the deconstruction of positive theology.
>
> (Hart 1989: 202)

Hart goes on to connect Pseudo-Dionysius's negative use of '*hyperousios*' in *The Mystical Theology* with Marion's crossing out of the word 'God' in *God Without Being*: 'J-L Marion, for example, crosses out "*Dieu*" throughout *Dieu sans être* [sic]' (Hart 1989: 199n). Marion's subsequent essay 'In the Name' endorses Hart's non-metaphysical reading of '*hyperousios*' even though, as I have said, his earlier works make no mention of this interpretation of the term (Marion 1999: 27). If Hart's negative translation of '*hyperousios*' as 'otherwise than being' is correct – and, as we will see, this is by no means a simple matter to determine – then the possibility arises that Derrida's positive translation of 'beyond being' may be uncharacteristically inattentive to this ambiguity in the word's meaning. Perhaps Marion's 'without being' may be closer to the counter-metaphysical letter of Pseudo-Dionysius's text than Derrida's 'beyond being'.

Derrida, however, explicitly defends himself against this charge. He offers this alternative definition of the term '*hyperousios*' in 'How to Avoid Speaking': '*hyperousios, -ōs, hyperousiotes*. God as being beyond Being or also God as *without* [sans] Being' (Derrida 1989a: 8). It appears that this inclusion of an alternative translation represents a concession to Marion, but it quickly becomes clear that Derrida actually means something quite different by the term 'without' here. He goes on to argue, in a discussion of Eckhart's reading of Augustine, that 'without' still has an essentially positive and thus ontotheological sense:

> *Without* does not merely dissociate the singular attribution from the essential generality: wisdom as *being*-wise in general, goodness as *being*-good in general, power as *being*-powerful in general. It does not only avoid the abstraction tied to every compound noun and to the being implied in every essential generality. In the same word and in the same syntax it transmutes into affirmation its purely phenomenal negativity, which ordinary language, riveted to finitude, gives us to understand in a word such as *without*, or in other analogous words.
> (Derrida 1989a: 8–9)

The 'without being' should not ultimately be taken in the negative sense of 'outside' or 'lacking' general being, Derrida suggests, but in the hyper-affirmative sense of 'exceeding' or going 'beyond' being. This attempt to demonstrate that the negative interpretation of '*hyperousios*' as 'without being' ultimately leads back to a positive translation could be interpreted as yet another attempt by Derrida to counter and neutralize Marion's critique of his reading of negative theology. For Derrida, then, '*hyperousios*' remains fairly and squarely within the horizon of being and 'ontotheology to be deconstructed'.

Marion has, though, recently renewed his attack on Derrida. His response draws on Hart's recent suggestion that Derrida's affirmative translation of the term still ignores an essential ambiguity between the positive and negative forces at play within it: 'while Derrida acknowledges that the Greek prefix *hyper* can mean both "above" and "beyond" he dwells on the first of these when contemplating being, namely "that which is more" rather than "that which is beyond"' (Hart 1997: 275). Marion's response draws on Hart's point about the *hyper*'s distance from all categories of being to lend support to his own scepticism about Derrida's definition of the '*hyperousios*':

At this point, it is necessary that we be sure of the exact scope of the adverb or suffix υπερ [*hyper*]. First of all, is it equal to the ambiguity of 'without,' an adverb suspected of re-establishing an affirmation? This can be doubted: 'The prefix – υπερ has a negative rather than a positive form [Kevin Hart]'.

(Marion 1999: 27; square brackets mine)

The upshot of this interpretation, Marion suggests, is that Dionysius's negative theology is not 'metaphysics to be deconstructed' but nothing other than deconstruction *itself* fifteen hundred years *avant la lettre*. This fact should give pause to triumphalist readings of deconstruction as a modern corrective to negative theology, Marion rather polemically implies, as if Derrida himself had ever suggested such a thing. In Marion's account, then, to say that God is *hyperousios* 'is to deny God is a being of any kind, even the highest or original being' (Marion 1999: 27).

What, to summarize, is the significance of this apparently rather dry and abstract semantic disagreement? It is not too much of an exaggeration to suggest that the Derrida–Marion debate about negative theology hinges upon their conflicting interpretations of this 'paradoxical writing of the word *without*'. First, Derrida argues that 'without being' carries a positive sense and means 'beyond being' whereas Marion argues that 'without being' carries a negative sense and means something like 'otherwise than being'. Second, Derrida uses his interpretation to argue that negative theology remains within the orbit of the metaphysics of presence whereas Marion uses his to respond that it exceeds the orbit of presence. Finally, Derrida concludes from this that negative theology may be an object of deconstruction whereas Marion comes to the opposite conclusion, namely, that it begins to look more like a subject of deconstruction, a discourse with deconstructive power. The problem with both Derrida's and Marion's accounts of negative theology from my perspective – particularly in the light of what we have witnessed in Chapter 1 – is that they appear to encourage an entirely *monolithic* reading of the *via negativa* as if it could only ever mean one thing. This kind of proprietorial reading – which tries to recruit negative theology to one position or another – entirely misses the pluralistic or hyperbolic dimension of the *via negativa* set out in essays like 'Sauf le nom'. In the remainder of this chapter, I would like to propose that it is impossible to choose between, or even dialectically sublate, the positive and negative dimensions of the '*hyperousios*' in Dionysius's discourse because it points to a radical plurality within negative theology itself.

Derrida and Marion on 'a paradoxical writing of the word '*without*'

I want to introduce my larger argument by situating Derrida's and Marion's reading of the '*hyperousios*' in the context of what Derrida calls a 'paradoxical writing of the word *without*' in Dionysius, Angelus Silesius and Maurice Blanchot. It will be my contention that this interpretation of the 'without' enables us to reconceptualize the Derrida–Marion debate in less dualistic and certainly more constructive terms. In my view, it might be more helpful to stop thinking about the Derrida–Marion debate about negative theology as a debate or even a dialogue – with their implications of logically or dialectically opposed positions which can be sublated or *aufgehoben* – and to start thinking of it as indicative of an aporia 'within' the *via negativa*.

'Pas'

Derrida introduces the quasi-concept of the 'without' or 'sans' in his essay on Maurice Blanchot's *Le Pas au delà* entitled 'Pas' (1986c). His contention is that the term 'without' does not just have the negative force of depriving or denying words of their old meanings but also the positive force of asymmetrically repeating or re-inscribing their old meanings in new contexts:

> If I write, for example: the water without water, what has happened? Or again, a reply without reply? The same word and the same thing seem removed from themselves, taken away from their reference and their identity, while continuing to be left to traverse, in their old body towards an entirely other dissimulated in them. But not [*pas*] more than in *pas*; this operation does not consist simply in depriving or denying, it is necessary in itself.
> (Derrida 1986c: 90; square brackets mine)

Derrida's essay identifies in Blanchot's concept of literature a moment of absolution or interruption at the heart of every identity that in his own work appears under the figure of *différance*, the promise or originary repetition. The 'same' word or thing – to employ the vocabulary Derrida is using here – can only be the 'same' if it is in a process of play between its old body and an entirely new other or 'without' itself. This slippage between positive and negative, old and new, meanings that is set in motion by the system named the 'without' is built into language from the start. There is no question of choosing one meaning over another or of dialectically sublating them in the form of a Hegelian *Aufhebung*. For example, Derrida employs the arresting tripartite negative of expressions like '*pas* without *pas*' and '*without* without *without*' in *The Postcard* (Derrida 1987a: 401) precisely in order to exceed the logic of the double negative, which leads back to the original term in classical logic, or progresses to a third term in Hegelian dialectics. In other words, Derrida argues that the phrase 'X without X' does not return to an original thesis, or proceed to a Hegelian third term but signifies that the thesis contains within it an absolute alterity or transcendence that cannot be re-appropriated by any logical system.

'How to Avoid Speaking: Denegations'

Derrida clearly makes use of this paradoxical logic in 'How to Avoid Speaking'. His reading of negative theology has been occasionally, and in my view rightly, taken to task for concentrating on the positive sense of the '*hyperousios*' at the expense of the negative but more generally he regards the equivocation between the two senses as *a priori*:

> As for the *beyond* (*hyper*) of that which is beyond Being (*hyperousios*), it has the double and ambiguous meaning of what is above in a hierarchy, thus both beyond and more. God (is) beyond Being but as such is more (being) than Being: *no more being* and *being more than Being*: being more.
> (Derrida 1989a: 20)

Derrida's argument makes explicit that the negative force of the term is no longer simply the inferior party in a hierarchy with the positive one but rather appears to have reached a parity of equivocation or undecidability: '*no more being and being more than Being*'. If Marion is sometimes justified in accusing him of concentrating on the positive side of this equivocation at the expense of the negative, Derrida is quite clear that here there is no question of opposing or hierarchizing the two terms: '[t]he French expression *plus d'être* (more being, no more being) formulates this equivocation in a fairly economical manner' (Derrida 1989a: 20). The reason why there is no question of choosing between the double senses of '*hyperousios*', I want to suggest, is that Dionysius's 'without being' is subject to the same aporetic logic as Blanchot's 'without'. There is an uncanny sense in which it remains within the promise of language, in other words, that interrupts or transcends its singular identity from within. This analysis appears to be confirmed by Derrida himself who explicitly mentions Dionysius's 'without' in the context of Blanchot's 'sans' in 'How to Avoid Speaking': '[c]oncerning a paradoxical writing of the word without [sans], notably in the work of Blanchot, I allow myself to refer to the essay "Pas"' (Derrida 1989a: 64n). What, though, are the wider implications of positing this essential undecidability between two radically different voices at the heart of negative theology?

'*Sauf le nom (Post-Scriptum)*'

Derrida explores the larger implications of this radical plurality 'within' negative theology in the fictional dialogue or polylogue 'Sauf le nom: (Post-Scriptum)' ([1993] 1995a). It finally delivers the pluralized, non-monolithic reading of negative theology hinted at in 'How to Avoid Speaking' that is broad enough to encompass the divergent readings of Heidegger, Lévinas, Von Balthasar, Marion and Derrida himself. It consistently argues, as we have already seen in Chapter 1, that negative theology is riven or bifurcated by at least two apparently contradictory set of values: 'How would what still comes to us under the domestic, European, Greek, and Christian term of negative theology, of negative way, of apophatic discourse, be the chance of an incomparable translatability in principle without limit?' (Derrida 1995a: 47). Derrida's text explores the relationship between the secret and the non-secret, the specific idiom and the translation, the ontotheological versus the non-ontotheological, and the European or Eurocentric versus an internationalism or universalism to come that refuses to gather itself into an identity. The essay makes absolutely clear that – whatever our own personal or political perspective might be on European or American imperialism – it is not possible to choose one set of oppositions over another here. There is no possibility of determining negative theology's name one way or another because, as Derrida goes on to confirm, its two different identities appear to inhere in one another in a continuous movement of grounding and deracination:

> [w]hat permits localizing negative theology in a historical site and identifying its very own idiom is also what uproots it from its rooting. What assigns it a proper place is what expropriates it and *engages* it thus in a movement of universalizing translation.
> (Derrida 1995a: 63)

This movement or rhythm of simultaneous appropriation and expropriation is both the basis of whatever more or less stable historical or theological status negative theology does possess and the reason why it can never simply be identical with that status. In the remainder of the text, Derrida goes on to explore the ramifications of this ambiguity in more detail.

Derrida's argument is once again that negative theology is animated by a hyperbolic or self-transgressive dimension that forces it out of its seemingly stable place and identity within Christian Neoplatonism and into new and unpredictable contexts. It is his contention that negative theology is ultimately a house divided against itself, in other words, both contesting and confirming its 'domestic, European, Greek and Christian' origins at the same time:

> In this sense, the principle of negative theology, in a movement of internal rebellion, radically contests the tradition from which it seems to come. Principle against principle. Parricide and uprooting, rupture of belonging, interruption of a sort of social contract, the one that gives rise to the State, the nation, more generally to the philosophical community as rational and logocentric community. Negative theology

uproots itself from there after the fact [*après coup*], in the torsion or conversion of a second movement of uprooting, as if a signature was not countersigned but contradicted in a codicil or in the remorse of a *post-scriptum* at the bottom of the contract. This contract rupture programmes a whole series of analogous and recurrent movements, a whole outbidding of the *nec plus ultra* that calls to witness the *epekeina tes ousias*, and at times without presenting itself as negative theology (Plotinus, Heidegger, Lévinas).

(Derrida 1995a: 67–8; square brackets mine)

It would take a book in itself to unpack the implications of this long and remarkable passage but let me attempt a very prosaic gloss. Derrida's argument is, crudely speaking, once again that negative theology is bifurcated by two contrary impulses, desires or voices that detach it from itself. Negative theology is enabled and disabled, counter-signed and contradicted by the repetition, the supplement or, as he puts it here, the essential *post-scriptum* that it carries within it. On the one hand, he argues that negative theology's faith in the truth of the name, the propriety of the place, the locality of the idiom and so on is the basis for the nation–state and the unified ontotheological and metaphysical community. On the other hand, its simultaneous interrupting, uprooting, or rupturing of the metaphysical principles or values from which it appears to come is the basis for the universalizing – if never absolutely universal – politics that he famously calls the democracy to come.[6] The *via negativa* is in a process of transit or motion between ontotheology and its other(s) but – as far as the Derrida–Marion debate is concerned – the crucial point is that there is no question of fixing its identity or destiny one way or the other. This is because Derrida's consistent argument is that negative theology is inhabited by a deconstructive hyperbolism or transgressiveness that, as we have seen, continually forces it to break with its ostensibly originating contexts and traditions.[7] For Derrida, to employ the logic we have been developing in this chapter, negative theology is without itself, without being, *hyperousios*, indeed, it is 'one of the most remarkable manifestations of this self-difference' (Derrida: 1995a: 71).

Why, to conclude, is negative theology in this seemingly permanent crisis of identity? Who or what gives rise to this paradoxical chorus of competing voices within it? Is it God Himself in all His generosity and goodness? Or is it the 'impassively foreign' non-place of *khōra*? Derrida gives the following remarkable answer in the conclusion to 'Sauf le nom':

– Do we have any choice? Why choose between the two? Is it possible? But it is true that these two 'places', these two experiences of place, these two ways are no doubt of an absolute heterogeneity. One place excludes the other, one (sur)passes the other, one does without the other, one is, absolutely, *without* the other. But what still relates them to each other is this strange preposition, this strange with-without or without-with, *without* [English in original].

(Derrida 1995a: 76; square brackets mine)

It is, Derrida, suggests, impossible to choose between the God of negative theology and the *khōra* of deconstruction. 'Sauf le nom' is one of a number of texts where – notwithstanding the distinctions set up in *Specters of Marx* ([1993] 1994) – Derrida indicates a certain undecidability between God and *khōra*, revelation and revealability and determined and general messianisms that needs to be respected in itself rather than foreclosed.[8] The two experiences of place are of an absolute heterogeneity and mutually exclude one another but *nonetheless* there is a point of chiasmus between them where it becomes impossible to determine which preconditions which. They are connected on a structural level by the 'paradoxical writing of the word *without*' we have been indicating throughout this chapter which – I would suggest – helps us to articulate their simultaneous identity and heterogeneity. There is an undecidability between them which can be accounted for by the logic of originary repetition we have already identified in Derrida's discussion of Blanchot: the same word and the same thing are taken away from themselves while continuing to traverse in their old body towards an entirely other dissimulated in them. This means that negative theology harbours the necessary possibility, the dissimulation of *khōra* within itself and – by the same token – *khōra* cannot completely exclude the ghost or spectre of the *via negativa*. Each is 'with-without or without-with, *without*' the other. Now this is not to suggest that God 'really' is *khōra* or *khōra* is God but that the attempt to identify and distinguish between the two very different forms of alterity forecloses the very otherness they mutually embody. What criteria could we use to safely distinguish between them? Could the God whom we *can* identify, whom we can see and live, the God who does *not* come like a thief in the night or a phenomenon that saturates our intention, still by definition *be* God? And how would it be possible to identify the 'impassively foreign' *khōra*, the non-place of absolute alterity that exceeds all concepts of being and non-being, donation, goodness and generosity, *as such* without turning it into exactly the kind of being beyond being that it opposes?

Jacques Derrida, to summarize, locates a point of undecidability 'inside' negative theology between *agathon*, and *khōra*, the Christian wilderness and the desert in the desert in his essay 'Sauf le nom'. It is this essential undecidability within negative theology itself, I would argue, that licenses Derrida and Marion's conflicting interpretations of the *via negativa* in their earlier work as either metaphysical or counter-metaphysical, ontotheological or non-ontotheological. It is impossible to determine the identity of negative theology – whether it is Christian or non-Christian, ontotheological or non-ontotheological, a determined messianism or a generalized messianic – without foreclosing the 'paradoxical hyperbole' that is its most characteristic feature. For Derrida, then, 'Sauf le nom' represents a move beyond dualistic or antagonistic readings of the *via negativa* and towards the radically pluralized 'interpretive discourse' promised at the end of 'How to Avoid Speaking'. The point of the essay is not to *settle* the meaning of negative theology once and for all, I would argue, but to *unsettle* it, to save negative theology's name for other contexts and other ways of reading. This act of salvation means that the concept of negative theology that emerges after the Derrida–Marion debate is very different from the one with which we began and I would like to conclude this chapter by sketching what form(s) it might potentially take. In Derrida's 'Sauf le nom', to conclude, negative theology is shown to be inherently *without* itself.

Without politics?

I want to conclude this discussion of Derrida and Marion, then, by briefly considering its ramifications for the future of negative theology. It is obvious that the Derrida–Marion debate has a number of still unfolding implications for any future discussion of negative theology from a re-evaluation of God as gift (Horner 2001) to a re-imagining of the liturgy as essentially non-predicative or even incarnational (Smith 2002) but the particular area I wish to focus on here is the political. My suggestion will be that 'the paradoxical logic of the without' we have located within Derrida and Marion's texts makes possible a re-siting of negative theology at the very heart of any responsible political thought or action whatsoever. In Derrida's dramatic and until now little considered words, there is no politics 'without' negative theology (Derrida 1995a: 81).

Marion and the politics of negative theology

Jean-Luc Marion raises the question of the political implications of negative theology in the Christian hermeneutics set out in the final sections of *God Without Being*. He begins with the seemingly tautologous point that Christian hermeneutics differs from all other modes of hermeneutic because they alone address Jesus Christ. Jesus Christ does not simply speak the word of God in the manner of an inspired prophet because He is Himself the Word of God and so He quite literally speaks Himself. Christ abolishes the distinction between the speaker and the spoken, on the one hand, and the text and the referent, on the other, because He is the Word made flesh. The task of Christian hermeneutics is not to attempt to speak the language of God or to propose its own language to speak of God – such as a literary, historical or scientific discourse – but rather to let the Word speak us (or make us speak) in the way that it speaks of and to God (Marion 1991: 143). This means that the basis of Marion's theological hermeneutics is to interpret the written text spoken solely from the perspective of its divine author – from the words to the Word as he neatly puts it – and his paradigm for the event that accomplishes this interpretative leap is the Eucharist.

Marion bases his concept of eucharistic hermeneutics around privileged mystical revelations of Christ such as Luke's account of Jesus's appearance to the disciples on the road to Emmaus (Luke 24:39). He begins by emphasizing the strikingly hermeneutical dimensions of this particular scene in which the two disciples are shown the true meaning of the Paschal event by the revelation and teaching of Jesus Himself. He lays particular stress, however, on the fact that it is only after the disciples have broken bread with Jesus that they stop seeing Him as a stranger and their eyes are opened to His true identity. Marion's argument is that the sharing of the Eucharist is the decisive moment in theological hermeneutics because the presence of Christ alone ensures the passage from the text to its divine referent that he regards to be essential for the correct interpretation of scripture:

> The Eucharist alone completes the hermeneutic; the hermeneutic culminates in the Eucharist; the one assures the other its condition of possibility: the intervention in person of the referent of the text as centre of its meaning, of the Word, outside of the words, to reappropriate them to himself as 'what concerns him, *ta peri heautou*' (24:27).
> (Marion 1991: 150–1)

So Marion's argument is that the Eucharist accomplishes the hermeneutic leap from the text to the Word but his fascinating account nonetheless raises a number of problems that have markedly political implications. The argument that only Christ is qualified to interpret scripture correctly – because He alone is that of which he speaks – raises the question of whether anyone human is capable of understanding His interpretation. There is also the question of where exactly Marion's emphasis on a decidedly transubstantive concept of the Eucharist as the only means to bring about correct theological interpretation leaves non-Catholics. Finally, and more generally, we might ask whether Marion is justified in telescoping all theological hermeneutics into the figure of Christ and in marginalizing literary, historical or political modes of interpretation: is the theological referent simply something to be received rather than something to be taught, debated or even – God forbid – questioned?

Marion's account does go on to provide a number of further criteria whereby the theologian may approach a correct theological hermeneutics but these do not really address the problems raised above. He argues that the theologian must participate fully in the hermeneutical community which, of course, must be defined by participation in the Eucharist. He locates Eucharistic participation within an identifiably Catholic

106 *Theologies*

ecclesiastical hierarchy that reaches its apex with the person Marion calls the 'theologian *par excellence*' (Marion 1991: 152) or the Bishop. It is Marion's view that the Bishop is what we might call the hypertheologian because His authority guarantees the legitimacy of the celebrant, the celebrant's performing of the Eucharist, and the theological hermeneutics that the Eucharistic sacrament makes possible:

> If, first, theology, as *theo*logy attempts the hermeneutic of the words in view, hence also, from the point of view of the Word, if the Eucharist offers the only correct hermeneutic site where the Word can be said in person in the blessing, if finally only the celebrant receives authority to go beyond the words as far as the Word, because He alone finds himself invested by the *persona Christi*, then one must conclude that *only the bishop merits, in the full sense, the title of theologian.*
> (Marion 1991: 153)

Marion goes on to explain what he recognizes is a controversial position by drawing on Pseudo-Dionysius's claim in *The Divine Names* that the divine Hierotheus became a theologian not simply through training but through experience and suffering (Marion 1991: 155). The ground of correct theological interpretation is not a social, pedagogical or communal relationship with others, to put it another way, but a real relationship with the living referent Himself. There is no way of teaching or learning theological hermeneutics, Marion insists, because they can only be received in a mystical encounter with Christ: 'the referent is not taught, since it is encountered by mystical union' (Marion 1991: 155). This mystical experience can only take place in the ritual of the Eucharist that is performed by the celebrant who is, in turn, legitimized by the authority of the Bishop:

> [w]ith this mystical experience, the morality or private virtues of the theologian are not first at stake, but above all his competence acquired in the matter of charity, in short of knowing the Word nonverbally, in flesh and Eucharist. *Only the saintly person knows whereof he speaks in theology, only he that a bishop delegates knows whereof he speaks.*
> (Marion 1991: 155)

Why, to beg the obvious question, is Marion so sure that the bishop always necessarily knows whereof he speaks in the first place?

Jean-Luc Marion's eucharistic hermeneutics are arguably the single most controversial aspect of a deeply controversial theological project. Its insistence on the primacy of the bishop as the anchor of eucharistic hermeneutics has been strongly criticized for advocating a certain mystical or theological authoritarianism by John D. Caputo, Richard Kearney and others.[9] The argument displays such an enormous confidence that the ecclesiastical leaders of the Church will always be the best hermeneutic readers and will not abuse their positions of interpretative authority that it may seem at best naïve and at worst a kind of apologia for theological absolutism to more sceptical eyes. There is no doubt that Marion would accept that eucharistic participation, ecclesiastical communities and authorities are just as vulnerable to abuse as any other structure but this makes it all the more strange that he should depend on them so exclusively as his hermeneutical insurance policy. This raises the question of whether a kind of politico-theological absolutism – in which the mystical encounter with Gxd without Being is shielded by a praetorian guard of priests and bishops – is the *only* politics of negative theology on offer here. Does negative theology's investment in the *hyperousios* always lead it to a hyperpolitics, a disturbingly absolutist political certitude or might there be another way of reading the *via negativa* politically?

Derrida and the politics of negative theology

Jacques Derrida focuses in detail on the political implications of negative theology in the essay 'How to Avoid Speaking'. He begins by rehearsing a charge that has historically been laid at the door of negative theology, and more recently of deconstruction, namely, that it is a form of secret society, clique, or brotherhood that reserves a secret truth or pseudo-truth for itself and excludes all those who do not share that secret. His claim is that, in the eyes of their accusers, negative theologians are 'terrorists' who 'organize themselves around a social power founded on the magic of a speech that is suited to speaking in order to say nothing' and whose 'alleged secret belongs to sham, mystification, or at best to a politics of grammar' (Derrida 1989a: 19). Derrida is keen to disassociate himself from the pejorative nature of these remarks but, like Marion, he is not averse to reading negative theology as the site for a potentially authoritarian politics of identity in the remainder of the essay. Derrida's essay refers to negative theology as a 'politopology' (Derrida 1989a: 21) and a 'topolitology of the secret' (Derrida 1989a: 23) in which the allegorical figures of theological rhetoric are 'a political shield, the solid barrier of a social division; or, if you prefer, a *shibboleth*' (Derrida 1989a: 24). The danger of negative theology is that it gives rise to a hierarchical and ultimately authoritarian politics, Derrida argues, in which the sacred truth divides bishops and priests, priests and laity, Christians and non-Christians, believers and non-believers. This Derridaean scepticism about the political power that resides within theological hermeneutics obviously stands in sharp contrast, although he does not mention this, to Marion's faith in the Bishop as the master Hermeneut.

Derrida does not simply identify negative theology with this authoritarian mode of politics, however, but characteristically seeks to uncover other political resources within it that are worth recovering and re-evaluating. He opposes Marion's reading of a monolithic theological hermeneutic that is guaranteed by an ecclesiastical hierarchy with a more fluid and multi-faceted *polis*. It is Derrida's consistent argument, as we have already seen, that negative theology is never singular, always multiple, spreading in different directions at the same time and this case is no exception. He argues that negative theology's 'topolitology of the secret' intersects with another *topos*, and another *polis*, that does not place such a high political price upon secrecy. Negative theology is consistently bifurcated by 'a double tradition, a double mode of transmission [*ditten paradosin*]' of secrecy and non-secrecy. On the one hand, negative theology is 'unspeakable, secret, prohibited, reserved, inaccessible', with all the political implications of exclusivity this involves. On the other hand, it must be 'philosophic, demonstrative [*apodeiktiken*], capable of being shown' (Derrida 1989a: 24) and this, too, has obvious political implications. Finally, and most importantly of all, Derrida again insists that the critical question here is not a matter of *choosing* between these two modes of politics but of inventing another mode, law, or politics that does justice to their contradictory imperatives: 'The critical question evidently becomes: How do these two modes relate to each other? What is the law of their reciprocal translation or of their hierarchy? What would be its institutional or political figure?' (Derrida 1989a: 24).

Derrida's 'Sauf le nom' picks up this – unanswered – question of what we might even call a 'third way' between the two modes of politics that bifurcate negative theology. He expands the idea of the double politics of secrecy and non-secrecy to encompass the political relationships between the local and the universal, the European and the international, between current democracy and what Derrida increasingly calls the democracy to come (Derrida 1995a: 47). It is clear from the preceding discussion that Derrida again sees no possibility of *choosing* between the European, Greek and Christian politics of negative theology, on the one hand, and the universalizing politics of negative theology, on the other, but of *inventing* a new mode of the political that does justice to both. Derrida goes on, however, to make the dramatic, unprecedented and rather dangerous claim that this new kind of *politics* (*la politique*) of negative theology might even constitute a model for the *political* (*le politique*) as such:

> – Would you go as far as to say that today there is a 'politics' and a 'law' of negative theology? A juridico-political lesson to be drawn from the possibility of this theology?
> – No, not to be drawn, not to be deduced as from a program, from premises or axioms. But there would no more be any 'politics', 'law', or 'morals' *without* this possibility, the very possibility that obliges us from now on to place these words between quotation marks. Their sense will have trembled.

– But you admit at the same time that 'without' and 'not without' [*pas sans*] are the most difficult words to say and to hear/understand, the most unthinkable or most impossible.

(Derrida 1995a: 81)

What does Derrida mean when he says that there would be no politics 'without' negative theology? First, he makes absolutely clear that he is not canvassing for any simple political theology and indeed his work consistently criticizes such gestures in Patočka (Derrida 1995b), Schmitt (Derrida 1997b), or Lévinas (Derrida 1999a), not to mention Marion. He contends that it is precisely because negative theology does not offer one simple ethical, juridical or theological message to be deduced or implemented that it is of political value, because if it did so it would turn the political into an automatic gesture of administrative or application and thereby deprive it of all responsibility for its decision-making. Far from sponsoring some specious political theology, negative theology represents the chance of a politics precisely because it does not offer a simple pathway between the contradictory and irreconcilable dimensions of the singular and the universal, the hegemonic and the democratic or, more generally, the conditional and the unconditional that constitute the field of the political. If negative theology contains a juridico-political lesson, it is because it represents an obligation to respect a multiple, irreconcilable and yet inseparable set of imperatives in a way that does the least violence to any of them. Finally and most importantly, Derrida sees negative theology as offering the chance of what we have called a politics of the 'mad' decision, 'impossible decision' or decision without criteria which does not subsume itself under a pre-determined concept of the political but rather seeks to invent the criteria by which it can do justice to the other:

> The difficulty of the 'without' spreads into what is still called politics, morals, or law, which are just as threatened as promised by apophasis. Take the example of democracy, of the idea of democracy, of democracy to come (neither the Idea in the Kantian sense, nor the current, limited, and determined concept of democracy, but democracy as the inheritance of a promise). Its path passes perhaps today in the world through (across) the aporias of negative theology that we just analysed so schematically.
> – How can a path pass through aporias?
> – What would a path be without aporia? Would there be a way [*voie*] without what clears the way there where the way is not opened, whether it is blocked or still buried in the nonway? I cannot think the notion of the way without the necessity of deciding there where the decision seems impossible. Nor can I think the decision and thus the responsibility there where the decision is already possible and

programmable. And would one speak, could one only speak of this thing? Would there be a voice (*voix*) for that? A name?

(Derrida 1995a: 83)

The radically undecidable status of negative theology – permanently caught between the singularity of God and the universality of being, the demand for secrecy and the necessity of pedagogy, the fidelity to theological tradition and the hyperbole that suspends every thesis, belief or doxa – cannot be resolved and calls for a decision. There is an exemplary sense in which negative theology offers a model for negotiating between the contradictory demands of the political more generally – the singular and the universal, the current juridico-political concept of democracy and a democracy to come that exceeds every concept of the term, the conditional contexts in which politics must take place and the unconditional appeal to justice that stops it from ossifying into a simple *realpolitik* – by making possible a politics of this decision. This decision is the only responsible mode of the political because it seeks to suspend any criteria to which it could have recourse and accede to the absolute singularity and contingency of the event that demands decision: 'Would there be a voice (voix) for that? A name?'. For Derrida, as we will see in Chapter 6, this politics could be described under the figure of hospitality to the totally other.

Jacques Derrida does not offer a *politics* of negative theology, to summarize, so much as introduce a certain *apophasis* into the political as such. He argues that (1) negative theology is the basis for a Graeco-Christian political desire for a secret or exclusive community governed by a secret that is entrusted only to those who understand it correctly; (2) negative theology is also the basis for a more radical political desire for a universal community or democracy that exceeds the still too limited political interpretations of those terms; and, more generally, (3) negative theology is in some sense the basis for a reconceptualization of the political as the impossible decision between the singular and the universal, the finite and the infinite and the conditional and the unconditional. If we might half-seriously describe this as Derrida's own third way – to rival the tripartite structure of Pseudo-Dionyius's own theology – it does not posit a *hyperousios*, a hypertheology and a hyperpolitics but attempts to maintain the plurality, contingency and undecidability of the politics of negative theology. The politics of negative theology handed down part and parcel from an ultimate referent and guaranteed by an ecclesiastical hierarchy, in other words, is translated into a *via negativa* of politics whose premises and *telos* cannot be determined as such but only more or less contingently decided and invented every time. This gesture transforms negative theology from a political absolutism designed to be followed unquestioningly and therefore irresponsibly by a select few because '*only he that a bishop delegates knows whereof he speaks*' (Marion 1991: 155) into a task that lies at the heart of all responsible political thought and action whatsoever. In Derrida's words, there is no politics 'without' negative theology.

Conclusion

Jean-Luc Marion's thought contains within it what Derrida calls a 'paradoxical writing of the word *without*'. It is my contention, to paraphrase Derrida, that Marion's reading of negative theology is removed from itself, taken away from its reference and identity, while continuing to be left to traverse in its old body towards an entirely other dissimulated within it. Marion's attempt to imagine an absolutely heterological concept of God without Being, in other words, is permanently vulnerable to collapsing back into being, into language, into the possibility of repetition in contexts not of its choosing. The fact that Marion's thought could be said to succumb to the very mode of ontotheological idolatry he has so brilliantly diagnosed in others is not so much a criticism of his account of the *via negativa* – there is no question of a choice here – as an invitation to imagine it differently. There is a sense in which Derrida saves Marion's reading of negative theology from the philosophical and ultimately political absolutism of the saturating givenness of the *hyperousios* by opening it up to non-Catholics, non-Christians, to 'an incomparable translatability in principle without limit' (Derrida 1995a: 47). This reading demonstrates that there is no simple way to draw the line between what is negative theology and what is not, who negative theology belongs to and who it does not, which sphere it belongs to and which it does not, and that such a situation does not simply represent a challenge to purely theological readings of the *via negativa* but also an opportunity to re-locate it within nominally secular areas of debate from which it has long since been evacuated: 'each time it leaves you without ever going away from you' (Derrida 1995a: 85). In Jean-Luc Marion's theology, this 'paradoxical writing of the word *without*' resonates.

Part III
Atheologies

This Part moves on to examine the impact of negative theology on the work of the philosopher and historian of ideas, Michel Foucault, and the pyschoanalyst and linguist, Julia Kristeva. It argues that Foucault and Kristeva seek to distinguish their own discourses from any implication of negative theology by attempting to historicize or psychoanalyse what they see as the transcendental implications of the *via negativa*. Just as Certeau and Marion are unable to save negative theology for Christian orthodoxy, however, Foucault and Kristeva are unable to preserve their own ostensibly secular discourses from any trace of the *via negativa*. The argument of this Part is that Foucault and Kristeva's work prematurely forecloses the relationship between their work and the *via negativa* and that their projects contain traces of the same transcendental assumptions they attribute to negative theology. In this Part, then, saving the name of negative theology means saving it from a secularism that is every bit as violent as its theological counterpart and, once again, opening the *via negativa* to a future that remains to come.

4 Foucault and 'the thought from the outside'

> It will one day be necessary to try to define the fundamental forms and categories of this 'thought from the outside'. It will also be necessary to try to retrace its path, to find out where it comes to us from and in what direction it is moving. One might assume that it was born of the mystical thinking that has prowled the confines of Christianity since the texts of the Pseudo-Dionysius: perhaps it survived for a millennium or so in the various forms of negative theology.
>
> (Foucault 1987a: 16)

Michel Foucault describes Maurice Blanchot's work as a 'thought from the outside' in his famous 1966 essay on the novelist and philosopher. He briefly ponders whether Blanchot's thought is a modern form of negative theology before going on to emphatically reject the charge. Foucault's own work from the 1960s onwards invites superficial comparisons with negative theology on a number of levels. It frequently concerns itself with what is negated or repressed within rational discourses on madness, illness, knowledge or sexuality. It often takes the form of a negative work, or as Foucault himself puts it, an archaeological labour, painstakingly stripping away layer upon layer of discourse in order to arrive at its object. More interestingly still, it is becoming increasingly possible to detect a 'theological turn' in Foucault's own work with, say, the exploration of Christian confession in the first volume of the *History of Sexuality* ([1976] 1979a). The suggestion that Foucault's historical archaeologies could be described as modern versions of Christian negative theologies has, however, been rejected by Foucault himself on the grounds that the two discourses are in fact diametrically opposed to each other. This chapter seeks to explore Foucault's relationship to negative theology across a range of texts from his earliest analysis of the *via negativa* in his archaeologies of madness and knowledge to his later work on the politics of confession. If we want to get a firmer purchase on Foucault's relation to negative theology, we need to set some perimeters for our enquiry at the outset. What exactly does Foucault mean by the 'thought from the outside'? How

116   *Atheologies*

does it differ from that thought from the inside 'that has prowled the confines of Christianity since the texts of the Pseudo-Dionysius'? And, perhaps most importantly of all, can the distinction between exteriority and interiority be maintained in the way Foucault suggests it can? In this chapter, I want to suggest that Foucault's attempt to develop a thought from the outside has a tendency to *turn into* a thought from the inside and that this situation has implications for our understanding of the relationship between his work and negative theology.

Foucault on negative theology

I want to begin this chapter by briefly introducing Foucault's reading of negative theology. It is first vital to place Foucault's understanding of the negative way within the context of his overall reading of religion. My main intention, however, will be to focus on Foucault's critique of the *via negativa* in 'The Thought from the Outside' ([1966] 1987a) and other contemporaneous work. The argument will make explicit a number of potentially interesting – and previously undiscussed – parallels between Foucault and Derrida's readings of negative theology in the late 1960s. They both see negative theology as a form of dialectical negation which is concerned with uncovering a superior affirmation; both try to disassociate it from supposedly non-dialectical discourses by members of the French literary avant-garde such as Georges Bataille and Maurice Blanchot and, perhaps most importantly, both posit it as a thought from the interiority of metaphysics that must therefore be opposed to their own respective thoughts from the 'outside'. This is not quite the whole story, however, because there are also a number of important differences between the two thinkers on the topic of negative theology which, as we will see, hinge on the question of whether it is ever entirely possible to establish a mode of thought that is simply *outside* metaphysics. In Foucault's account, negative theology is a thought from the inside that must be opposed to his own thought from the outside but the veracity of this claim needs to be tested.

Foucault and religion

Michel Foucault is undoubtedly one of the most famous and influential French thinkers of the past 30 years or so but his work on religion has been neglected until recently. It seems that his journalistic reputation as the contemporary Marx or Nietzsche, the ultimate 'death of God' atheist, is now beginning to be revised thanks to the labours of critics like Bernauer (1990), Caputo (1993) and Carrette (2000). First, it is becoming increasingly clear just how much Foucault's work is the product of a strong Christian and more particularly a Catholic intellectual background as much as a neo-Hegelian or Nietzschean one. More generally, his many local arguments about the question of religion across a wide range of texts from the

1960s to the 1980s are now finally beginning to merit the same attention as the readings of madness, illness, history, and so forth: Foucault's analysis of religion stretches from explorations of mysticism and negative theology as experiences of the 'outside' roughly analogous to the avant-garde literature of Blanchot, Philippe Sollers and the *nouvelle romanciers* in the 1960s to (published and unpublished) studies of the politics of Christian confession as a technology of subjectivity in the late 1970s and 1980s. Perhaps most importantly, however, these myriad local arguments are now gradually beginning to be pieced together into what seems to be a remarkably ambitious and wide-ranging reading of 'the question of religion' as such. Foucault's reading of religion has, as we will see, been described as an attempt to re-evaluate and atomize 'the religious' as less a set of beliefs and more as an immanent political experience that attempts to govern or regulate human life. The religious reading of Michel Foucault affirms the remarkable depth and generosity of his engagement with religious questions – and rescues it from an increasingly ossified, predictable set of readings and interpretations – but it falls far short of converting Foucault to Christianity or any other religion. There is no doubt that Foucault's work on the Christian tradition reveals a thinker more deeply committed to religious questions than anyone had previously imagined but it is characterized throughout by a very familiar hermeneutics of suspicion. This philosopher remains a self-confessed atheist, suspicious of the transcendental truth claims of Christianity and the power structures that inevitably lie behind them, and keen to develop a site of potential opposition to them that does not merely reinforce or collapse back into what it opposes. For Foucault, as we will see, Christianity is an essentially socio-political institution that requires a correspondingly socio-political critique.

'*Maurice Blanchot: The Thought from the Outside*'

Foucault begins his reading of negative theology, and by extension Christianity more generally, in the essay 'Maurice Blanchot: The Thought from the Outside' ([1966] 1987a). It is part of a larger discussion of transgression in contemporary French literature that encompasses Blanchot, Bataille, Roussel, Robbe-Grillet and Sollers among other writers. He begins by toying with the idea that Blanchot's thought might be a modern form of negative theology in the essay before quickly going on to dismiss the idea out of hand:

> Yet nothing is less certain: although this experience involves going 'outside of oneself,' this is done ultimately in order to find oneself, to wrap and gather oneself in the dazzling interiority of a thought that is rightfully Being and Speech, in other words, Discourse, even if it is the silence beyond all language and the nothingness beyond all being.
> (Foucault 1987a: 16)

Foucault's brief but tantalizing critique of negative theology here is worth teasing out in a little more detail because it offers an excellent insight into his critique of religion more generally. First, it is worth noting that it shares a number of important parallels with Derrida's roughly contemporaneous reading of negative theology as merely 'a phase of positive ontotheology' (Derrida 1978c: 337n). Negative theology, Foucault argues, goes outside itself purely in order to find itself again. The negative way transgresses the order of being, speech and the interiority of the subject, he suggests, purely in order to reinforce them as divinely orientated. There is a sense in which negative theology's abjection or dissolution of the self before God is merely a means towards re-affirming and re-unifying that self as grounded in God, Foucault implies, and it could certainly be argued that Julian of Norwich, Teresa of Avila and John of the Cross describe how the self must be negated, detached or annihilated in order to reach its true centre or ground as a soul that exists in a non-differentiated union with God. This means that the *via negativa* is not ultimately negative or transgressive at all because it is always concerned with dialectically re-appropriating its negations into a higher positivity, or, as Foucault puts it, to wrap and gather oneself in the dazzling interiority of a thought that is rightfully Being and Speech.[1] So Foucault sees negative theology as what he would later call a technology or politics of the self whose supposed movement outside language, the subject and the object only serves to confirm the unity and integrity of the interiority of being, speech and the individual.

Foucault's argument goes on to expand this critique of negative theology or mysticism (he seems, rather problematically, to use the terms interchangeably) by comparing Pseudo-Dionysius and Maurice Blanchot's respective discourses in a little more detail. It is an interesting comparison not so much for the accuracy or inaccuracy of Foucault's account of the two authors but for his own thoughts on the relationship between them. His uncompromising position is that, despite certain superficial similarities which he does not go into, Dionysius's negative theology could not be more different from Blanchot's thought from the outside:

> Despite several consonances, we are quite far from the experience through which some are wont to lose themselves in order to find themselves. The characteristic movement of mysticism is to attempt to join – even if it means crossing the night – the positivity of an existence by opening a difficult line of communication with it. Even when that existence contents itself, hollows itself out in the labour of its own negativity, infinitely withdrawing into a lightless day, a shadowless night, a visibility devoid of shape, it is still a shelter in which experience can rest. The shelter is created as much by the law of a Word as by the open expanse of silence. For in the form of the experience, silence is the immeasurable, inaudible, primal breath

from which all manifest discourse issues; or speech is a reign with the power to hold itself in silent suspense.

The experience of the outside has nothing to do with that. The movement of attraction and the withdrawal of the companion lay bare what precedes all speech, what underlies all silence: the continuous streaming of language. A language spoken by no-one: any subject it may have is no more than a grammatical fold.

(Foucault 1987a: 53–4)

Foucault sets up an opposition between negative theology and the thought from the outside here that helps to clarify our understanding of both. First, it is clear that there is a *historical* distinction to be drawn between the two: Dionysius's thought has survived for two millennia whereas Blanchot's is still in the process of being born. Second, there is a key *linguistic* difference between the mode of transgression they affirm: Dionysius's thought confirms the silent interiority of a subject, as we have already seen, while Blanchot's is the subjectless and objectless anonymity of 'the continuous streaming of language'. Finally, and more generally, there is a larger *philosophical* divergence between the two forms of negativity: Dionysius's negative theology dialectically converts negativity into positivity whereas Blanchot's is what we might call a Bataillean negativity without reserve. The two forms of thoughts are historically, linguistically and philosophically opposed to one another upon Foucault's reading, then, and this explains his reluctance to entertain any hasty comparison or identity between them. There are again clear points of comparison between Foucault's critique of mysticism as a mode of dialectics (which ultimately serves to affirm rather than negate) and Derrida's critique of negative theology as a Bataillean restricted economy (which spends its funds only in order to recoup them further down the line) although we should be wary of forcing the parallel. For Foucault, to summarize, Pseudo-Dionysius's negative theology is a thought from the inside that is diametrically opposed to Blanchot's thought from the outside and this is why comparisons between the two discourses cannot be allowed to stand.

Foucault's critique of negative theology

Michel Foucault's critique of negative theology went almost unnoticed for 30 years but it has provoked considerable controversy in the past decade or so. It has been interpreted as everything from an explicit disavowal of the *via negativa* to an attempt to re-appropriate it for secular ends and Foucault himself has been styled as everything from a contemporary *Aufklärer* to – as unlikely as it sounds – some kind of *soi-disant* 'modern mystic'. My intention at this stage is simply to get as good a purchase on Foucault's reading of the *via negativa* as possible, however, and postpone any questions of judgement until later on. Let me set out some questions to be picked up and considered in more detail in the remainder of the chapter.

First, I think we need to at least register a concern about Foucault's particular reading of the *via negativa* as merely confirming the unity and integrity of the subject. I am not suggesting for one moment that negative theology is not on some level a question of socio-political power – it would be stupid to pretend otherwise – but it is possible to take issue with the blanket nature of Foucault's assertions. It is striking that Foucault of all people should make such a sweepingly a-historical claim about negative theology – as if there were only ever one and it remained the same throughout history – but he repeats it even more starkly and polemically in an interview with a Buddhist priest more than ten years later: 'Christian mysticism concentrates on individualization' (Carrette 1999: 112). Foucault seems to argue that the supposed mystic escape from the self into a union with God is merely a means of divinely validating the subject as a unitary individual, but there has to be some question about whether mysticism provides the kind of transcendental anchor for essentially immanent epistemological beliefs that he claims it does. Foucault's implication is that Christian mysticism can be read as confirming a transcendentalized and individualized subjectivity but it is not at all clear that mysticism is as monolithic as he wants it to be. The assertion of a fundamental non-contradiction or identity between self and other – where I am not what I am – is not necessarily recuperable in terms of an accepted or enforced individualization. This mystical concept of the self's ground *being* an other is absolutely central to Christian mysticism but it is one that could only appear paradoxical to an accepted or imposed concept of individual subjectivity (Certeau 1986: 96). There are grounds for developing a structural comparison between the mystical subject of Pseudo-Dionysius, St John of the Cross, St Teresa and others – in which the basis of subjectivity is a divine alterity that calls the subject's own self-understanding into question rather than confirms it – and the continental subject of Derrida, Kristeva and even Foucault – in which the basis of subjectivity is a linguistic, psychoanalytic or socio-historical alterity that confounds the logic of subject and object (Jantzen 1995; Carlson 1998). Could Foucault's concept of mysticism as a technology of the self possibly miss a potential *critique* of subjectivity within the mystical experience that ironically bears certain resemblances to his own?

Second, I would also want to raise a question about Foucault's possibly simplistic definition of negative theology as a discourse by a subject directed towards an object that supposedly stands in contrast to Blanchot's subjectless and objectless streaming of language. I think Foucault is absolutely correct to characterize Blanchot's theory and practice of literature in this way but my concern is once again whether there is a tendentious understanding of the linguistics of the *via negativa* going on here.

Negative theology is frequently criticized by Derrida and other philosophers as a mode of positive theology or ontotheology that remains absolutely committed to a system whereby a subject predicates an object. But negative theology, as we have already seen, is a complex and multi-faceted phenomenon that resists such simple and reductive readings. The negative theological discourse is almost definitively sceptical of the credibility of metaphysical concepts that simply assume a transparent relationship between signifier and signified, name and thing, *logos* and *theos*, and so on. This is particularly explicit in the case of Pseudo-Dionysius's 'third way' which seeks to bypass the concept of language as a predicative or instrumental discourse by a subject on an object, as we have seen in the discussion of Jean-Luc Marion, by positing a subject overtaken by an intuition that exceeds all intention who speaks pragmatically of an object who can never be predicated as such (Marion 1999: 32). If it is premature to assume that Dionysius's third way achieves what it sets out to do, Foucault's admittedly brief critique of negative theology is still vulnerable to the accusation that Marion later levels so famously (and incorrectly) against Derrida, namely, that he does not even notice that there *is* a third way beyond the kataphatic and apophatic approaches. More positively, it is again possible to contend that Foucault misses – whether intentionally or unintentionally – potential points of converse between the *via negativa* and historical archaeology: both advertise themselves as a highly pragmatic, historically contingent mode of discourse that would never wish to be mistaken (even if they sometimes are) for universal descriptions of a prior, a-historical 'real'. Could we offer a more positive account of the relationship between negative theological discourse and Foucault's own avowedly anti-theological archaeological or genealogical method?

Finally, let me raise another concern about Foucault's more general account of the opposition between negative theology and its other(s). I want to consider Foucault's account of negative theology at face value rather than question it from any external theological perspective because my contention will be that *even on his own uncompromising terms* the *via negativa* is closer to his own work than he might think. It is first necessary to place Foucault's reading of the *via negativa* against the more general backdrop of the relationship between the thought from the inside and the thought from the outside in Western philosophy and literature. My claim will be that it is possible to detect an interesting oscillation between two different accounts of the relationship between interiority and exteriority in Foucault's text which we might designate as 'historical' and 'transcendental' respectively.

On the one hand, Foucault is concerned to define the relationship between the inside and the outside *historically* by demonstrating that the difference between the two appears at a determinate historical moment or moments. To begin with, Foucault is apparently quite willing to offer what is, in this supposedly non-dialectical context, a very Hegelian history of the thought from the outside that stretches from Sade through Nietzsche before reaching its culmination in Blanchot. Foucault goes on to discuss twentieth-century avant-garde literature in a remarkably restless, urgent and even apocalyptic tone that insists on the absolute contemporaneity – the here and now – in which he is writing (Foucault 1987a: 16). Foucault's argument is that the thought from the outside possesses an identifiable historical genealogy which sees it gradually begin to gather force throughout the nineteenth century before decisively breaking through the interior at a specific historical moment in the contemporary period with Blanchot: 'he is that thought itself' (Foucault 1987a: 16). If Foucault often seems to be describing the birth of the outside in historical terms, though, there are also occasions in his texts when it resists such precise historical identification with a particular time, place or event and this is where the interesting hesitation in his texts I just mentioned begins to make itself felt.

On the other hand, Foucault often expresses a certain unease about whether the relationship between the inside and the outside can be accounted for in such simple empirical terms and suggests that it is extremely difficult to find a language faithful to this thought without 'leading the experience of the outside back to the dimension of interiority' (Foucault 1987a: 21). Foucault expresses similar concerns in 'A Preface to Transgression' (1999a), 'The Prose of Acteon' (1999b) and other contemporaneous texts about the difficulty of maintaining or articulating the force of exteriority without lapsing back into the interiority it seeks to transgress. Foucault's admission about the extreme difficulty of doing justice to the thought from the outside in language certainly sits uneasily alongside his earlier claim that this thought is now finding multiple expression at diverse points of culture including even the 'simple gesture of writing' and suggests another less explicit and normative set of criteria for definition at work (Foucault 1987a: 16). The real or apparent contradiction between 'historical' and 'trans-historical' or 'transcendental' accounts tends to be glossed over by Foucault himself in 'The Thought from the Outside' – inasmuch as he seems to see it as simply a question of imprecise use of language which can be corrected if only we take a little more care – but it does seem to encroach upon his work with a frequency that seems more than accidental. This results in a situation in which the outside always seems to exist in a *tension* with the inside and, as we have perhaps already begun to see, Foucault is compelled to maintain a permanent vigilance to stop the one collapsing into the other. Why, to raise one final question we will have to come back to later on, does this strange oscillation between *historical* and what we might call *quasi-transcendental* conditions of possibility occur in Foucault's account of negative theology?

Michel Foucault argues, to summarize, that Blanchot's thought from the outside stands in linguistic, philosophical and historical opposition to a dialectical thought from the inside that includes negative theology. My claim, however, will be that the opposition between the two is fraught with difficulty as Foucault draws it here and requires further consideration. It is my intention in the next section to pursue the comparison between Foucault and Derrida's analyses in a more sustained fashion by considering their famous debate about Descartes and madness. For me, Derrida's insistence on the impossibility of a thought that is simply 'outside' metaphysics calls Foucault's historical opposition between the outside and the inside into question. The Derridaean approach sees the tensions in Foucault's historicist philosophy less as empirical accidents to be admitted and thus resolved or neutralized and more as structural necessities. This complex relationship between the outside and the inside in Foucault and Derrida has, I think, potentially important implications for our understanding of the relationship between Michel Foucault's work and negative theology. In summary, I have suggested that Foucault fends off negative theology as a thought from the inside which is linguistically, philosophically and historically opposed to his own thought from the outside, but in the next section I want to show how Derrida argues that Foucault's outside is always already *inside* (Derrida 1976: 46–55).

Derrida on madness

I want to continue, then, by re-visiting the famous Foucault–Derrida debate albeit from a slightly different perspective. Michel Foucault's book *Folie et déraison: Histoire de la folie à l'âge classique* (1961) is an attempt to write a history of the exclusion or incarceration of madness by reason. It generally, but not, as we will see, consistently, dates this rational exclusion of madness to the seventeenth century or what it calls the 'classical age'. The now celebrated argument of Foucault's book is that post-Enlightenment discourse historically defines *la folie* (madness) as *déraison* (unreason) or merely the absence, negative or opposite of reason. This process of exclusion reaches its political apotheosis with what Foucault calls the 'great confinement' of 1657 when the destitute and insane of Paris were incarcerated in the new *Hôpital Générale*. In philosophical history, the Foucault–Derrida exchange about the meaning of these events is usually read as a defining moment in the debate between structuralism and the emergent 'post'-structuralism – and it clearly is – but my contention will be that it also significantly clarifies Michel Foucault's problematic relationship with the *via negativa*.

'Cogito and the History of Madness'

Jacques Derrida's critique of Foucault's book in his essay 'Cogito and the History of Madness' ([1964] 1978e) is extremely well known. He greatly admires Foucault's work but suggests that its real value lies in raising questions beyond its own reach. Derrida argues that Foucault's attempt to write a history of reason's exclusion of madness is simply impossible. His consistent charge is that Foucault's self-professedly 'difficult' attempt to write a history of madness itself without falling into the language of reason is futile and only ends up perpetuating the rational suppression of madness it seeks to denounce: 'it is also, in all seriousness, the *maddest* aspect of his project' (Derrida 1978e: 34).

Derrida begins with the relatively basic point that it is impossible to write a *history* of reason because reason itself must be presupposed in such a project. He goes on to note a series of inconsistencies in Foucault's argument that problematize his historical account of the relationship between reason and madness. If he intends to write a history of reason's exclusion of madness, Derrida argues, Foucault must re-trace the relationship between the two to a 'zero point' where this division first comes into effect. The onus is thus on Foucault to identify the point in history when madness was first excluded by reason but, when called upon to do so, Derrida identifies the same hesitation between historical and transcendental analyses in Foucault's account of madness that we noted earlier. There are a number of inconsistencies in Foucault's chronology of madness that lead him to imply that the exclusion of madness began as early as the advent of Western philosophy with the *logos* of Socrates (Derrida 1978e: 39–40), on the one hand, and that it started much later, in what he calls the classical age, with Descartes's *Meditations on First Philosophy* (1641), on the other. This chronological inconsistency is exacerbated by Foucault's claim that the historic point at which the exclusion of madness by reason happens is also the point at which the 'possibility of history' begins (Derrida 1978e: 42) because history is itself a corollary of reason, which leads Derrida to point out that, if reason's exclusion of madness is what makes history *possible*, then clearly that exclusion cannot be an event that occurs at a specific moment *in* history. For Derrida, Foucault's claim that the possibility of history begins at a specific historical point – whether in the first century BC or the seventeenth century AD – puts the historical cart before the horse.

Descartes and the Cogito

Derrida goes on to substitute Foucault's historicist account of the relationship between reason and madness for a quasi-transcendental one via an analysis of Foucault's reading of Descartes's *Meditations on First Philosophy* (1641). It is with Derrida's reading of Foucault's critique of Descartes – which occupies a mere two pages in Foucault's large book – that 'Cogito and the History of Madness' really begins to get its teeth into Foucault. Descartes's *Meditations on First Philosophy* famously begin by rejecting everything that he has hitherto believed, assumed or taken on trust about himself in order to start over again on firmer ground. He rejects all prior sensible and intelligible knowledge he has gained about the world in the effort to reach a *tabula rasa* from which he can begin to construct his own transcendental theory of the subject. He begins by raising the question of whether what his senses tell him is real or illusory and Foucault argues that at this point Descartes makes a crucial distinction between the rational doubt of the senses and the far more radical sensory doubt of madness. Rational man will reasonably doubt *some* of the things that his senses tell him, to be sure, but only a madman would doubt *everything* his senses tell him (Descartes 1986: 13). Foucault argues that Descartes does not see madness as offering any insight into the trustworthiness of sensory knowledge because it is a form of illusion that bears no relation to truth whatsoever. The thought of the mad is thus excluded from the category of thought that can be reasonably called into doubt and eventually from the sphere of thought itself: 'thought, as the exercise of the sovereignty of a subject who puts himself in the service of the perception of truth, cannot be thought insane' (Foucault 1961: 58). This decisive act or event – in which reason and madness are for the first time opposed to one another – is instrumental in the foundation of reason and the incarceration of madness. So, upon Foucault's reading, Descartes's exclusion of madness is one small but significant step on the road that leads to the *Hôpital Générale*.

Derrida's critique of Foucault targets this small but apparently pivotal moment in the history of madness. He offers what superficially seems to be a very classical, traditional defence of Descartes against his contemporary critic. His position is that Foucault's reading of Descartes is wrong on a number of quite basic levels. It not only misreads the analysis of madness in the *Meditations* but it wrongly attributes a historical significance to that analysis that it simply does not possess. Its main charge is that – *pace* Foucault – Descartes does not reject the figure of the madman because he represents *too* radical a form of doubt to cast doubt on sensible knowledge but because he is *nowhere near* radical *enough* to provide the philosophical 'ground zero' he needs. Derrida argues that Foucault's reading conveniently stops before Descartes goes on to draw a crucial parallel between the illusions of the madman and the illusions of the sleeper or dreamer. Descartes, Derrida insists, sees a dreamer as the victim of a far more radical version of sensory illusion than a madman because a madman is not wrong all the time whereas the dreamer is *always* wrong to believe what he sees: '*from this point of view*, the sleeper, or the dreamer, is madder than the madman' (Derrida 1978e: 51). If the dreamer is seen as 'madder' than the madman, Derrida suggests, then here is an example of how madness, if taken to its absolute limits, can indeed be of use in casting all sensory knowledge into doubt. Perhaps even the dreamer is not 'mad' enough for Descartes's needs, though, because he quickly leaves this figure behind in the search for an even more radical form of doubt from which to construct the Cogito. The dreamer may call the veracity of *sensible* knowledge into doubt even more radically than the madman but even he is not completely mad because in dreaming he still adheres to certain non-sensible, *intelligible* assumptions about the world like geometry and arithmetic (Descartes 1986: 14). There is a sense in which even the dreamer is not mad enough to provide an absolute ground zero from which to build the Cogito because Descartes has not managed to cast *all* sensible and intelligible knowledge into doubt. This is why Descartes goes on to embrace what seems to be the *even madder* hypothesis that the whole world – the world of *both* sensible *and* intelligible truths in other words – is an illusion perpetrated by an Evil Genius (Descartes 1986: 15). For Derrida, Descartes's embrace of the absolute madness of hyperbolic doubt finally enables him to reach the philosophical *prima fundamentis* from which he can go on to build his theory of the Cogito.

The history of madness

Derrida makes a number of specific objections to Foucault's reading of Descartes, then, but their larger implications are only beginning to emerge. It is simply not the case that Descartes takes a historical, foundational decision to exclude madness from the interiority of thought. He clearly cannot reject madness because, in doing so, he would be rejecting the very radical or hyperbolic doubt by which he seeks to prove his own subjectivity. Far from excluding madness, Derrida argues, Descartes *embraces* it as an essential element in constructing meaning: 'everything that was previously set aside as insanity is now welcomed into the most essential interiority of thought' (Derrida 1978e: 53). Derrida memorably contends that 'Cogito ergo sum' means what it means regardless of whether the person saying it is mad or not, being serious or not, a machine, a talking parrot and so on (Derrida 1978e: 56). If madness and reason are not to be seen as economically or dialectically opposed, then the relationship between the two discourses needs to be explored in such a way as to bring out their paradoxical complicity.

Derrida's essay maintains that this chiasmus of madness and sanity in Cartesian thought necessitates a new definition of the Cogito as a paradoxical point of origin which exceeds the distinction between historically determined reason and unreason while at the same time setting it in motion:

> The hyperbolic audacity of the Cartesian Cogito, its mad audacity, which we perhaps no longer perceive as such because, unlike Descartes's contemporary, we are too well assured of ourselves and too well accustomed to the framework of the Cogito – rather than to the critical experience of it – its mad audacity would consist in the return to an original point which no longer belongs to either a *determined* reason or a *determined* unreason, no longer belongs to them as

opposition or alternative. Whether I am mad or not, *Cogito, sum.* Madness is therefore, in every sense of the word, only one *case* of thought (*within* thought). It is therefore a question of drawing back toward a point at which all determined contradictions, in the form of given, factual, historical structures, can appear, and appear as relative to this zero point at which determined meaning and nonmeaning come together in their common origin.

(Derrida 1978e: 56)

Derrida's re-reading of the Cogito argues that it precedes reason and madness as the common condition of possibility and impossibility for their determined meanings and thereby calls into question Foucault's account of reason's origin as a historical gesture of self-definition accomplished by excluding madness as its other. Reason cannot be said to exclude madness as its constitutive other because it already carries *within itself* its possibility of being otherwise, or to put it another way, its outside is *already* inside. The classical decision to separate reason and madness into interior and exterior is not the historic, foundational act Foucault claims it is but rather an internal dissension or cleavage within meaning itself. There is no way in which Descartes can simply 'decide' to exclude madness from thought, as Foucault forcefully argues that he does, any more than he can 'decide' to stop thinking altogether. This zero point of undecidability between reason and madness exceeds the realm of history 'in the direction of the nondetermined' (Derrida 1978e: 54) but – or so Derrida famously argues – the problem with Foucault's structuralist reading is that it continually seeks to reduce that undecidability to a historically determined event, totality or economy. Now this leads Derrida to conclude that the Foucauldian reduction of the nondetermined to the determined, the non-historical to the historical, and play or excess to structure or economy ironically repeats the supposed Cartesian reduction of meaning-in-general to reason, madness to unreason, and unreason to deviancy. For Derrida, to summarize his most famous and controversial charge, Foucault merely reinforces the violent division and internment of reason and madness that he mistakenly denounces in Descartes: 'I say that this reduction to intraworldliness is the origin and very meaning of what is called violence, making possible all straitjackets' (Derrida 1978e: 57).

Derrida's dispute with Foucault is not simply about the meaning of madness, then, but of reason, history and ultimately of meaning itself. It points to a significant divergence of approach that is made explicit in the final, most demanding and least analysed pages of 'Cogito and the History of Madness'. It becomes increasingly apparent that the difference between Foucault and Derrida's concepts of history is the difference between a static, foundational event or crisis, on the one hand, and a tension or process, on the other:

> The historicity proper to philosophy is located and constituted in the transition, the dialogue between hyperbole and the finite structure, between that which exceeds the totality and the closed totality, in the difference between history and historicity; that is, in the place where, or rather at the moment when, the Cogito and all that it symbolizes here (madness, derangement, hyperbole, etc.) pronounce and reassure themselves then to fall, necessarily forgetting themselves until their reactivation, their reawakening in another statement of the excess which also later will become another decline and another crisis.
>
> (Derrida 1978e: 60)

Derrida here posits a concept of history as the process of transition between history and historicity, between the determined concepts of history and that which exceeds them. Derrida's history is neither Foucault's determined historical event or crisis nor a Kantian transcendental 'other world' but the rhythm or movement between the finite structures of history and the infinite nondetermination that exceeds them. The negotiation of a point of chiasmus or middle ground between the empirical and the transcendental which belongs to neither – Derrida later calls it 'quasi-transcendental' (Derrida 1986a: 151–62a) – is a characteristic move in his 1960s' work on both philosophy and the human sciences. There is no way in which the transcendental gesture of philosophy can divorce itself from the empirical world valorized by structuralism but – by the same token – there is no way in which the empirical event so beloved of structuralists can separate itself from the transcendental gesture of philosophy or theology. This paradoxical logic of spectral possession or contamination – in which the transcendental gesture is haunted by the ghost of what it attempts to transcend and the empirical thrust by the spirit of what it tries to empiricize – is of course nothing other than the logic of deconstruction. Now deconstruction demands a decision which does not seek to arrest or stabilize this flux by referring it back to some prior non-existent 'real' but which, as we have already seen, recognizes the contingency or decisiveness of its own legislative force. In 'Cogito and the History of Madness', Derrida is emphatically not asking us to choose between the historical and the transcendental – as if such a choice were possible – but to go through the 'madness' of a decision that attempts – however impossibly – to do justice to both (Derrida 1978e: 31).

What, to summarize, are the differences between Foucault and Derrida's analyses of Descartes? I think it is possible to set them out in fairly stark and uncompromising terms. First, Foucault argues that Descartes excludes madness from the interiority of reason into the exteriority of deviancy whereas Derrida argues that Descartes does not exclude madness in favour of reason but embraces it wholeheartedly because reason and madness are both intrinsic to meaning in general. Second,

Foucault suggests that the distinction between reason and madness is a decisive and foundational act of division between the interiority of reason and the exteriority of madness whereas Derrida maintains that it is not a historical decision but a dissension or cleavage that is internal to meaning in general. Third, Foucault argues that reason is formed through a dialectic or economy with its other whereas Derrida argues that reason is produced through the creation of an excess or expenditure without reserve. Finally, Foucault sees history as the product of a determined empirical event, crisis or economy whereas Derrida sees history as the process of play or transition between the empirical and the transcendental, the historical and the a-historical. Perhaps the best way to summarize the Derrida–Foucault debate, then, is as a debate about where to draw the line between history and historicity, the empirical and the transcendental or the inside and the outside: Foucault attempts to *overturn* what he sees as an unwarranted hierarchy of the transcendental over the empirical by empiricizing the transcendental so that it becomes nothing more than a series of more or less disguised power gestures whereas Derrida does not simply overturn that hierarchy but *displaces* it to demonstrate that any attempt to empiricize the transcendental remains indebted to its other and vice versa. Now we need to consider the theological implications of this disagreement – which have never really been examined before – in greater depth but the basic dispute between Foucault and Derrida is hopefully clear. In the simplest terms, Michel Foucault sees madness as a thought from the outside whereas Jacques Derrida says that Foucault's concept of madness is *already* inside reason.[2]

Foucault, madness and religion

I now want to consider the theological implications of Foucault's reading of madness in more detail before focusing on some specific examples from his later texts. It is surprising that religion or theology hardly figures at all in the literally hundreds of pages of commentary that have been written on this subject by figures such as Boyne, Flaherty and others. My feeling is that Foucault's work on madness not only contributes significantly to his critique of religion and negative theology but also highlights some of the problems inherent in his attempt to articulate a philosophy that is absolutely outside the *via negativa*. In my view, Foucault is certainly not a negative theologian or 'modern mystic' but the relationship between archaeology and negative theology is more complex than he makes out.

Christianity and madness

First, Foucault himself stresses throughout the text that the Christian Church played a pivotal role in the history of the internment of madness by reason. He often makes clear the ways in which Christianity operates

130 *Atheologies*

within and alongside secular technologies of the self in the classical period. Christian modes of discipline such as the monastic order – with their emphasis on silence, obedience and individual renunciation – are replicated and reinforced in secular disciplinary regimes such as the prison and the hospital system. So Foucault would see religion not so much as a rival to Cartesian rationalism in this sense as an intellectual precursor to it which provides it with the model of the individual rational subject safely anchored in the idea of the transcendental God: it 'safeguards the old secrets of reason' and 'constitutes the concrete form of what cannot go mad' (Foucault 1965: 244).

Negative theology and madness

Given this perspective, Christian mysticism or negative theology's relationship to madness would seem to be equally disciplinary in orientation. It is not clear from the text itself but my impression is that it would be very premature to rank Foucault alongside critics such as Michel de Certeau, Julia Kristeva and others who see Christian mysticism as occupying a marginal, subversive role within institutional Christianity. Foucault draws his examples of madness from secular sources such as Bosch, Nietzsche and Artaud and – given everything he has said about it elsewhere – it is unlikely that he would see Christian mysticism as anything other than an integral part of classical technologies of the self. The techniques he identifies as central to Christian mysticism – silence, self-sacrifice and obedience as a means of reaching the true ground of the individual – are all the more powerful as modes of discipline for not appearing to be so. Perhaps we might again point to a missed opportunity in Foucault's text here – which has been brilliantly filled in recent years by critics such as Grace Jantzen – to construct a politics of mysticism that does not simply confirm the status quo: couldn't the work of Christian mystics like Julian of Norwich or Teresa of Avila offer a means of critiquing social and particularly gendered technologies of the self?

Negative theology and historical archaeology

Finally, and most importantly, however, I want to revisit Foucault's attempt to articulate a thought that is extrinsic to negative theology in the light of Derrida's critique of his apparently naïve methodology. I want to hazard the suggestion that Foucault's legacy to religion is neither the wholesale rejection of religion as a series of more or less disguised power moves nor the embrace of religion as a form of political or gender subversion but the articulation of a central problem about deciding exactly where religion begins and ends, what is and is not religious.

Derrida's reading of Foucault, we have seen, demonstrates that the latter's analysis of madness remains within the transcendental philosophical concepts of history, reason and the subject it purports to attack. It argues that Foucault's history of the transcendental concept of reason does not recognize its own complicity in the rationality it seeks to historicize and only ends up perpetuating its violence under another name. Deconstruction's critique of Foucault's doomed attempt to historicize or empiricize the transcendental is replicated in numerous other critiques of Marxist, historicist or structuralist thought. Marxism, for instance, seeks to reduce the transcendental drive of religion to a set of material conditions as, crudely speaking, the opiate of the people but in doing so elevates materialism into an unimpeachable transcendental law. Structuralism, by the same token, seeks to circumscribe the transcendental reach of philosophy but it cannot think the structurality of its own structure and so elevates it into its own transcendental without realizing it. The slippage from the empirical to the transcendental is not necessarily due to any empirical error – although it is entirely characteristic that Foucault would see it that way – but is rather a sign that the empirical and the transcendental dimensions exist in a differential rather than essential relation with each other. This process by which humanist or structuralist attempts to historicize or empiricize the transcendental inevitably end up repeating transcendental gestures in empirical forms is described most succinctly by Derrida in the labyrinthine text *Glas* ([1974] 1986a) under the name of 'transcendental contraband' (Derrida 1986a: 244a). For Derrida, 'transcendental contraband' signifies a common metaphysical situation whereby discourses that seek to exclude the transcendental dimension of philosophy end up smuggling it back in again under a non-transcendental guise. In Derrida's account, the transcendental keeps turning up like Banquo's ghost at the empirical feast: absent, present, present because it is so massively, absolutely, transcendentally absent.

Foucault famously seeks to historicize the transcendental truth claims of reason but I would argue that the *Histoire de la folie* is vulnerable to the accusation that it surreptitiously elevates history itself into the role of what Derrida calls 'transcendental contraband'. His ostentatiously historical discourse often seems to rely on some oddly unhistorical definitions. He disowns the language of psychiatry as if reason adhered to that discipline alone (Derrida 1978e: 34–5). He claims to write an archaeology rather than a history of madness – as if the discipline of archaeology were any less indebted to reason than history (Derrida 1978e: 35). His suspicion of psychiatry forces him to rely on popular definitions of madness that overlap with 'everything that can be put under the rubric of *negativity*' including, we might logically conclude, negative theology (Derrida 1978e: 41). His project is a conveniently circumscribed history of the reason of 'yesterday' rather than of reason as meaning in general (Derrida 1978e: 55). His concept of history, in short, begins to assume the very uncritical, unhistorical and transcendental status that it calls into question in others. It is this indebtedness to the transcendental even in the act of denying it that also explains why his readings so often end up reproducing the very gestures they criticize. If we want to get the best purchase on the ironies inherent in Foucault's position, it is worth closing this section by looking at an important footnote in Derrida's critique of Foucault which places his ostensibly anti-Hegelian project firmly back within the orbit of Hegelian dialectic and economy:

> And if there is no history, except of rationality and meaning in general, this means that philosophical language, as soon as it speaks, reappropriates negativity – or forgets it, which is the same thing – even when it allegedly affirms or recognizes negativity. More surely then, perhaps. The history of truth is therefore the history of this *economy* of the negative. It is necessary, and it is perhaps time to come back to the ahistorical in a sense radically opposed to that of classical philosophy: not to misconstrue negativity, but this time to affirm it – silently. It is negativity and not positive truth that is the nonhistorical capital of history. In question then would be a negativity so negative that it could not even be called such any longer. Negativity has always been determined by dialectics – that is to say, by metaphysics as *work* in the service of the constitution of meaning.
>
> (Derrida 1978a: 308n)

Derrida effectively argues that Foucault cannot conceive of a concept of history outside reason and so his attempt to write the *history* of reason's exclusion of madness inevitably recruits madness into the service of reason. Derrida's quite devastating point is that the thinker who did so much to warn against the dangers of anti-Hegelianism merely collapsing back into Hegelianism ends up defining madness as simply the reassuring negative of reason that can be dialectically converted into a positivity via the familiar gesture of the *Aufhebung*. The history of madness is what Derrida – in language heavily indebted to 'A Hegelianism without Reserve' (1978d) – would call a restricted rather than a general economy. This is not a problem that arises in Derrida's case because he never proposes an *opposition* between positivity and negativity, like Foucault, so much as an undecidability at the heart of that opposition which calls for a re-thinking of its oppositionality: '[i]n question then would be a negativity so negative that it could not even be called such any longer'. Now I want to suggest that Foucault's discourse on madness in *Folie et déraison* – with all its attendant problems – casts a new light on his discourse on mysticism in 'The Thought from the Outside'. Does his unintended propensity to put negativity to work in the service of transcendental concepts of truth and reason force us to reconsider his critique of negative theology as a dialectical economy that merely serves to reconfirm being and speech? Could this inevitable tendency to *dialecticize* negativity in Foucault suggest that there is a closer link than we might think between his work and that

Foucault and 'the thought from the outside' 133

branch of dialectics he calls negative theology? Is Foucault's discourse on negative theology a case of the historical pot calling the theological kettle black?

Michel Foucault's critique of negative theology, to summarize, does not work on its own historical terms but I would argue that his failure to adequately distinguish between the thought of the inside and the outside raises important questions in its own right. It could ironically be suggested that Foucault's critique of negative theology contains a great deal of what – fairly or unfairly – *he himself* criticizes as negative theological. Foucault criticizes negative theology for negating being and speech only in order to reaffirm their integrity but he finds himself accused of reappropriating the negativity of madness into the interiority of reason. Foucault's history of madness is vulnerable to the very charges that he levels against negative theology, namely, that it dialectically converts negation into work, self-sacrifice into self-affirmation and a space that is nominally beyond reason into a new colony for the interiority of the rational individual. The conclusion must be drawn that Foucault – however contrary to commendable intentions – ends up perpetuating the negative theological technology of the self as silent, obedient and self-sacrificing individual that he so forcefully criticizes. This is not to make the patently absurd claim that Foucault is some sort of mystic *manqué* or that historical archaeology is really negative theology in disguise but to point out the difficulty Foucault finds in identifying a space that is absolutely outside the *via negativa*. Now we will unpack the implications of this tentative conclusion in the remainder of this chapter – beginning with an examination of Foucault's *Archaeology of Knowledge* ([1969] 1972) – but the problem itself is at least clear. In summary, Foucault's thought from the outside is still 'inside' the problematic he names negative theology.

Foucault's archaeology of knowledge

I think that what is at stake in my argument can best be seen by looking at Foucault's little discussed but crucial transitional text *The Archaeology of Knowledge* ([1969] 1972). It is with this text that the entire critical debate about Foucault's relation to negative theology comes to a head. My contention is once again less to try and settle this debate one way or the other but to use it to highlight a point of chiasmus between what Foucault calls the thoughts from the inside and those from the outside. In my reading, Foucault's project of historical archaeology is obviously not indebted to negative theology in any historical, thematic or doctrinal sense but there may be a larger structural relationship between the two discourses.

The Archaeology of Knowledge

Michel Foucault's *Archaeology of Knowledge* is his most painstaking attempt to formulate theoretically the archaeological project begun in *Folie et*

134 *Atheologies*

déraison. It consists of a series of definitions of technical terms which comprise the archaeological project like the statement or *énoncé*, discourse, the historical a priori and the archive. He introduces his text by saying – again in language recalling Blanchot – that archaeology is an attempt to 'define a particular site by the exteriority of its vicinity' (Foucault 1972: 17). He goes on to explore this exteriority in what is, by his standards, remarkably hesitant and self-effacing but at the same time highly rhetorical language:

> What, do you imagine that I would take so much trouble and so much pleasure in writing, do you think that I would keep so persistently to my task, if I were not preparing – with a rather shaky hand – a labyrinth into which I can venture, in which I can move my discourse, opening up underground passages, forcing it to go far from itself, finding overhangs that reduce and deform its itinerary, in which I can lose myself and appear at last to eyes that I will never have to meet again. I am no doubt not the only one who writes in order to have no face. Do not ask me who I am and do not ask me to remain the same: leave it to our bureaucrats and our police to see that our papers are in order. At least spare us their morality when we write.
> (Foucault 1972: 17)

Foucault's famous rejection of the identity politics of academics who seek to reduce his œuvre to a proper name and a body of unified writings is a salutary warning to anyone who wishes to write on him. The Blanchotesque claim that he writes in order to 'lose myself and appear at last to eyes that I will never have to meet again' also brings to mind his earlier suggestion that Pseudo-Dionysius writes only in order to gather himself once again in the interiority of a thought that is being and speech. There is an implicit promise here that Foucault's own work actually accomplishes the sacrifice of the individual, identity and truth floated in the various forms of negative theology whereas Pseudo-Dionsyius's work collapses back into the identity politics that leads to the modern bureaucratic state. This is a promise we have heard before in Foucault's texts – to negotiate a thought that is outside negative theology – but I would argue that it is most clearly articulated in *The Archaeology of Knowledge*.

Foucault interestingly describes the first stage of his archaeological project as a negative one: (Foucault 1972: 21). He seeks to define archaeology according to what it is not and 'neither ... nor' formulations of the kind favoured by Pseudo-Dionysius and other negative theologians abound. He stresses that what he calls 'discourse' is neither history nor anthropology (Foucault 1972: 21–30), neither a word nor a thing (Foucault 1972: 40–9), neither the property of a transcendental nor a psychological subject (Foucault 1972: 50–5), neither idealist nor empiricist (Foucault 1972: 56–63). Moreover, the *énoncé* is neither a proposition, a sentence nor a speech act (Foucault 1972: 79–105), the historical a priori, which we will return to later, is not a Kantian condition of possibility (Foucault 1972: 127) whereas the historical archive cannot be described in its totality at all (Foucault 1972: 130). Finally, Foucault is keen to stress that the entire project of historical archaeology should neither be conceived as a discipline belonging to the history of ideas (Foucault 1972: 135–40) nor science (Foucault 1972: 178–95).

Foucault's intricate attempts to formulate a theoretical framework in which to couch the archaeological project without falling back on received ideas has, as we will see, encouraged many critics to draw comparisons with negative theology but in fact his own aims could not be more clear:

> What, in short, we wish to do is to dispense with 'things'. To 'depresentify' them. To conjure up their rich, heavy, immediate plenitude, which we usually regard as the primitive law of a discourse that has become divorced from it through error, oblivion, illusion, ignorance, or the inertia of beliefs and traditions, or even the perhaps unconscious desire not to see and not to speak. To substitute for the enigmatic treasure of 'things' anterior to discourse, the regular formation of objects that emerge only in discourse. To define these *objects* without reference to the ground, the *foundation of things*, but by relating them to the body of rules that enable them to form as objects of a discourse and thus constitute the conditions of their historical appearance.
> (Foucault 1972: 47–8)

Michel Foucault's project in this text is emphatically not, then, a theological attempt to negate all metaphysical images of the *causa sui* in order to praise the transcendental God, but a philosophical effort to dispense with the traditional concept of archaeology as uncovering the ontological reality of things in order to analyse the immanent, historical field of discourse. The difference between the two projects would again appear to be that negative theology is a dialectical negativity that seeks to reappropriate its negations into some higher transcendental positivity whereas archaeology is an unreserved negativity that calls the very existence of that transcendental into question. This is because negative theology negates in order to affirm the authority of the *transcendental* over discourse – the real presence of God over and against all images of Him – whereas archaeology negates in order to affirm the authority of *discourse* over the transcendental – the discursive rules that allow God to appear as a real presence. In Foucault's own admirably clear terms, negative theology is a discourse that seeks to renounce words whereas '[w]hat ... we wish to do is to dispense with "things"' (Foucault 1972: 47).

Foucault criticism

Foucault implicitly and explicitly rejects any theological motive for his work but this has not stopped a whole host of critics from identifying the project of historical archaeology with negative theology. It was ironically – given Foucault's own willingness to defend *him* against unwanted charges of mysticism – Maurice Blanchot who first floated the idea that there may be some relationship between the two discourses in his essay 'Michel Foucault as I Imagine Him' (1987b). Blanchot somewhat gnomically suggested: 'read and re-read *The Archaeology of Knowledge* ... and you will be surprised to rediscover in it many a formula from negative theology' (Foucault 1987a: 74). In recent years, Blanchot's invitation has been taken up with alacrity by a group of critics who have read Foucault as everything from a negative theologian *manqué* to a committed atheist.

First, James Bernauer has offered what is arguably the most sophisticated analysis of the relationship between Foucault and negative theology to date in his book *Michel Foucault's Force of Flight* (1990). Bernauer drew inspiration from a private meeting with Foucault himself in Paris in 1980 where the latter generously informed him that his work could perhaps be compared to negative theology if only insofar as it related to the human rather than the divine sciences. Bernauer's text goes on to draw an important parallel between historical archaeology's negations of essentialist concepts of Man and negative theology's negation of essentialist concepts of God: 'Foucault's negative theology is a critique not of the conceptualization employed for God but of that modern figure of finite man whose identity was put forward as capturing the essence of the human being' (Bernauer 1990: 178).

Bernauer's conclusion is that Foucault's work contains what he calls 'worldly mysticism' but at the same time he is at pains to stress that the negative theological and archaeological discourses do not share any intrinsic identity. *The Archaeology of Knowledge* may use the same linguistic and formal techniques as negative theology but it is not a theological work and thus any theological significance it might possess is a strictly secondary concern (Bernauer 1990: 178).

Second, John D. Caputo broadly supports Bernauer's position in his essay 'On Not Knowing Who We Are: Madness, Hermeneutics and the Night of Truth in Foucault' (1993). Caputo suggests that Foucault's work constitutes a kind of immanent negative theology that struggles against any 'kataphatic' discourse about the individual (which tries to say what the individual is or should be) in the name of an 'apophatic' freedom (which preserves the right of the individual to be different):

> Foucault wants to keep open the negative space of what the individual is *not*, of what we *cannot* say the individual is, to preserve the space of a

certain negativity that refuses all positivity, all identification, that is always in the end a historical trap.

(Caputo 1993: 251)

Caputo's essay only departs from Bernauer's original thesis when it takes issue with his choice of the word 'transcendence' to describe the freedom the individual achieves as it escapes essentialist conceptualizations of the subject: 'Foucault has in mind a more modest freedom from below, a refusal, a resistance, a certain stepping back, not so much a *trans*cendence, let us say, as a *res*cendence' (Caputo 1993: 255).

Jeremy R. Carrette is, if anything, even more cautious than Bernauer and Caputo about overstepping the mark when comparing archaeology and negative theology in his ground-breaking book *Foucault and Religion* (2000). Carrette explicitly sets out to correct what he calls the 'misleading assumption that there is a "mystical discourse" within Foucault's work' and rehearses many of the same arguments as his predecessors (Carrette 2000: 85). Carrette's book stresses Foucault's own personal atheism, insists that his references to 'mysticism' must not be taken out of their historical context and relegates the apparent similarities between his work and negative theology to a question of 'style', language and metaphor rather than content (Carrette 2000: 94).

Foucault's religious critics deserve immense credit for opening up the debate between archaeology and negative theology – and moving beyond the simple either/or distinctions that have bedevilled it in the past – but there are still unanswered questions here. It is obvious that Bernauer *et al.* represent an important advance upon Foucault's own blanket rejections of any connection between his project and negative theology in his early work, but contemporary Foucault scholarship still allocates theology an essentially marginal position at the fringes of his texts. It is interesting, for example, that current Foucault criticism relies on many of the same historicist gestures that Foucault himself used to marginalize the *via negativa*: Foucault's work can only be seen in its specific historical context, the similarities between it and negative theology are a superficial matter of style rather than content and Pseudo-Dionysius and Foucault's discourses are diametrically opposed to each other as thoughts of the inside and the outside, the transcendent and the immanent, the theological and the material, and so forth. If it is certainly no crime to give such a Foucauldian reading of Foucault, my concern would be that this interpretation is just as vulnerable to the Derridaean objections developed earlier. First, Foucault's atheism obviously influences his approach to negative theology but that context cannot totally determine the meaning of his texts for all time any more than Foucault's own attempt to contextualize Descartes's *First Meditations* within the history of reason and madness could adequately describe what was going on in the Cogito. The similarities between mysticism and archaeology may be a question of style rather than substance but given the fact that Foucault cannot help but use the language and concepts of the metaphysical tradition to which negative theology itself belongs – inside and outside, immanent and transcendent, even the distinction between form and content – it does not take a Derridaean to see that it is hardly a straightforward matter to separate the argument of Foucault's texts from the language in which it is expressed. There is a sense in which Bernauer, Carrette *et al.* exhibit a thoroughly Foucauldian desire to expel negative theology to the exterior of Foucault's texts, then, but the problem with this is that the distinction between the interior and the exterior will not stay where they want it to be. Finally, and most importantly, I think the originary complication of the transcendental and the empirical that Derrida introduces towards the end of 'Cogito and the History of Madness' would also force us to raise a concern about whether Foucault's self-styled 'immanent negative theology' is really that different from the 'transcendental negative theology' he rejects. Is historical archaeology really able to preserve the space of a certain negativity for the subject that refuses all positivity, all identification, as historical traps or does he himself fall into the historical trap he consistently accuses transcendental negative theology of setting up, namely, affirming the individual as silent, unified self-sacrificial subject?

The historical a priori

Foucault is not a negative theologian, then, but it may be that his relationship to negative theology is more complex than has previously been suggested. It is possible to see this problem most clearly by looking more closely at certain passages of argument from *The Archaeology of Knowledge*. I want to look in particular detail at his account of what he famously – if a little confusingly – calls the 'historical a priori'. My contention is that it is here that Foucault's difficulties in separating the inside and the outside from each other become most explicit. Let me cite his account of the historical a priori in full:

> Juxtaposed these two words [historical a priori] produce a rather startling effect; what I mean by the term is an a priori that is not a condition of validity for judgements, but a condition of reality for statements. It is not a question of rediscovering what might legitimize an assertion, but of freeing the conditions of emergence of statements, the law of their coexistence with others, the specific form of their mode of being, the principles according to which they survive, become transformed, and disappear. An a priori not of truths that might never be said, or really given to experience; but the a priori of a history that is given, since it is that of things actually said. The reason for using this rather barbarous term is that this a priori must take account of statements in their dispersion, in all the flaws opened up

by their non-coherence, in their overlapping and mutual replacement, in their simultaneity, which is not unifiable, and in their succession, which is not deductible; in short, it has to take account of the fact that discourse has not only a meaning or a truth, but a history, and a specific history that does not refer back to the laws of an alien development.

(Foucault 1972: 127)

It is with Foucault's account of the historical a priori that we reach the logical culmination of that oscillation between the historical and transcendental we have already observed in his texts from 'The Thought from the Outside' onwards. On the one hand, the historical a priori still sounds – despite his protestations – like a terribly Kantian business of 'freeing the conditions of emergence of statements, the law of their coexistence with others' and 'the principles according to which they survive'. On the other hand, it is closer to a Nietzschean exercise in recognizing that the 'dispersion' of statements is neither 'unifiable' not 'deductible' but belongs to a specific history that 'does not refer back to the laws of an alien development'. Foucault seems to oscillate between saying that every discourse is the product of a specific history that pertains only to itself and saying that every discourse is the product of a body of apparently a-historical rules that make possible its relation to other discourses.

Foucault's argument would again seem to be vulnerable to the old Derridaean objection that he wants to have his transcendental cake and eat it, then, by developing a ground for argumentation that is both transcendental all the way up and historical all the way down. His position in *The Archaeology of Knowledge* is much subtler than the one advanced in the *Histoire de folie*, however, because he actually proceeds to tackle the objection that historical archaeology relies on a residual transcendentalism in his methodology head on:

[T]his a priori does not elude historicity: it does not constitute, above events, and in an unmoving heaven, an atemporal structure; it is defined as the group of rules that characterize a discursive practice: but these rules are not imposed from the outside on the elements that they relate together; they are caught up in the very things that they connect; and if they are not modified with the least of them, they modify them, and are transformed with them into certain decisive thresholds.

(Foucault 1972: 127)

The argument is that the a priori rules that govern the history of discourse are – contrary to appearances – not *actually* a-historical at all: 'this a priori does not elude historicity: it does not constitute, above events, and in an unmoving heaven, an atemporal structure'. They do not constitute a timeless structure far above the flux of human events because they are themselves subject to the same historical shifts they organize and relate: 'they are caught up in the very things that they connect; and if they are not modified with the least of them, they modify them, and are transformed with them into certain decisive thresholds'. There are already signs of the famous turn from archaeology to genealogy that so defines Foucault's later work here where the conditions of possibility for a discourse are no longer examined in isolation – as if they existed in some historical vacuum – and discourse becomes something to be analysed as an event that is deployed in a particular historical context. This argument seems to mark the point where Foucault finally stops tacking between the historical and the transcendental, then, and decides to come down squarely on the historical side of the equation. In the *Archaeology of Knowledge*, to put it another way, Foucault begins the process of historicizing the remaining transcendental implications of his *own* project, but does he succeed?

Foucault's radically historicized version of archaeology is obviously an important advance over the deeply structuralist methodology of his earlier texts but it is still possible to express a reservation about whether it represents the decisive break with transcendental philosophy he claims it does. It may be that even at this apparently decisive moment his commitment to historicism is not historical all the way down. It is beyond question that Foucault is willing to historicize the rules of the historical a priori but there is still something in his account which eludes historicization and this is what in the above passage he calls 'historicity' itself. Foucault writes that the historical a priori remains part of the historical processes it tries to account for because even it 'does not elude historicity' and the notion that the concept of the historical a priori is subject to historicity is a decisive and influential one on later critical schools such as new historicism and cultural materialism. But it also raises an inevitable set of Foucauldian questions about what historicity *itself* is subject to, how it has managed to acquire this privileged position as the value according to which all values are judged, and from whence its power, meaning and authority derive. If this concept ensures that Foucault's project is subject to the historical forces it tries to thematize, it also means that, crucially, the truth value of historicity *itself* can never be subject to those forces without setting in motion an infinite regress which calls the entirety of Foucault's analysis into question. The problem is that Foucault's attempt to historicize any lingering transcendentalism in his archaeological project is still carried out under the auspices of a concept that is not apparently historical because what Foucault calls historicity historicizes everything except itself. There may be a sense in which the historical a priori does constitute a Kantian 'unmoving heaven' above the ebb and flow of human time after all; there may yet be an 'a-temporal structure' at the heart of temporality. This well-documented inability to completely historicize his own appeal to history is perhaps the underlying cause of many of the common criticisms of his early work as either relativist, objectivist, or most commonly of all, some self-contradictory combination of both (Dews 1995: 55; Jantzen 1995: 347–8). In other words, Foucault's historicizing of the transcendental goes hand in hand with his transcendentalizing of the historical in a way that vindicates Derrida's 'transcendental contraband' argument that any discourse against the transcendental ends up elevating some nominally non-transcendental concept into a transcendental position.

So Foucault's historical archaeology cannot succeed, then, and this failure has important implications for his historical critique of negative theology as well. Michel Foucault, as we have seen, seeks to historicize negative theology as part of a broader Christian technology that subjectifies the self as silent, independent and unified subject (Carrette 1999: 113). He sees negative theology as a historical construction of oppressive power relations that requires a correspondingly historical act of exposure, refusal and resistance. His archaeological and genealogical methodologies offer an important ethico-political corrective to the undoubted violence of Christian transcendental truth claims but the question remains of whether his own discourse merely reproduces that violence on an immanent level. His discourse posits a purely immanent historicity from which the transcendental can be endlessly criticized but this cannot fail to throw up new transcendental terms his discourse is unable to adequately deal with. Its tendency to see negative theology as nothing more than a social construction does not simply lead it to a misleadingly monolithic concept of the *via negativa* which ignores the ways in which it can function as a subversive or resistant discourse within the status quo but also means that it fails to recognize the philosophical similarities between it and his own discourse. Foucault himself can be seen to ironically fall victim to his own critique of negative theology as a technology of the self whose negativity merely serves to reinforce a certain positivity of the subject. Foucault's attempts 'to keep open the negative space of what the individual is *not*, of what we *cannot* say the individual is', in the words of Caputo, cannot entirely succeed because his account depends on the presumption that individual identity can never be *anything* other than historically located. If Foucault wants to affirm a non-transcendental, contingent and relative concept of the individual, he ends up elevating the historical into a universal, timeless transcendental horizon against which the individual must exclusively and perpetually be situated. The question again arises of the precise *history* of the concept that everything is historical or – if it does not have one – of the difference between it and any other transcendental theory of the individual. This is emphatically not a call on my part for a return to some essentialist concept of the human as biological, rational or religious subject but – on the contrary – a critique of a concept of non-essentialism that assumes the same privileged status as the essentialisms it criticizes. In summary, Foucault's self-styled historical negative theology – 'of what the individual is *not*, of what we *cannot* say the individual is' – actually ends up positing the same idolatries about the subject as he accuses its transcendental equivalent of doing about God.

Foucault's negative theology

Michel Foucault's attempt to articulate a space outside negative theology remains, then, at least partially in fee to that transcendental interiority he associates with the *via negativa*. He is clearly not a mystic of any description. He opposes negative theology at every turn and neither the sincerity nor the philosophical integrity of this opposition is in doubt. It is more a question of whether it is possible to have a philosophical discourse that positions itself *absolutely* outside the transcendental. Foucault constructs the concept of historical archaeology as a radically immanent and historical discourse in opposition to the transcendental truth claims of metaphysical theology and philosophy. Foucault's distinction between historical archaeology and negative theology becomes increasingly difficult to make good, however, as their shared faith in the omniscient power of a transcendentalized value beyond all negation – whether it be God or History – becomes increasingly apparent. If negative theology loses itself only in order to find itself again, Foucault's own attempt to 'lose myself and appear at last to eyes that I will never have to meet again' (Foucault 1972: 17) only ends up finding him in a position of similar metaphysical and, according to his own account, historico-political privilege. The problem is that Foucault's historicization of the transcendental cannot historicize its own appeal to historicity without licensing an infinite regress and so surreptitiously sets history up as what Derrida would call a 'transcendental contraband'. This re-admission of the transcendental via the back door may not be enough in itself to justify the comparisons between archaeology and negative theology – not every transcendental has to be theological nor every theology transcendental of course – but the fact that negative theology is one of the transcendentals Foucault most frequently outlaws from his own texts suggests that there is a certain aptness in identifying it as the concept that puts the backbone into supposedly historical concepts like archaeology. Now this situation has important implications for Foucault's historico-political analysis of negative theology and I would like to consider some of these in the final section of this chapter. In summary, Foucault's thought from the outside becomes difficult to tell apart from the thought from the inside and I would like to conclude by suggesting that this fate is an opportunity to understand the history of negative theology differently.

True confessions?

I want to conclude, then, by trying to imagine what a 'history' of negative theology might look like after Foucault. It is obvious that this will have to be a fairly speculative enterprise in the aftermath of Foucault's own death and the continuing absence of crucial works on Christianity such as the fourth volume of *The History of Sexuality* from his published canon. My intention is less to try to predict what Foucault would have written had he lived (what would be the point of that?) nor even to tease out the logical conclusions of his original positions (which has already been done very convincingly by critics like Bernauer and Carrette) but rather to take up Foucault's own invitation to imagine him differently: '[d]o not ask me who I am and do not ask me to remain the same' (Foucault 1972: 17). The focus for this discussion will be a brief comparison between Foucault and Derrida's approaches to the question of Christian confession. This discussion will enable us to sharpen up the differences between Foucault's concept of a negative theology that can always be reduced to certain historical contexts and Derrida's concept of a *via negativa* that is defined by its transgressive, hyperbolic nature. In summary, I want to suggest that Derrida shows that any history of negative theology – whether theological or atheological – will always produce a reductive and ultimately violent reading of the *via negativa*.

Foucault on confession

Michel Foucault's work on Christian confession is in a fragmentary form but the overall direction of his argument appears relatively clear. It is clear that his analysis of the practice of confession is part of a general recognition on Foucault's part that the study of *oppressive* power needed to be complemented with a study of *productive* power. His analysis of Christianity as a silencing force in early works like the *Folie et déraison* (1961) goes hand in hand with the analysis of Christianity as a verbalizing force in mature studies such as the *History of Sexuality* ([1976] 1979a). Foucault provides a very sketchy overview of confession in Church history from the Lateran Council onwards in the first volume of this text. Foucault's famous argument is that from its Christian origins the confession goes on to become one of Western society's most highly valued techniques for subjectification of the individual by imposing a truth upon him/her in the guise of the articulation of self-knowledge:

> The confession is a ritual of discourse in which the speaking subject is also the subject of the statement; it is also a ritual that unfolds within a power relationship, for one does not confess without the presence (or virtual presence) of a partner who is not simply the interlocutor but the authority who requires the confession, prescribes and appreciates it, and intervenes in order to judge, punish, forgive, console, and reconcile; a ritual in which the truth is corroborated by the obstacles and resistances it has had to surmount in order to be formulated; and finally, a ritual in which the expression alone, independently of its

144 *Atheologies*

>external consequences, produces intrinsic modifications in the person who articulates it: it exonerates, redeems, and purifies him; it unburdens him of his wrongs, liberates him, and promises him salvation.
>
>(Foucault 1979a: 61–2)

Confession, Foucault goes on to argue, is codified and institutionalized as a practice from the Lateran Council onwards and becomes an increasingly central part of civic and religious society in the Middle Ages. Protestantism and the scientific and medical developments of the Enlightenment, he suggests, turn it from a ritualistic and centralized power into one that is dispersed across a whole range of fields including pedagogy, medicine and psychology. The cumulative effect of this long history is the transformation of sexuality into discourse, Foucault famously argues, and the subsequent deployment of this '*scientia sexualis*' as a means of establishing a normative concept of the individual. This work concludes with the tantalizing suggestion by Foucault that a 'different economy of bodies and pleasures' (Foucault 1979a: 159) might one day enable us to understand and counter the deployment of sexuality that stretches from medieval Christian history to twentieth-century medicine but the tantalizing idea of a politics of opposition or resistance is not really pursued. Now Foucault's admittedly brief and incomplete history of confession has been subjected to a number of attacks from historians over the years – accusing it of historical inaccuracy, incoherence and an unwarranted trans-historical essentialization of confession (Tambling 1990) – but my concern here is less with correcting Foucault's position than questioning its basic premises. To what extent is it possible to write a *history* – in the singular – of the institutionalization of confession?

Derrida on confession

Jacques Derrida focuses in detail on the subject of Christian confession at the beginning of the essay 'Sauf le nom'. It focuses on St Augustine's *Confessions* rather than the medieval or Renaissance models but despite the vast historical differences between the two, I do not think a comparison of approaches is necessarily invalid. First, it is important to note that Derrida sees confession as having its roots in the radically plural resources of the *via negativa*. He starts by rehearsing his argument from 'How to Avoid Speaking' that negative theology is characterized by a contradictory drive to both address God in absolute secret, on the one hand, and to perform a pedagogic, initiatory role to the mystical and larger Christian community, on the other: 'Dionysius the Areopagite, for example, articulates a certain prayer, turned towards God; he links it with an address to the disciple, more precisely to the becoming-disciple of him who is thus called to hear' (Derrida 1995a: 38). He then goes on to suggest that precisely the same structure of conversion is at work in the *Confessions* of St Augustine

Foucault and 'the thought from the outside' 145

(Derrida 1995a: 38). His argument is that Augustine's *Confessions* share a destiny with negative theology because they are not primarily a predicative statement where something is said about something but an address to those brothers who are called to hear in an attempt to generate a Christian community or fraternity in a spirit of love and charity:

> – When he asks (himself), when he asks in truth of God and already of his readers why he confesses himself to God when he knows everything, the response makes it clear that what is essential to the avowal or testimony does not consist in an experience of knowledge. Its act is not reduced to informing, teaching, making known. Stranger to knowing, thus to every determination or to every predicative attribution, confession shares [*partage*] this destiny with the apophatic movement. Augustine's response is inscribed from the outset in the Christian order of love or charity: as fraternity.
> (Derrida 1995a: 38–9)

Derrida introduces a concept of confession here that is suggestively different from Foucault's in *The History of Sexuality* on a number of levels. Derrida's concept of confession is not a new technology of the self as a speaking subject, designed to succeed the mystical technology of silence, but a further extension of the apophatic mode that speaks no truth about the subject whatsoever. If Foucault's concept of confession is concerned with the subjectification of the self via the establishment of a set of constative (or rather constativized) truths about his/her identity, Derrida's is more interested in the confessional mode as the performative creation of a community or fraternity of believers that did not pre-exist its articulation: '[t]he avowal is destined to God and to creatures, to the Father and to the brothers in order to "stir up" love, to augment an affect, love among them, among us' (Derrida 1995a: 39). The emphasis on the communitarian rather than individual structure of the confessional act does not mean that it is a politics-free zone, of course, for Derrida is quite clear about the elitist and patriarchal implications within the notion of the fraternity of the initiated both here and in the essay 'How to Avoid Speaking'. There is no doubt that Foucault would look upon the potential violence implicit in such notions as Christian fraternity with a suitably cold archaeological eye – and he would of course be quite right to do so – but this fact does not necessarily vindicate Foucault's attempt to resist or counter such notions as any more peaceful. This is because Derrida's analysis of Augustinian confession is not content to see it as a purely empirical violence but as part of a much larger structure of originary or structural violence that cannot be opposed or made good by Foucault's correspondingly empirical account of a 'different economy of bodies and pleasures'.

Derrida's discussion of confession moves on to consider in more detail the way in which Augustine seeks to establish the Christian fraternity. It is absolutely crucial to the success of this exercise that Augustine's confession be put down in writing if it is to survive as an act of testamentary attestation (Derrida 1995a: 39). He uses writing, to put it another way, in order to ensure the permanence of his original speech act of confession, its repetition outside its original historical context and its widespread publicization as a means of generating the fraternity he has in mind. But Derrida's classic point will be that the ability to put that speech act into writing is not simply a contingency that *befalls* Augustine's confession after the event but something that is *built into* the very structure of that event in the first place:

> I want 'to do the truth' he says, in my heart, in front of you, in my confession, but also 'in my writing before many witnesses' (*in stilo autem meo coram multis testibus*) (10.1.1). And if he confesses in writing (*in litteris, per has litteras*) (9.12.33; 10.3.4), it is because he wants to leave a trace for his brothers to come in charity in order to stir up also, at the same time as his, the love of readers (*qui haec legunt*) (11.1.1). This moment of writing is done for 'afterwards' [*après*]. But it also follows the conversion. It remains the trace of a present moment that would have no sense without such a conversion, without this address to the brother readers: as if the act of confession and conversion having *already* taken place between God and him, being as it were written (it is an *act* in the sense of archive or memory), it was necessary to add a *post-scriptum* – the *Confessions*, nothing less – addressed to brothers, to those who are called to recognize themselves as the sons of God and brothers among themselves. Friendship here has to be interpreted as charity and as fraternity. But the address to God itself already implies the possibility and the necessity of this *post-scriptum* that is originarily essential to it.
>
> (Derrida 1995a: 39–40)

Derrida here begins to introduce what is a very different model of confession to the Foucauldian technology of the self advanced in the *History of Sexuality* and other related texts. Derrida's main point is that the *speaking* subject of confession is preceded by the *writing* subject of confession and this, as we will see, has clear implications for Foucault's history of confession. If the historical act of Augustine's confession to God is contingent upon its capacity to be written as such, then this calls into question the whole matter of the *time* of the confessional act.[3] Augustine seeks to preserve the trace of his original act of confession to God in writing for his brothers but that moment is already inscribed within a code of repeatability that is immemorial. The *Confessions* are no longer simply the record of a historical speech act, in other words, because they 'were already, in their wildest present, in their date, in their place, an act of memory' (Derrida 1995a: 40). There is also a sense in which the *Confessions* are no less the testament to an infinite future, as well, because their status as a written text also ensures that they can be read in contexts outside the historical intention of their author to create a Christian fraternity such as the secular tradition of autobiography (Derrida 1995a: 40) and indeed Derrida's own decidedly heterodox quasi-autobiography *Circumfession* ([1990] 1993). For Derrida, Augustine's 'original' act of confession is dispersed across a past that has always already happened and a future that will never absolutely arrive so it can never be present or re-presented as such.

What, to summarize, is Derrida's challenge to Foucault's attempt to historicize confession? First, Derrida argues that it is impossible to identify a real or originary act of confession in Augustine because it depends on an immemorial possibility of inscription. He contends that Augustine's *Confessions* can be understood only to the extent that they are written texts but that at the same time this means that they necessarily *escape* any singular historical or empirical determination. Derrida contends, then, that the very structure that makes possible the institutionalization of confession by Augustine and his successors – writing, the trace, repetition – also means that such a process of institutionalization will never be complete because no institution could ever claim to embody it without arbitrarily fixing or arresting something that remains inherently protean.

Second, Derrida's argument makes clear that confession's possible or necessary inscription as such forbids the possibility of any simple *history* of the confessional act. It is clear that Augustine's *Confessions* cannot be reduced to a simple event in time because they are contingent upon a structure that exceeds temporality and this has obvious implications for any attempt to write the history of confession. If writing forms the basis for any history of confession whatsoever, it is also what ensures that confession can never be traced back to any simple historical or empirical context(s) without reducing it to that which it permanently exceeds. The important point to grasp here is that Derrida would make no distinction between a history of confession that *supports* or *contests* the concept of subjectivity or community to which confession gives rise because both illicitly reduce the confessional act to an empirical event and negate the more originary structure of inscription and repetition in which it exists. This means that there is no essential difference between the empirical violence Foucault convicts Christianity of practising in the name of confession and the correspondingly empirical opposition or resistance he offers under the guise of a 'different economy of bodies and pleasures' because both are guilty of what Derrida elsewhere calls the 'reduction to intraworldliness' that is 'the origin and meaning of what is called violence' (Derrida 1978e: 57).

Finally, and more generally, then, I would argue that Derrida can be seen to situate all empirical or political histories of confession against a larger quasi-transcendental background of originary trace, repetition or writing that requires a complete re-evaluation of the relationship between

148 *Atheologies*

its alleged violence or non-violence. It may appear that Derrida's concept of confession represents a quietist *retreat* from the account of empirical violence described in *The History of Sexuality* but we are beginning to see that in fact it posits a massive *generalization* and *transcendentalization* of violence to include *both* Christianity's violence *and* Foucault's attempts to oppose that violence alike. Derrida is canvassing for a situation of what he famously calls 'originary violence', in other words, the state of originary undecidability or groundlessness to which all empirical concepts of violence, whether in the form of law, illegality or transgression or institutionalization, are a response (Derrida 1976: 112). Derrida's insistence upon this absolute inescapability of violence in both supposedly empirical violence and the attempts to oppose that violence does not necessarily commit him to a relativism or fatalism because, as we have already seen, it is the means of bringing into view his concept of the ethico-political decision. For Derrida, it is only by recognizing the very inescapability of violence that it becomes possible to offer an ethico-political response to the empirical or political violence Foucault is describing that avoids the twin dangers of simply accepting such violence as natural or succumbing to consolatory fantasies of resistance, reparation or non-violence. The first task of any future history of confession, sexuality or negative theology that seeks to genuinely bear witness to the undoubted abuses, injustices and violences that have been done in their names is the acceptance of this general economy of violence. There is no possibility of doing without violence altogether but – according to the economy of 'greater' and 'lesser' violence traced in Chapter 1 – it is possible to minimize it by acknowledging the inevitable contingency and finitude that haunts all decision-making. This is the instant of Kierkegaardian madness that every history must go through (Derrida 1978e: 31) if it is to stand a chance of avoiding the institutionalized violence of reason that Foucault so powerfully warns us against in *Folie et déraison*. In Derrida's account of confession, we begin to glimpse what such a history might look like.

Conclusion

Michel Foucault's attempt to develop a thought from the outside negative theology demands re-thinking. It has been my contention throughout this chapter that Foucault's thought from the outside is always already inside. He seeks to articulate some space outside the transcendental but his archaeological projects are always carried out in the name of some newly transcendentalized concept such as history. His critiques of mysticism, madness, knowledge, confession, and so on can be criticized for situating the individual against the same transcendentalized horizons as the technologies of subjectivity he criticizes. If Foucault's archaeologies inevitably collapse back into the 'interiority of a thought that is rightfully Being and Speech', as he puts it in 'The Thought from the Outside', my contention is that this fatality might also be an opportunity to understand that interiority in less monolithic, a-historical and, well, internal, terms. Negative theology is not simply a tradition that has 'prowled the confines of Christianity since the texts of the Pseudo-Dionysius' (Foucault) but something that is permanently capable of 'crossing a frontier, including that of a community, thus of a sociopolitical, institutional, ecclesial reason or raison d'être' (Derrida 1995a: 36). The surprising legacy of Foucault's problematic historicist critique of negative theology might, then, be a re-evaluation of the *via negativa* as something that necessarily exceeds its Christian and Neoplatonic context and spills over into an indeterminable and potentially infinite number of new contexts, both Christian and non-Christian. This hyperbolic concept of negative theology would require a history which is just as prepared to re-think its own 'sociopolitical, institutional, ecclesial reason or raison d'être' to do justice to it. In all these ways, Foucault's thought from the outside will remain within the thinking that has 'survived for a millennium or so in the various forms of negative theology'.

5 Kristeva and 'the original *technē*'

> I like to imagine, however, that human beings were able to 'think' ... a beginning before the beginning. I like to hear, in their ramblings about 'virginity', a proto-space, a timelessness, whatever was here before the Word was. Before the Beginning: a non-imprint, a non-place beyond the grasp of the original *technē*, the primordial furrow?
>
> (Kristeva 1999a: 119)

Julia Kristeva's thought could be described as an attempt to think 'a beginning before the beginning'. It is possible to detect this paradoxical thought in all her work from her earliest texts on psycholinguistics to her later work on religion. It can be found in her famous concepts of the chora, the semiotic, abjection, melancholia and what most recently – together with the anthropologist Catherine Clément – she calls 'the sacred'. Kristeva defines 'the sacred' in *Le féminin et le sacré* (1999a) as the desire to understand the true meaning of religious myths of the origin such as the act of 'original *technē*' by which God supposedly created the world. Kristeva's argument seeks to uncover what she takes to be the genuine psycho-sexual origins of Christian doctrines like God's creation, the Virgin Mary's immaculate conception and the incarnation, death and resurrection of Christ. If the sacred represents a psychoanalytic critique of Christian dogma, however, it also represents an attempt to get underneath the skin of a secular modernity that is no less in thrall to the myth of original *technē*. The myth of the all-powerful Christian God who creates the world *ex nihilo* is increasingly realized, Kristeva argues, in the equally omnipotent secular figure of the chemist, scientist or genetic engineer. This belief in an original all-powerful manufacturing cause – whether it is the ancient Christian God or the modern genetic engineer – has the deleterious effect of reducing the human to nothing more than an instrument or tool to be exploited for ulterior ends. For Kristeva, then, the attempt to think a beginning before the beginning could be described as an attempt to uncover the sacred behind the religious, the psychoanalytic behind the Christian and the originary sexuality behind originary *technē*. Now in this chapter I want to consider Kristeva's analysis of the relation between the sacred and *technē* in *Le féminin et le sacré* – which is an admirable, necessary but underexplored one – alongside Derrida's suggestively analogous analysis of faith and the question of technology in 'Faith and Knowledge' ([1996] 1998a). My guiding questions will be these. What exactly is the sacred? How does Kristeva see the relationship between it and Christian theology and particularly negative theology? To what extent is she able to negotiate a concept of the sacred that is more original than original *technē*? In this chapter, I want to argue that Kristeva's sacred is *itself* technological and that this state of affairs necessitates not only a re-thinking of her attempt to distance herself from negative theology but a re-thinking of the relationship between religion and technology more generally.

Kristeva and psychoanalysis

I want to begin with a very brief overview of Kristeva's theory of psychoanalysis. Julia Kristeva is arguably best known for her research in the field of psycholinguistics. Kristeva develops a famous distinction between the semiotic and the symbolic in *Revolution in Poetic Language* ([1974] 1984). Kristeva's semiotic and symbolic are the pre-linguistic and linguistic stages of the subject that go together to form a dynamic process of subjectivity. The semiotic is the pre-linguistic biological and psychic energy which exists when the bodies of mother and infant share a common maternal space whereas the symbolic is the post-linguistic signifying order that comes into being when the infant acquires language and a sense of separate identity. This pre-linguistic semiotic space does not simply disappear upon the entry into language but continues to make itself manifest as a rupturing or subversive force within the symbolic order. For Kristeva, 'semanalysis' is a mode of psychoanalytic reading which can register and articulate the traces of the semiotic in symbolic representations such as modernist poetry, abstract expressionist art and other creative activities.

Abjection

Kristeva supplemented her original analysis of the semiotic and the symbolic with explorations of what, in highly influential later texts like *Powers of Horror* ([1980] 1982), she famously calls the abject. It is this key term that Kristeva uses to describe the first attempt by the nascent subject to differentiate itself from its mother. It would not exactly be true to describe the abject as a thing – because, like the semiotic, it precedes the distinction between subject and object – but once again it is a process of developing subjectivity. The abject is the process by which the infant begins to separate itself from the maternal union and create a space where it can negotiate a distinct identity and subjectivity for itself. This infant can only complete the process of entering language and becoming a speaking subject when it ceases to simply abject or abandon the mother and starts to identify with the father of individual pre-history. For Kristeva, this pre-linguistic process of abjection and identification again continues to exist in the symbolic order through works of art and religion.

Religion

So Kristeva offers a subject in process, then, fissured between the competing demands of the semiotic and the symbolic. Her work identifies various cultural examples of this libidinal economy including the poetry of Lautrémont, the art of Jackson Pollock and more recently the politics of immigration in Europe. She has increasingly turned to religious subjects in recent years, however, and particularly towards the question of how the fissured subject of psychoanalysis can be thought of in Christian terms. She first begins to read Christianity psychoanalytically in *Tales of Love* ([1983] 1987b) but the process accelerates with the essays *In the Beginning Was Love* ([1985] 1987a) and the cultural analysis *New Maladies of the Soul* ([1993] 1995) before reaching a conclusion in *Le féminin et le sacré* (1999a). Kristeva has been both criticized and congratulated for this apparent 'theological turn' in her work over the past 20 years or so (Jardine 1981; Spivak 1988; Hill 1990; Kearns 1993; Chopp 1997; Ward 1999) but her project remains unambiguously an atheist one. The abiding thesis of these texts is that Christianity is merely the historical stage on which essentially psychoanalytic desires are played out. This means that Christianity may well be an important historical precursor to psychoanalysis but – more crucially – that psychoanalysis is the true successor and replacement of Christianity. For Kristeva, the Christian desire for loving, ecstatic fusion with a transcendental other reflects the semiotic drive for unity with the immanent other who is not simply within the world but within ourselves. In a recent interview, Kristeva describes her psychoanalytic project as a mode of internalizing the transcendent:

> For me, the Some Thing is immanent to man. It's the possibility of speaking, of creating, of making meaning and putting meaning into question. Where does the need come from to set up some authority beyond the human? That is what psychoanalysis asks.
>
> (Kristeva 2002b: 54)

Kristeva and Christianity

I now want to look in a little more detail at Kristeva's work on Christianity. Kristeva's *In the Beginning was Love: Psychoanalysis and Faith* ([1985] 1987a) is her first exploration of the relationship between the two discourses. It revises Freud's understanding of the relation in *The Future of an Illusion* as essentially one between pathological illusion (religion) and reason or atheism (psychoanalysis) towards one between two different approaches to illusion (Freud 1975). The two discourses are the product of the same essential psychic illusions or fantasies, Kristeva insists, and they both recognize that those illusions are necessary and unavoidable in the development of the subject. They are separated by the crucial fact that religion dogmatizes those illusions as mythologies whereas psychoanalysis helps the subject understand the sexual drives that create them. In other words, religion transcendentalizes the immanent whereas psychoanalysis internalizes the transcendent.

In the Beginning was Love

Kristeva argues that religion and psychoanalysis are both the fantastic expressions of the desire of a destabilized subject to gain stability through loving identification and ultimately fusion with an all-powerful father figure (Kristeva 1987a: 19). It is her contention that both discourses begin in an act of trust or faith in which the believer/analysand transfers his or her trauma or suffering into a relationship with the other whether it be God or the analyst. It is not the psychoanalyst's job to work out whether those fantasies have any basis in fact or not – because this would constitute nothing more than another form of repression – but rather to understand the drives that create them (Kristeva 1987a: 26). The difference between the two discourses is that religion is a 'macro-fantasy' that projects or dogmatizes these psychic desires in the form of a fundamental mythology whereas psychoanalysis is a 'micro-fantasy' that grounds those desires in the individual life of the subject (Kristeva 1987a: 44). This means that psychoanalysis is ultimately 'not less than religion, but more' (Kristeva 1987a: 52) because it helps the subject to renounce the dogmatic fantasies of religion by analysing and understanding their underlying psycho-sexual nature. So psychoanalysis becomes a kind of immanent religion and the analyst a sort of secular priest in the confessional box: 'the analyst, like Dante in hell, hears them all' (Kristeva 1987a: 53).

Kristeva backs up her argument with a 'semanalysis' of the Credo of AD 381. She highlights five features of the Credo which embody basic human fantasies. First, she again says that the desire for loving identification and fusion with the Almighty Father is a basic psychoanalytic fantasy. Second, the expression of belief in Christ's Passion symbolizes the guilt and suffering that spring from the incestuous desire for union with a parent. Third, the emphasis on Christ's suffering also represents the profound depression or abjection that necessarily precedes the entrance into language and subjectivity. Fourth, the concept of the Trinitarian God is not merely Christian dogma but representative of the psychoanalytic Holy Trinity of the Imaginary, Symbolic and Real. Fifth, and finally, Kristeva turns to the figure of the Virgin Mary and I would like to consider this point in a little more detail because it brings out some interesting tensions in her account.

The Virgin Mary

Kristeva's argument points to a number of ways in which the Virgin Mary is a potent symbol of basic psychic fantasies. She fulfils the Oedipal fantasy of a loving relationship with a mother and no father to act as a rival. She also fulfils what Kristeva calls the common women's narcissistic fantasy of having a child without the need of a father. She is, moreover, the only human being that does not have to die because her life ends in Dormition according to Orthodox doctrine and Assumption according to Catholic doctrine. It is not surprising, however, to learn that Kristeva thinks fantastic identification with the figure of the virgin mother came at a great cost:

> Unfortunately the censorship of female sexuality helped to infantilize half the human race by hampering its sexual and intellectual expression. However, that censure (only lifted by advances in contraception) was generously compensated for by praise of motherhood and its narcissistic benefits.
> (Kristeva 1987a: 43)

But interestingly Kristeva does not believe that the symbolic potency of the figure of the Virgin Mary declined following the technological repeal of this religious prescription on female sexuality – as one might think it would – for she goes on to say that Mary continues to resonate with women in the age of contraception, artificial insemination, and so forth:

> Thus today, now that so-called artificial pregnancies have given reality to the distinction between sexuality and procreation, femininity and maternity, the image of the virgin mother resonates with the daydreams of modern women of no particular religiosity in the absence of any secular discourse on the psychology of motherhood.
> (Kristeva 1987a: 43)

So Kristeva argues that the virgin mother remains a potent image for secular women not because she symbolizes various sexual fantasies but because, in the absence of any secular alternative, she represents what is now sexual reality. The woman who procreated without having sex psychically resonates with the women who have sex without procreating. The woman who underwent the first artificial insemination, so to speak, inevitably speaks to the women who now experience *in utero* fertilization and other insemination technologies. The woman who was once the fantastic symbol of the prohibition of female sexuality strangely becomes the symbol of the liberation of female sexuality qua sexuality. We are all, it seems, Marys now.

Julia Kristeva's interest in the figure of the Virgin Mary is well documented in a number of texts but the argument she gives here seems to be particularly surprising. I am less interested in considering it in empirical terms or even in terms of Kristeva's own theological views than in putting it in the context of her own overall thesis. It is my view that in this characteristic discussion we can identify a number of tensions in Kristeva's account of religion. First, I think it is odd to see her suggest that the religious discourse on the psychology of motherhood persists simply because there is no secular alternative to it when the entire thesis of her book is that psychoanalysis constitutes precisely that secular alternative (Kristeva 1987a: 3). Is her self-professedly excessive faith in the centrality of the psychoanalytic relationship perhaps, as she often fears it is, misplaced in the era of Prozac and 'pop' psychology?

Second, Kristeva's reading of Mary impacts in a problematic way on her psychoanalytic critique of religion. She consistently argues, as we have seen, that religion does not enable the subject to understand and articulate the sexual origins of its dogma so it is striking to find the religious performing exactly that role here. Women in modern secular society presumably do not fantasize about the Virgin Mary because they believe in the doctrine of the immaculate conception – Kristeva explicitly says they have no particular religiosity – but because Mary provides the only means of articulating the psychology of contemporary female sexuality and maternity. Why, then, does Kristeva insist that religious discourse has to be renounced or at the very least transferred, into psychoanalytic discourse? Are we going to have to re-consider her construal of the relative positions of religion and psychoanalysis when – as Kristeva herself points out in *New Maladies of the Soul* ([1993] 1995) – it now appears that the latter is more likely to die out than the former?

Finally, however, I want to flag up another, apparently tangential, question about the relationship between psychoanalysis and faith that will become more and more central as this chapter goes on. It concerns Kristeva's critique of technology. It is the central thesis of *In the Beginning was Love*, remember, that sexuality constitutes the primal scene of all fantasy whether it be the religious discourse of believer and God or the secular discourse of analyst and analysand. The passage on the virgin birth makes the interesting point, however, that the distinction between sexuality and procreation – the very gesture that allows sexuality qua sexuality to emerge as itself – only becomes concrete in modernity with the advent of birth control, artificial insemination, and so on. This presumably means that whereas sexuality has always existed as a psycho-biological economy – Kristeva is not saying, like Philip Larkin, that sexual intercourse began in 1963 – its physical appearance as such was contingent upon technology. So Kristeva posits a non-technological essence of sexuality – in the form of the semiotic – that precedes its technological actualization as such in modernity. Now later on I want to consider this reading of technology – which locates Kristeva within a tradition that stretches from Aristotle to Heidegger – in the light of Derrida's argument that 'the question of

156 *Atheologies*

technology (a new name must perhaps be found in order to remove it from its traditional problematic) may not be derived from an assumed opposition between the psychical and the nonpsychical, life and death' (Derrida 1978: 228). What if technology belongs more originarily to the concept of sexuality than Kristeva allows? How would the originary technicity of sexuality affect her psychoanalytic critique of religious faith? If technology is what makes sexuality possible, and sexuality is what makes religion possible, then what would a religion after originary *technē* look like? In the next section, I would like to pursue all these questions in more detail by looking at Kristeva's concept of the sacred.

Kristeva and the sacred

I want to give an overview of Clément and Kristeva's book *Le féminin et le sacré* (1999a). It takes the form of a correspondence between the two writers in the late 1990s on the following question: 'Does there exist a sacred that is distinctively feminine?' (Kristeva 1999a: 8). Its answers to this question range from Christianity to Buddhism, mysticism to psychoanalysis, Teresa of Avila to Princess Diana. The epistolary and dialogic form of *Le féminin et le sacré* means that its arguments are generally impressionistic, and its conclusions provisional, but certain key themes still emerge. There is once again a distinction between a declaredly 'religious' drive to transcendentalize the immanent and a sacred mission to interiorize the transcendent. For Kristeva, I think, the sacred represents her most explicit attempt to affirm a semiotic origin for religious experience that overcomes the prohibition on sexuality originally imposed by Christianity and, as we will see, perfected by technological modernity.

The sacred

Kristeva begins by defining the sacred very provisionally as 'a point of crossing between sexuality and thought, the body and meaning that is realized most intensely by women' (Kristeva 1999a: 8). She argues that women have a privileged – but not exclusive – access to the sacred because their bodies are at a strange crossroads between '*zoē* and *bios*, physiology and narration, genetics and biography' (Kristeva 1999a: 28). She goes on to draw a crucial distinction between 'the sacred', on the one hand, and 'religion and belief' (which appears to include everything from Catholicism to communism), on the other:

> Beliefs and religion can be imaginary constructions (as in the case of [Kristeva's analysand] Marianne or [Freud's] Clara), ideological (such as atheism or communism), scientific (where we believe in the all-powerful status of science). All deny the sexual pleasure [jouissance] and the narcissistic dependence of the infant's relationship

Kristeva and 'the original technē' 157

> with his/her parents and also our dependence on nature, biology, genetics. They propose consolatory figures and all-powerful means of healing ... It remains to say that the sacred may not be the religious ... What if the sacred was the human being's unconscious recognition of an unsustainable eroticism: always on the frontiers of nature and culture, the animal and the verbal, the sensible and the nameable? What if the sacred was not a religious *need* for protection and the absolute power of institutions of recuperation but the *pleasure* of that *cleavage* between power and powerlessness, that exquisite weakness?
> (Kristeva 1999a: 46–7; square brackets mine)

Kristeva's argument recasts the debate as less one between theism versus atheism or faith and rationalism – all forms of repression in the above case – towards one between two different sorts of discourse on desire. It is the subject's semiotic desire for loving fusion with an all-powerful father or mother that produces both the sacred and the religious but the difference between them again concerns their *response* to that constitutive sexuality. On the one hand, the religious represses sexuality by proposing ever more reified or dogmatized ego-ideals for identification and fusion such as God, Revolution or Progress. On the other hand, the sacred unconsciously recognizes the 'unsustainable eroticism' that pre-exists impossible consolatory fantasies of this nature and subverts their supposedly all-powerful authority. This leads to a situation where the religious inheres in the visible means of power in society from political institutions to the media whereas the sacred exists almost silently and invisibly on the margins of that society and makes itself felt as a 'resistance' (Kristeva 1999a: 48) to its symbolic order. For Kristeva, to borrow a phrase from *In the Beginning was Love*, the religious 'heals the wounds of Narcissus' (Kristeva 1987a: 25) whereas the sacred exists in the cleavage of that wound.

Christian mysticism

Kristeva's text then goes on to analyse various examples of the feminine sacred from Church history. It is interesting to note that, like so many of her contemporaries, she accords a privileged status to Christian mystics. She sees the attempt to articulate 'unrepresentable experience' (Kristeva 1999a: 59) in the texts of Teresa of Avila, Hildegarde of Bingen and Angele de Foligno as an instance of the erotic resistance of the sacred. She suspects that Angele de Foligno's description of the mystic God as a 'thing without name' is the product of what she calls a mystic – as opposed to rational – atheism:

> I would say that the sacred – that 'thing without name' – perhaps betrays, beyond the depressive silences of our mystic, a suspicion of disbelief. If it doesn't have a name, does the divine really exist? One

might believe so, one might not. The hidden traces of a mystic atheism (perhaps the only one, which certainly has nothing to do with the atheist religion of those intellectuals who call themselves materialists, that I spoke of last time) and, as I think of it, a subtle, specifically feminine atheism rooted in that suspicion carried aloft on the power of the Word, in that withdrawal to the abyssal continent, hidden from the feeling body.

(Kristeva 1999a: 63)

Kristeva argues that Foligno's mystic discourse is atheist as opposed to religious because the transcendence it describes is wholly immanent. The negative theological discourse negates the capacity of language to account for the immanence of the body rather than the transcendence of God. This discourse articulates the basic abjection of the body without seeking – like the religious fusion offered in either its Christian or atheist/materialist forms – to repress or objectify that internal alienation. For Kristeva, then, mystical discourse merits the status of sacred rather than religious because it gives women the creative space to turn the abjection of their body into pleasure and its negation into glory (Kristeva 1999a: 63).

So Kristeva goes on to offer a kind of archaeology of the sacred which stretches from Christian mysticism to her own psychoanalytic discourse. It is clear that the mystical tradition represents a kind of sacred auto-critique of the religious which paves the way for Freudian psychoanalysis, Heideggerian fundamental ontology and her own semiotic. Kristeva continually recruits one of Eckhart's most famous prayers to her own project of thinking the sexual origins of religious purity or virginity: 'When Meister Eckhart asks God "to free him from God" (would I say from the "Virgin of God"?) isn't he also imagining a non-place, an unthinkable outside?' (Kristeva 1999a: 119). Kristeva's attempt to posit psychoanalysis as exactly that unthinkable space outside of all religious fantasies is again set out in Eckhartesque terms: 'I am persuaded that the philosophical tradition we have called "atheist" may well be an angle capable of bringing together a humanity that wants to be "free of God" without losing meaning or the work of meaning' (Kristeva 1999a: 266). More recently, Kristeva has gone so far as to call St Augustine '*le premier analyste*': 'with St Augustine, faith is open to interrogation, since I have "become a question for myself", the All, the Absolute is called into question' (Kristeva 2002b: 53). The mystic attempt to put the absolute under the interrogation of the subjective, as Kristeva would see it, anticipates the analyst's desire to situate the macro-fantasy of religion clearly within the micro-fantasies of the analysand's own life. This passage from a transcendent work of meaning to an immanent one – which begins in Christian mysticism and is completed in modern psychoanalysis – is nothing other than the passage from the religious to the sacred. Now what is remarkable about all this is less the attempt to read religion in atheist or psychoanalytic terms as a pathology – Christian mysticism, in particular, has been read this way throughout its turbulent history and not least by some Christians themselves – than the attempt to read psychoanalysis in quasi-religious or what she would call 'sacred' terms. We can see Kristeva effectively turning Freud's definition of religion as a beautiful illusion in comparison to the hard scientific reality of psychoanalysis on its head, for example, when she speaks of the feminine sacred as 'une mystique laïque' (Kristeva 2002b: 53).

Julia Kristeva, to summarize, sees the sacred as a kind of secular mysticism or negative theology that is irreducible to the religious in all its ancient and modern forms. It internalizes the transcendental whereas the religious transcendentalizes the immanent. It can be detected in Christian mysticism, fundamental ontology and psychoanalysis and stands in opposition to – and often within – a dominant philosophical tradition that stretches from Christendom through communism to late capitalism. It upholds the constitutive sexuality that the other 'religions' deny, dogmatize and exploit in the form of all-powerful maternal or paternal figures like God or Science. My contention, however, will be that the sacred is above all the resistance to the religious valorization of *technology* because the technological is what makes possible the belief that sexuality is something capable of being *exploited* in the first place. The sacred tradition of *sexualizing* the body that runs from Christian mysticism to psychoanalysis is opposed to a religious tradition of *technologizing* the body that stretches from the doctrine of the immaculate conception to contemporary biotechnologies and genetics. This question of what Kristeva calls original *technē* is what we now need to consider in more detail. To understand the sacred – and, more importantly, its limits – we need to understand the *technological* threat of the religious.

Kristeva and technology

I want to continue, then, by considering Kristeva's reading of technology in greater depth. It has to be admitted at the outset that Kristeva never actually offers an explicit *reading* of technology as such but her local arguments on a range of bewildering and seemingly unconnected issues – the Virgin Mary, National Socialism, Princess Diana and Prozac – add up to a remarkably wide-ranging critique of this question. Kristeva, I want to argue, sees the technological in clearly Heideggerian terms as not primarily an empirical matter of power stations, communication advances and atomic bombs but as an ontological question that is coterminous with human thought (Heidegger 1997). Kristeva's account follows Heidegger in seeing the technological as a *Gestell* or enframing of the world which turns it into an object or 'standing reserve' of energy to be calculated and exploited accordingly. Moreover, Kristeva's account is certainly also indebted to Freud's thinking in *Civilization and its Discontents* on the connection between religion and technology as manifestations of the human desire for omnipotence and omniscience (Freud 1961).[1] For Kristeva – and here her thinking also betrays a major debt to the critics of the Frankfurt School – the technological reaches its apotheosis in what she calls the 'hard' and 'soft' totalitarianisms of National Socialism and genetic engineering respectively because a habit of thought that sees the world as an object to be exploited will inevitably tend to see the human in such terms as well. So Kristeva's argument goes on to posit the sacred as precisely the means of countering the originary claim of the technological and the implicitly totalitarian threat it carries within it. The sacred must resist the 'soft totalitarianism' (Kristeva 1999a: 26) of technological bio-determinism without – and here is the rub – itself succumbing to violence and repression. This leads Kristeva to define the sacred as a non-technological essence but my feeling is that – like Heidegger's own thought – this critique of technology may still remain vulnerable to the technological thinking it criticizes. Now this is certainly not intended as a criticism of Kristeva's fears about a bio-determinist agenda in geneticism, neurology and evolutionary theory – which are, I repeat, unquestionably well founded – but of whether it is possible to oppose that agenda as if we were somehow outside it and its influence. In Kristeva's account, the sacred supposedly precedes the reach of original *technē* but I want to show that this beginning before the beginning remains in fee to the technological.

'Is Psychoanalysis a Form of Nihilism?'

Kristeva begins to pave the way for her sacred critique of the technological in the short text *In the Beginning was Love*. She introduces the topic in the chapter entitled 'Is Psychoanalysis a Form of Nihilism?'(Kristeva 1987a: 59–63). She begins with a brief but telling definition of nihilism before going on to consider the role of psychoanalysis. Kristeva's argument defines nihilism in Heideggerian terms as the belief that Being no longer exists as a value outside of subjective beings (Heidegger 1997: 99–107). Kristeva's argument is that nihilism begins when the existing subject becomes the object of its own enquiry or, as she more tendentiously puts it, when human beings begin to objectify their own being (Kristeva 1987a: 58). If nihilism begins with the Christian doctrine of the Incarnation, Kristeva argues that it carries on through to Cartesian rationalism before reaching its logical conclusion in the scientific dogmatism of contemporary bio-technology:

> As one hears all too often nowadays, life in the midst of modern technology has itself become an object, a product of the work of chemists, surgeons and genetic engineers serving power-hungry men and women. As the 'rights of man' are expanded to embrace the

power of a Being, even a supreme Being, the analyst detects the manic cry of the nihilist: 'The Creator is dead, and I have taken his place.'

(Kristeva 1987a: 62)

Psychoanalysis, however, occupies an exceptional place both inside and outside the history of nihilism, Kristeva suggests. The psychoanalytic discourse is *both* a nihilistic process of objectification that leads the analysand to understand his or her self more clearly *and* an anti-nihilistic process that cannot be reduced to objective terms because it leads the analysand to understand that his or her self is constituted by the other (Kristeva 1987a: 62). This leads Kristeva to conclude that psychoanalytic discourse occupies a fascinating autocritical position within rationalism that enables it to endorse the rationalist drive to *understand* the subject while renouncing the rational will to *dominate* or objectify that subject: 'In my opinion, therefore, psychoanalysis is the modest, if tenacious antidote to nihilism in its most courageously and insolently scientific and vitalist forms. It is the ethical shield, the superman's safeguard. But for how much longer?' (Kristeva 1987a: 63).

Kristeva's critique of technology is already becoming clear in this passage but I would like to make three quick points about it. First, Kristeva again argues that there is a dominant philosophical tradition that brings together Christianity and the so-called 'modern technology' in the project of objectifying or reifying the immanent. Second, Kristeva posits a philosophical counter-tradition – that will be later identified as the sacred – that performs a kind of autocritique of the dominant one from the position of a threshold between the body and thought, sexuality and meaning. Finally, however, I would like to raise a question about how Kristeva chooses to describe the relationship between the two discourses: 'psychoanalysis is the modest, if tenacious *antidote* to nihilism' (stress mine). The pharmacological metaphor of the 'antidote' here is to say the least an unfortunate one – given that the supposed 'disease' is the work of 'chemists, surgeons and genetic engineers' – and my feeling is that there might be an issue worth exploring more generally here. There is a sense in which Kristeva's thought might be exposed to the disease it is attempting to remedy – a case of 'Physician, heal thyself!' perhaps? – without being able to recognize or acknowledge the fact. This psychoanalytic antidote to the technological disease is itself made possible by what it seeks to cure and my argument will be that this very Derridaean logic of supplementation can be traced throughout Kristeva's critique of technology. What if – to ask the now very clichéd Derridaean question – Kristeva's *pharmakon* for technology is a poison as well as a cure?

Le féminin et le sacré

Kristeva's critique of technology becomes most clear – and, as we will see, most problematic – in *Le féminin et le sacré* (1999a). She begins by rehearsing her by now familiar opposition between the sacred, on the one hand,

and religion and belief, on the other. It becomes increasingly clear that this opposition derives from two different understandings of the originary claims of technology. The religious espouses the view that the technological precedes the psychoanalytic whereas the sacred holds that the psychoanalytic precedes the technological. This leads Kristeva to oppose a philosophy of *technē* that stretches from the immaculate conception to modern genetics with a philosophy of *psychē* that stretches from Renaissance mysticism to, however improbably, the funeral of Princess Diana. In my view, however, Kristeva's attempt to oppose *technē* and *psychē* becomes increasingly problematic and the two traditions she sets up become harder and harder to tell apart.

Genetics

First, Kristeva tackles the question of genetics and bio-determinism. She begins with a discussion of the Virgin Mary that again notes the paradox that Mary should simultaneously be at the centre of a cult of maternity and a cult of birth control (Kristeva 1999a: 25). She quickly moves from this ancient act of religious *technē* to the political *technē* of totalitarianism and contemporary technocratic societies: 'Moreover, the technological progress of the advanced democracies, which have the ambition to "manage" life in all innocence, is heavy with the same totalitarian menace: the menace that destroys life after having devalued the question of its meaning' (Kristeva 1999a: 25). Kristeva again shows that there is a philosophical continuity between religious doctrine and modern genetics that stems from the reduction of the maternal to a biological tool manipulated by a divine or divinized technician. If we do not want technology alone to be responsible for the future of the species, Kristeva argues, then it becomes more essential than ever to celebrate maternity as the product of a loving desire to have children that cannot be reduced to a simple biological or technological process (Kristeva 1999a: 25). To counter the culture that tries to programme destiny into the genetic code itself, Kristeva argues, we need to turn to the women who are active participants in the technological 'upheavals' of modern society (Kristeva 1995: 221). So Kristeva goes on to argue that technological advances such as birth control and artificial insemination have – far from contributing to the ever-increasing technological management of life – been essential in maintaining the psychoanalytic dimension of *giving* life:

> Since they are more skilled than ever at controlling their life, thanks to technology, women are also more ready than ever not to be simple genitors [*génitrices*] (assuming that being a genitor could ever be simple) but to *give meaning* to the act of *giving* [donation] that is life.
> (Kristeva 1999a: 26)

The basic point is that technological advances in birth control – which have effectively guaranteed that no woman needs to have a baby unless she actually chooses to – mean than maternity is 'more ... than ever' invested with a psychoanalytic rather a simply biological meaning. This is fair enough but it does not explain why the presumably originary psychoanalytic desire to give life should stand in need of technology's 'help' in the first place – why were women apparently *less* ready to be anything other than genitors *before* the advent of contraception? – or whether that technology can be easily exempted from the accusations of technological management levelled elsewhere. There is a weird sense in Kristeva's argument – that we first noticed in the discussion of the Virgin Mary from *In the Beginning was Love* – that technological supplementation is necessary to fulfil an unexplained lack in a supposedly primary psycho-sexuality. For Kristeva, the feminine sacred is – quite commendably – conceived as a response to 'the new kind of *soft* [English in text] totalitarianism which, after the celebrated "loss of values", lifts up life as the "supreme value", but life for itself, life without questions, with women/mothers being the natural instruments of that "zoology"' (Kristeva 1999a: 26). What if – however unwittingly – the sacred is *itself* the product of the 'totalitarianism *soft*' of technology?

Totalitarianism

Second, Kristeva's text moves on to consider the political implications of the sacred in more detail. She begins by asking the question of whether the sacred could ever form the basis for a politics (Kristeva 1999a: 66). It is again clear that the shadow of 'hard' as well as 'soft' totalitarianism hangs over this debate with discussions ranging from Hitler's Germany to Peron's Argentina. My view is that this critique of totalitarianism again goes hand in hand with a critique of the technology that in Kristeva's analysis makes totalitarianism possible. If we follow Kristeva's argument through, we will see that the question of technology again refuses to remain a merely secondary, instrumental or indeed 'technical' question. Kristeva categorically states at one point that the sacred cannot form the basis for a politics: '[n]one has for me the singular lucidity to carry that word "sacred"' (Kristeva 1999a: 218). But her argument goes on to demonstrate the incompatibility of the sacred and the political by drawing a very interesting contrast between the 'exception' of French Republicanism and the 'rule' of National Socialism or Argentinian military dictatorship:

> The 14th July Celebration. Just yesterday, in front of the TV, I was overwhelmed by the *Marseillaise* on the Champs, I got up out of my chair, a lump in my throat. A republican religion? Of course. But I would maintain that it succeeds best where the others fail: in

164 *Atheologies*

> preserving the community, and the individual, and in the practical and concrete improvement of the human condition. Not enough, never enough, with too many mistakes, but what's better?
>
> I know that there is no lack of people who see the same sacred in Hitler, especially in Hitler, who has himself been on TV recently. Well, not me. In my view, the fascination with the feeble body (Hitler's), or with that of a woman who didn't hang around on political platforms but who was all the more exciting for that [Eva Peron], and manages to get a hard-on to ensure the power and coherence of a group, stems from a secular religion. It is so much more dangerous when it carries neither the prospect of Hell nor a morality. It is a political religion that seems to me to end up in the most pernicious religion of all, in the most illusory sense of the term, and it has nothing to do with the sacred.
>
> (Kristeva 1999a: 219)

Kristeva's argument here is obviously commendable but my feeling is that it is rather vulnerable in the context of her overall argument. The obvious political difference between the French republic and the Nazi state is that one is liberal democratic whereas the other was totalitarian but – given everything Kristeva has said about psychoanalysis and belief – this is surely outweighed by their abundant similarities. There is such a deep psychoanalytic identity between Christianity, totalitarianism and modern technocracy in Kristeva's analysis that her attempt to distinguish between secular political belief systems like liberal democracy and fascism on such limited grounds looks like splitting hairs. They are both secular religions, primarily sexual fantasies of fusion with an all-powerful paternal or maternal figure (whether it be Marianne or the Führer) and both inherently technological in their fabrication of an identity for the people or *Volk* (no coincidence that both are/were principally mediated experiences either). This is obviously not to suggest for one moment that there is no meaningful *ethical* or *political* difference between liberal democracies and totalitarian states – and of course Kristeva knows this better than anyone – but that the entirely separate *psychoanalytic* distinction between the two does not stand up. Now this point is also very well made by Catherine Clément who insists that Kristeva cannot make simple distinctions between the politics of the sacred and the politics of totalitarianism because they are mutually implicated: 'Hitler almost certainly experimented with the sacred' (Kristeva 1999a: 232). So Kristeva's attempt to distinguish between the sacred and the religious and technological again proves difficult to maintain, then, and instead we can see the makings of a very dubious distinction between what we might call 'sacred technology' – democratic technocracies, the pill, artificial insemination, and so forth, on the one hand – and 'religious technology' – totalitarian technocracies, genetic determinism and indeed all other forms of technological life or thought – on the other. What I would want to ask, though, is how – to put it more bluntly than she deserves – anyone other than Kristeva is supposed to tell the difference between the two?

The media

Finally, Kristeva moves on to examine in more detail what form this pre-technological politics of the sacred might take. I have already suggested that by definition the sacred resists the demands of what, with a nod to Guy Debord, Kristeva calls '*la société du spectacle*'. It is found on the margins of the symbolic order and its defining gesture is resistance, bluff and ruse against its authority. It is Kristeva's conclusion that the sacred can only protect itself against the threat of totalitarianism and the technology inherent within it by remaining *secret*: 'the rehabilitation of secrecy can be a salutary counterpoint to such tendencies, to such dangers' (Kristeva 1999a: 227). If this sounds reasonable enough, the onus is still on Kristeva to nominate an example of an absolutely secret space within the public arena of the spectacle society. Kristeva floats a number of candidates for sacralization such as the voice of Maria Callas but perhaps her most interesting proposal concerns the then-recently dead Princess Diana. Kristeva's argument is that Princess Diana's status as a sacred figure is not so much due to her mass media appeal but because she embodies the universal but essentially unrepresentable lack that is melancholia: '[t]he spectacle society cries for a woman who died from an absence of communication' (Kristeva 1999a: 277). For Kristeva, humanity projects on to the lacking figure of Diana its own essential lack of love or as she dramatically puts it 'men and women, we are all an unloved Diana' (Kristeva 1999a: 277). More generally, Kristeva asks whether Diana's life and death constitute the final triumph of the religious over the sacred or – perhaps – a sacred intervention into the sphere of the religious:

> Is it the ultimate triumph of the spectacle society, which adds death itself to its false set of accounts? What if – on the contrary – the virtual universe has been fissured by the time of the sensible, by the feminine timelessness? That would be a sacred ruse of the sacred.
> (Kristeva 1999a: 278)

Now even if we take Kristeva's obviously contentious view of Diana as a kind of modern-day Mary or Angele de Foligno at face value, we immediately encounter the same problems we found earlier. The argument seems to be that Diana is sacred because she encapsulates the unrepresentable absence that is melancholia but it is difficult to see what the basis for our supposed identification with her could be if not the mass *representation* of that absence. There is no way in which the spectacle society can project itself onto a 'women who died from the absence of communication' unless that absence is itself somehow communicated as a spectacle. This means that the Diana phenomenon is another example of that paradoxical logic whereby Kristeva's distinction between the sacred critique of technology and the religious exploitation of it turns into a perilous distinction between sacred technology and religious technology. We need to explain why this ostensibly originary sexuality always requires a technological prosthesis at the primal scene to make it what it should be in itself anyway and my argument in what follows will be that Derrida helps us to answer that question. Why – to pose the question yet again – does the sacred appear to depend on the very technics it simultaneously decries?

Sacred technologies

Julia Kristeva's attempt to elaborate a non-technological concept of the sacred is, then, an important but ultimately problematic one. Its failure has a number of implications that we will develop in the remainder of this chapter. First, technology is not just a set of empirical objects to be used or not by human beings as the case may be but something that plays a part in constructing what we understand as the human. Second, technology is neither a particular period nor even an epoch in a history of being whose essence is, as Heidegger famously put it, nothing technological but something that is intrinsic to being in general. Finally, this means that the question of technology must therefore be re-thought in terms that do not assume a simple distinction between the human and the non-human, being and non-being, life and death. The upshot of this radicalization of technology is Derrida's claim of nearly 40 years ago that 'a new name must perhaps be found in order to remove it from its traditional problematic' and the catechretic term that suggests itself is 'originary technicity'. This Derridean concept of a technics more original than any particular technological object or historical epoch will have important implications for the Kristevan critique of technology. In summary, I want to suggest that Derrida's account of originary technicity helps us to understand why Kristeva's concept of the sacred remains technological all the way down.

Derrida and originary technicity

I want to give a brief overview of Jacques Derrida's reading of technics with particular reference to the relationship between religion and technology. It will be my contention that Derrida's and Kristeva's readings of technology share a number of key features although they are ultimately very different. First, they both follow Heidegger in extending the question of technology far beyond the empirical realm of modern techno-science into the dimension of thought in general. Second, they both conflate the question of technology with the question of religion so that the two ostensibly opposed discourses are shown to be inseparable. Finally, Derrida and Kristeva both posit their respective discourses of deconstruction and the sacred in opposition to the triumphalism of contemporary or techno-scientific positivism in which the human is reduced to an effect or object of the technological. The big difference between them is that Kristeva posits the psychoanalytic primacy of the human *over* the technological whereas Derrida posits what could be called an 'originary technicity' that *precedes* all concepts of the human and technological alike. This dispute about the relative merits of *phusis* and *technē* comes to a head in Derrida and Kristeva's respective readings of religion – *Le féminin et le sacré* (1999a) and 'Faith and Knowledge' ([1996] 1998a) – where we see two quite different accounts of the relationship between religion and technology. In Derrida's reading of originary technicity, I think we glimpse a more complex account of the relationship between religion and technology where they are no longer held to be mutually antagonistic concepts.

Philosophy and technology

Jacques Derrida's deconstruction of technology needs to be seen against the background of a larger understanding of the technological that is synonymous with Western philosophy itself. Philosophy has almost always distinguished between human nature and technology on the grounds that the latter is a secondary tool or instrument of the former. Plato's *Meno* arguably brings metaphysics into existence with a distinction between the immortal soul and the body, the transcendental and the empirical, form and matter and *logos* and *technē* (Plato 1961). Aristotle's famous position in the *Physics* is that the relationship between the human and the technological is an essentially extrinsic one in which the former uses the latter as an instrument or means to bring about certain ends (Aristotle 1984). Martin Heidegger occupies a slightly anomalous place in this tradition because instead of reducing technology to an instrumental status, he sees a meditation on the *Gestell* or enframing of the technological as holding within it a revelation of Being. But even Heidegger valorizes only certain forms of *technē* – such as handwriting – as authentic and revelatory of *Dasein*'s Being and relegates others – like typewriting – as secondary and reifying (Derrida 1989b: 10).[2] For all its avant-garde status, the work of cybercultural theorists like Donna Haraway often merely confirms the Aristotelian tradition by negative example: Haraway's celebration of technology inverts the traditional supremacy of the organic but leaves the essential opposition between the human and the technological intact (Haraway 1991). In Derrida's deconstruction, however, philosophy brings this reading of technology to – if not an end – then at least a closure.

Deconstruction and technology

Derrida offers a remarkably consistent reading of technology throughout his work that has only recently begun to receive critical attention. It goes without saying that his texts are 'interested' in technology on even the most banal and empirical level if we think of the numerous references to machines, computers, telephones, television and email that litter his texts. It is possible to trace a particular analysis of technology from his earliest interventions on writing and textuality as the condition of possibility of the voice (Derrida 1973; 1976; 1978a) to his current concerns on media and spectrality as the condition of ontology (Derrida 1994; 1998a; 2002b). The consistent position of these texts is to resist the traditional philosophical reduction of the technological to a secondary status by insisting on what Bernard Stiegler has called 'originary technicity' (1994: 30).[3] This is not simply due to the fact that the technological objects under discussion cannot be reduced to the status of mere tools because – like writing – they have the capacity to operate in the absence of any human intention whatsoever. More generally, Derrida's radical and ambitious claim will be that the technological is not just an inauthentic derivation that is secondary to the human but – in a sense that needs to be defined carefully to avoid mistaken allegations of humanist fatalism or techno-scientific triumphalism – the condition of possibility for being in general:

> There is no naturally originary body: technology has not simply added itself, from the outside or after the fact, as a foreign body. Or at least this foreign or dangerous supplement is 'originarily' at work and in place in the supposedly ideal interiority of the 'body and soul'.
> (Derrida 1995c: 244–5)

Derrida's argument runs largely as follows. Humanity – whether it is understood theologically, philosophically or, as is increasingly the case, bio-genetically – necessarily involves a negotiation with technology – whether it takes the form of sign systems, writing, or empirical technology like machines – in order to authenticate itself. The human must negotiate with the technological to be itself in the first place but – and here of course is the classic Derridaean twist – this negotiation with technology is also the ruination of any pure, essential concept of the human. This argument does not entail a simple *inversion* of the traditional hierarchy so that technology begins to assume an 'essential' status over humanity but – as is the case with Derrida's famous analysis of writing, for example – an *overturning* of the opposition in which the empirical concept of technology assumes the more radical and generalized status of 'originary technicity'. There is an important sense in which the entirety of being should be described as 'technical', Derrida wants to suggest, because it is structured along the same lines of delay, difference and supplementation as the traditional concept of technology in metaphysics. So this 'originary technicity' is neither human or technological in the empirical sense of the terms but another quasi-transcendental name – following such strategically-deployed predecessors as 'arche-writing' or the general text – for the generalized system of differences in which the opposition between the two terms is (de-)constituted. For Derrida, then, 'originary technicity' does not simply require 'the re-siting of the technical within the human' (Beardsworth 1996: 149) – to use Richard Beardsworth's striking but perhaps still slightly too anthropocentric formula – but rather an attempt to articulate an *internal* relation between everything that goes under the categories of the human and the non-human, the living and the non-living and more generally even being and non-being.

Now Derrida's concept of being as 'originary technicity' necessarily involves a re-thinking of the history of the philosophy of technology. It resists all attempts to essentialize the distinction between the human and the technological whether they come from one side or the other. Derrida holds that metaphysical humanism and techno-scientific positivism – to take only the two most obvious contemporary readings of technology – simply represent different sides of the same attempt to make good the human/technological distinction. Derrida's readings of 'originary technicity' habitually involve a double move against valorizations of *psychē* or human consciousness, on the one hand, and valorizations of technology, on the other. On the one hand, religious or philosophical humanism is seen to entail an originary negotiation with mechanicity, automation or repetition in its attempt to valorize the human: Freud's uncannily successful comparison between the supposedly spontaneous processes of human memory and that of a mere writing machine reveals the finitude of mnemic spontaneity (Derrida 1978b: 196–231). On the other hand, scientific or technological positivism depend on a prior commitment to transcendental philosophical values without being able to think the fact: even Stiegler's more anthropological attempts to see philosophy as the simple *effect* of empirical technological developments are vulnerable to the 'transcendental contraband' objection that philosophical claims – about universality, causality and truth – are essential to the argument they are advancing (Bennington 2000: 162–79). The point is once again to show that the attempt to determine or programme the meaning of being according to a single value – whether it be 'nature' or 'technology' – must always fail because it depends upon and inevitably reproduces a residue or remainder that cannot be contained or conceptualized as such. This concept of 'original technicity' enables Derrida to resist both the totalizing claims of a theological or philosophical humanism (which would reduce the technological to a mere tool of the human) and a scientific positivism (which would reduce the human to an effect or object of the technological) by showing that both claims violently foreclose what we have seen to be the arrival of the other as justice. If we begin with a simple concept of the human or the technological as primary, then there is simply nothing to decide in absolutely singular ethical situations such as that presented by, say, the human genome project. For Derrida, as we have constantly seen throughout this book, deconstruction is an incalculable experience of alterity as justice that is ultimately as foreign to all humanisms as it is to all techno-scientific positivisms:

> It's better to let the future open – this is the axiom of deconstruction, the thing from which it always starts out and which binds it, like the future itself, to alterity, to the priceless dignity of alterity, that is to say, to justice.
> (Derrida 2002b: 21)

Religion and technology

Derrida's concept of the originary technicity of the human, to conclude, clearly necessitates a massive re-thinking of the relationship between being and non-being at every level (Stiegler: 1994; Beardsworth 1996; Critchley 1999: 143–83; Clark 2000: 238–58). It is Derrida's hitherto little-discussed analysis of the relationship between religion and technics, however, that I want to focus on in more detail in the remainder of this discussion. Religion and technics are historically and conceptually opposed concepts throughout Western philosophy regardless of whether the distinction is construed from the perspective of Christian theology, on the one side, or Enlightenment metaphysics, on the other. More obviously, the opposition between religion and technology still manifests itself in a whole host of associated philosophical oppositions (religion versus reason), political configurations (Christian versus non-Christian, Church versus State, and so on), and ethical questions (fundamentalism, questions about women's rights, abortion, contraception, the human genome project). Derrida's concept of 'originary technicity' is remarkable, however, because it is the first explicit attempt, to my knowledge, to think religion and technology together as part of the same phenomenon: 'at stake is doubtless everything which *today* links Religion and Technics in a singular configuration' (Derrida 1994: 167).[4] The concept of originary technics necessarily precedes the distinction between religion and technology because neither exists without the system of differential relations or supplementation it lends its name to. There would be no religion whatsoever if it did not originarily differentiate itself from technology and no technology if it did not differentiate itself from the religious. This makes it impossible to analyse religion without analysing technology and vice versa because the two terms are inseparable even in their most obvious empirical or institutional forms. In Derrida's 'Faith and Knowledge' ([1996] 1998a), what we might call this originary technicity of the religious is set out in more detail.

Derrida, religion and technology

I want to focus in more depth, then, on Derrida's remarkable text 'Faith and Knowledge: The Two Sources of "Religion" at the Limits of Reason

Alone' ([1996] 1998a). It takes as its starting point the following question: '[h]ow "to talk" religion? Of religion? Singularly of religion, today?' (Derrida 1998a: 1). The essay performs the characteristic Derridaean reading of theology (Derrida 1989a; 1995a) of locating a point of undecidability between the ostensibly theological and the non-theological, the theist and atheist. This middle ground between religion and reason – which is variously figured in Derrida's texts as *khōra*, the promise and the messianic without messianisms (Derrida 1998a: 16–20) – is interestingly figured in technological terms here. In 'Faith and Knowledge', the religious is originarily technical and it is that paradoxical logic that I wish to explain.

'Faith and Knowledge'

Jacques Derrida's starting point is the meaning of the word 'religion': '[r]eligion? *In the singular?*' (Derrida 1998a: 25). 'Religion' can never be singular for a number of reasons that go on to become major themes in the essay. First, 'religion' cannot easily be separated either historically or philosophically from the 'secular' (a concept which is itself religious of course): ostensibly non-theological concepts like the ethical, the economic or the political are the product of a theological heritage. Second, religion (let's assume the scare-quotes from now on) is originarily a *response*, an address or answer to a call from an other: a pre-originary openness or 'yes' that is the condition of my identity even if it is that to which I want to say 'no'. Third, religion is originally a word of Latin etymology (*re-ligare*, to re-bind) that inevitably raises questions about the extent to which it can be translated into non-European or non-Christian contexts.

Derrida's most important point about the irreducible plurality of the religious, however, lies in the Bergsonian claim that it has two main sources respectively called 'faith' and 'knowledge':

1 The experience of *belief*, on the one hand (believing or credit, the fiduciary or the trustworthy in the act of faith, fidelity, the appeal to blind confidence, the testimonial that is always beyond proof, demonstrative reason, intuition); and
2 The experience of the unscathed, of *sacredness* or of *holiness*, on the other.

(Derrida 1998a: 33)

Religions in the *plural*, then, are the subject of Derrida's essay. The irreducible plurality of a religion which is both religious and secular, call and response and faith and knowledge is pitted against the far too normative and simplistic concept of a monolithic 'return of the religious' in the remainder of the text. This 'return of the religious' today is neither simply 'religious' nor even a 'return' if everything Derrida says about religion holds and to understand it we need a more complex trope for the relationship between the historically and philosophically opposed concepts of the religious and the non-religious. For Derrida, that trope is (auto-) immunization.

(Auto-)immunization

Derrida's well-known argument is that religion and reason (associated, as he says, not only with philosophy, but with science as technoscience) are bound together in what he calls a 'terrifying but fatal logic' of (auto-) immunization (Derrida 1998a: 44). It is Derrida's major contention that the 'return' of the religious in techno-scientific modernity constitutes a particularly disturbing example of the 'logic' by which the human body will naturally or chemically (with the help of immuno-depressant drugs used in organ transplants) suppress its own immune system in order to allow foreign antigens to enter itself without being rejected:

> Religion today allies itself with tele-technoscience, to which it reacts with all its forces. It is, *on the one hand*, globalization: it produces, weds, exploits the capital and knowledge of tele-mediatization; neither the trips and global spectacularizing of the Pope, nor the interstate dimensions of the 'Rushdie affair', nor planetary terrorism would otherwise be possible, at this rhythm – and we could multiply such indications *ad infinitum*. But, *on the other hand*, it reacts immediately, *simultaneously*, declaring war against that which gives it this new power only at the cost of dislodging it from all its proper places, *in truth from place itself*, from the *taking-place* of its truth. It conducts a terrible war against that which protects it only by threatening it, according to this double and contradictory structure: immunitary and auto-immunitary.
> (Derrida 1998a: 46)

Religion suppresses its own 'natural' immunity to the foreign body of technology in order to better tolerate the artificial graft or prosthesis but at the same time it violently reacts against, and begins to reject, this foreign body in its system. The religious swallows the rational cure in order to heal itself but the technological *pharmakon* is also a poison which it is forced to vomit in a series of ever-more violent motions. This (un)holy alliance between the religious and the technological can be formulated as a logic or even as a kind of machine – '[e]ach time what is involved is a machine, a tele-machine' (Derrida 1998a: 42) – and to understand it we need to take that machine to pieces.

On the one hand, Derrida argues that religion and reason (as technoscience) are intimately connected with each other. He argues that the contemporary phenomenon labouring under the less-than-perfect name of the 'return of the religious' cannot be understood if we continue to naïvely oppose 'Reason *and* Religion, Critique or Science *and* Religion, technoscientific Modernity *and* Religion' (Derrida 1998a: 28). Derrida's argument is that religion and reason are both responses to the pre-originary 'yes' to the other we have already encountered in texts like 'How to Avoid Speaking'. Religion and reason are, in other words, the products of a language event that they did not choose but which they inherited as the condition of their identity and which they must automatically repeat regardless of whether they wish to do so or not. Religious and rational discourse necessarily take the form of a repeated pledge, promise or testimony to speak the truth – even or especially when they wish to lie or dissimulate – as the condition for addressing the other at all (Derrida 1998a: 44). The promise or guarantee to address the other faithfully and truthfully that Derrida is referring to here is as essential to Christian acts of prayer as it is to television programmes or to any other discourse that presupposes a shared knowledge or understanding. There would be no promise of good faith whatsoever if it was not capable of being repeated as such but – as Derrida shows at length in 'A Number of Yes'– this repetition always contains the threat of mechanical repetition or bad faith because it is capable of operating independently of our original intentions. This essential repeatability that precedes all empirical concepts of religion and technoscience exposes them to a quasi-transcendental 'originary technicity' as their condition of possibility (Derrida 1998a: 47). Now this (un)holy alliance between the ostensibly exclusive concepts of faith and technology manifests itself on the most empirical and institutional level possible in everything from the propagandizing of John Paul II to the appearance of Osama Bin Laden on television stations like Al-Jazeera. For Derrida, to summarize, religion and technology are allied in an unprecedented quasi-technical logic that characterizes – inasmuch as it can be characterized in a few pages – the phenomenon of the 'return' of the 'religious' today.

On the other hand, however, religion and reason reject one another in the same automatic, machine-like way in which they allied themselves (Derrida 1998a: 44). Religion finds that technology is a poison as well as a cure because it carries within it a generalized virtuality or spectrality of presence, identity and location that disrupts the purity of the holy or sacred on which the religious depends (Derrida 1994; 2002b). Technology generalizes religion on a global level at the cost of displacing or spectralizing its sense of identity (the individual, the community), its sense of place or territory (Christendom, the homeland, the promised land) and its attachment to the polis and the nation–state (Europe, Israel/Palestine or what is called 'the Gulf' or 'the Middle East'). Religion's immune system begins to kick in once again when it feels its commitment to the unscathed or sacred to be under threat and it starts to reject its foreign body by acts of violence designed to cleanse, preserve or re-establish the purity of the sacred once again (Derrida 1998a: 44). Religious (auto-) immunization gives rise to new forms of violence which either ally themselves more directly with technology (the implicitly hegemonic assumptions lying behind internationally broadcast Christian appeals for 'peace' or 'one world') or seek to return to a pre-technological archaic state (the return of ritualistic bodily violence in the form of sacrifice, torture and sexual mutilation) (Derrida 1998a: 52). The most horrifying example of religious (auto-)immunization today, however – a 'today' after September 11th 2001 of course – might be the explicit and contradictory conjunction of religious violence that is *both* hypersophisticated *and* archaic at the same time. This can be seen in the case of Islamic suicide bombers who communicate by video, email and the Internet, learn to fly jumbo jets, and wage chemical and biological warfare with the aim of protecting themselves against the godless, decadent, Western technocracy or Christian nations prosecuting a crusade against heathens or heretics with smart bombs, satellite technology and a weapon of mass destruction called a 'daisy-cutter'. For Derrida, to summarize again, religion and reason react against one another according to a logic that is every bit as automatic and technical as their coming together.

In summary, then, Derrida argues that religion and reason (as technoscience) are locked together in this logic of (auto-)immunization. It is important to stress that although he explains the relationship between the two concepts in what are for him unusually empirical terms – he continually makes reference to the fact that he is writing about religion *today* – the role played by technology here is a *quasi-transcendental* one as well. Derrida continually emphasizes that the relation between religion and technoscience is *originarily* a technical one in the sense that technics exceeds its empirical context to supply the name for the system of originary difference and supplementation that gives the two terms their more or less stable identity: '[t]he relation between these two motions or these two sources is ineluctable, and therefore automatic and mechanical' (Derrida 1998a: 46–7). Derrida's argument, then, complicates the relationship between the ostensibly opposed concepts and traditions of religion and technology by showing that they depend on the same original and predetermining generalized structure of alterity. The structure he is describing here goes under various well-known quasi-transcendental names in his text(s) – *khōra*, the promise, the messianic are just three of the most obvious – but my contention is that we need to add original technicity to that list: 'they ought to be thought *together*, as *one and the same possibility*: the machine-like and faith' (Derrida 1998a: 48). This Derridaean attempt to think the sacred and the technological together has – I want to argue – important implications for what we have seen to be the Kristevan attempt to think the sacred as unscathed of all technology. For Derrida, the religious – whether considered as faith or the sacred – is *originarily technical* and this state of affairs bring him into conflict with Kristeva's sacred critique of *technē*.

The originary technicity of the sacred

What, then, are the main implications of Derrida's reading of technology for Kristeva's concept of the sacred? I would argue that Derrida's argument about the originary technicity of the religious clarifies a number of problematic aspects we have located within Kristeva's sacred critique of *technē*.

First, Derrida situates Kristeva's critique – despite her careful attempts to distinguish psychoanalysis from other modes of rationalism – absolutely within the Aristotelian instrumentalist reading of the relationship between humanity and technology. Kristeva's attempt to negotiate a concept of the sacred as prior to all technology simply reproduces the opposition between *phusis* and *technē* as user and tool. The repeated fear in her texts that techno-science is reducing the human to an object merely represents an updated version of Mary Shelley's humanistic fear in *Frankenstein* (1818) that the secondary has become unnaturally primary or the monster has become the maker.

More generally, Derrida's concept of originary technicity possibly explains both why the sacred *has* to be opposed to technology and why Kristeva has such great difficulties in *making good* that opposition. Kristeva's critique of *technē* relies on surreptitiously technological or gestures throughout, as we have seen, but Derrida's concept of originary technicity makes it clear that this is a structural necessity rather than a simple accident. Derrida's thesis is that the human must run the technological gauntlet in order to establish itself but at the same time this technological prosthesis always makes it more – or less – than the human. So what Kristeva unfortunately calls the sacred 'antidote' to technology in its most bio-deterministic forms in fact invites another pharmacological metaphor because it is a perfect example of what Derrida calls the logic of (auto-)immunization.

The sacred must *suppress* its own immunity to technology in order to become sacred in the first place and we might speculate that it is precisely this process of (auto-)immunization that also produces the sacred's violent reaction *against* technology. There might of course be an objection here that Kristeva's psychoanalytic concept of a sacred experience immanent to the subject is very different from the religious version of the sacred as an experience of a transcendental object given by Derrida and so the logic of (auto-)immunization does not apply. This might well be true as far as it goes but what defines the sacred in the Derridaean sense is not its immanent or transcendental status but the fact that it is an experience of the *unscathed* (Derrida 1998a: 33) and everything we know about Kristeva's concept from the emphasis on the body, secrecy and the unnameable or unthinkable outside identifies it as just such an intimate experience of a pure interiority.

Jacques Derrida's concept of originary technicity undercuts Kristeva's concept of the pre-technological sacred, then, but this is not quite the whole story about the relationship between religion and technology. It is possible to argue that Derrida's re-siting of the technical back within Kristeva's concept of the sacred does not necessarily spell the end for Kristeva's immanent negative theology. My contention in the final part of this chapter will be that Derrida's concept of originary technicity enables us to begin a slightly more constructive dialogue between theology and technology by reinventing the sacred in less metaphysical terms. In Derrida's concept of originary technicity, we begin to glimpse the possibility of what might be called a 'theology after technics'.

Theology after technics?

I want to conclude this chapter, then, by offering some notes towards a future 'theology after technics'. It is important to establish at the outset that such a theology is theoretically possible in the first place and not simply a contradiction-in-terms and answers to this question are only beginning to appear at the time of writing (Stiegler 2001; de Vries 2002b). My contention will be that a theology after technics is not only possible but necessary as a theological response to a question that is too simply reduced to the status of 'modern technology', the 'information age' or 'the twenty-first century'. Let me stake out the territory.

Jacques Derrida emphatically claims that faith and knowledge, religion and technology, the sacred and science are not mutually exclusive concepts and the task for any theology of technicity is to think these two different possibilities together. It would thus be a mistake to identify the logic of originary technicity as either exclusively secular or theological because, as we have seen, it is precisely what allows them to appear as oppositions. It is the consistent argument of 'Faith and Knowledge' that the logic of originary technicity does not *destroy* religion by elevating technology to a God-like position but – on the contrary – acts as the very *condition* of its possibility. Technics violently intensifies religion's very commitment to the sanctity of the unscathed or sacred precisely because it always mediates or contaminates it at source. Religion's access to the sacred is not barred by technics, in other words, because originary technicity is the basis on which there is access to the sacred in the first place: no sacred without technics. If this is the case, then the question is not whether there still *can* be a concept of the sacred after technics – Pope John Paul II and Osama Bin Laden would seem to have settled that question pretty conclusively between them – but rather *which* concept of the sacred comes out the other end of technicity. Does theology after technics have to intensify its drive for a pure, unmediated experience of the sacred and the disturbing socio-political violence it carries with it or could it accept the impossibility of such an unmediated experience of presence and the drive for mastery it contains?

Derrida could license a theology that does not simply react automatically to the logic of originary technicity, in my view, but which harnesses that logic to the challenge of developing a post-ontotheological theology that seeks to think God beyond or outside human being or being in general. It is my proposal, then, that a theology after technics could take advantage of the technical critique of attempts to valorize either the human or the technological as originary. The logic of technicity refuses both theological and humanist claims to elevate the human to an autonomous status anchored in God or Reason and scientific/technological attempts to reduce it to a soft machine with a built-in self-destruct mechanism, we have seen, because both predetermine the undecidability on which the opposition between the human and the technological depends. There is a constitutive sense in which everything that goes under the categories of the human, the living and even of being in general exists in an intrinsic relation to the non-human, the non-living or non-being in general (whether animal, vegetable, mineral, machine, ghost, spectre or divinity) and so every attempt to essentialize that distinction must fail. This analysis of the relationship between being and non-being undoubtedly stands in historic contradiction to Christian theology of causality and creation – in which God plays the role of *causa efficiens* and Man the *ens creatum* – but at this point the very Heideggerian question arises of whether this theology is not in fact ontotheology: '[h]e then becomes even in theology the God of the philosophers, namely, of those who define the unconcealed and the concealed in terms of the causality of making, without ever considering the essential provenance of this causality' (Heidegger 1997: 26). If originary technicity enables us to deconstruct the concept of God as *causa efficiens*, does this necessarily count as an argument against the existence of God or could it perhaps be a means of liberating Him from ontotheology?

Derrrida's logic of originary technicity has theological potential, then, because the originary relation between being and non-being it entails offers a suggestive means of describing the relation between the human being and God in non-ontotheological terms. Its negotiation of an internal relation between being and non-being is not merely a means of re-articulating the relationship between the human and the animal, the prosthesis or the machine, but between the human and the divine as well because the task of any post-ontotheological theology is precisely to think the divine as otherwise than being. My proposal, then, is that a theology after technics could take the form of a modern negative theology that would vigorously police *all* attempts to reduce the alterity of the sacred – whether it be conceived religiously as the transcendent or psychoanalytically as the immanent – to a tool or instrument of being. The concept of theology after originary technics could contribute to a long theological tradition of criticizing metaphysical or ontotheological concepts of God and positing his irreducibility to a science of being. There is a potential sense in which this theology might offer a means of negating ontotheological concepts of God as being or essence *without* – and here is the rub – incurring the common accusation of re-affirming such concepts at a hyperessential or super-eminent level. This theology after technics might contribute to the development of a post-ontotheological theology that does not simply collapse back into the ontology it opposes – I want to suggest – because it would take the form of a moment of interruption or undecidability within ontology itself. Let me put some flesh on the bones of these speculations by briefly tracing its implications through twentieth-century theological readings of technology from Martin Heidegger to Julia Kristeva.

Martin Heidegger

First, I would like to consider Heidegger's famous critique of ontotheology in this context. Heidegger criticizes the ontotheological concept of God as *causa sui* because it 'corresponds to the reason-giving path back to the ultimate *ratio*' (Heidegger 1969: 60). Heidegger's fullest explanation of the royal road to the *causa sui* occurs in the collection entitled *The Principle of Reason* (1991). It shows how the principle of reason gradually develops from Plato through Leibniz to the position where 'God only exists insofar as the principle of reason holds' (Heidegger 1991: 28). The radical nature of this claim is not that reason is the only way to prove God's existence, Heidegger suggests, but that God exists purely and simply in order to prove reason. This means that God exists as nothing more than a kind of transcendental anchor for human understanding – or to put it in the terms of *The Question of Technology* – as a tool, means or instrument which the human may utilize to make the whole of being intelligible. There is a basic continuity between the ontotheological thought that sees God as a *causa efficiens* who can be put to work in the service of reason, in other words, and the technological thought that sees a river or forest as a potential dam or power station to be put to use in the production of energy. They are both products of the principle of reason that places the human at the centre of being and sees the world as existing purely in order to be calculated or exploited for the maximum possible yield. Now Heidegger's critique of ontotheology, then, is not simply that it is wrong nor that it is futile (though it is) but that it constitutes a Promethean act of presumption regarding man's place in relation to the entirety of Being. So the later Heidegger – the delimitations of theology in earlier essays like 'Phenomenology and Theology' notwithstanding – seeks to oppose the God of philosophy and metaphysical theology with the God of faith: '[w]ill Christian theology one day learn to take seriously the word of the apostle [St Paul] and thus also the conception of philosophy as foolishness?' (Heidegger 1998: 288).

Heidegger is historically vulnerable to the charge that his critique of ontotheology is as problematic as what it is criticizing. It is Lévinas's ground-breaking claim that Heidegger's prioritizing of ontological comprehension reduces the alterity of the other to the identity of the same (Lévinas: 1998: 5–10). Marion argues that Heidegger's critique of ontotheology takes God out of the ontic frying pan only to land him in the ontological fire (Marion 1991: 41). Derrida develops a critique of Heidegger's commitment to metaphysics across nearly 40 years of texts that take in the ontico-ontological distinction ('Différance'), his valorization of 'spirit' over and against technology (*Of Spirit*), and his famous improvised speech in front of a group of Zurich students about one day possibly writing a theology without the word 'being' ('How to Avoid Speaking'). Derrida's argument, as we have already seen, is that the philosophical attempt not to speak of God is always contaminated by the pre-originary 'promise' of language which has already quasi-mechanically committed us to speaking about the ineffable even if it is merely to say nothing (Derrida 1998a: 59). Heidegger's speech about perhaps one day writing a philosophy in which the word 'being' did not figure is compromised not merely by the nice irony that everything he said was *already* being written down by one of the students present but by his larger claim that the revelation of God (*Offenbarung*) can only flash or appear against the background of the revelation of Being (*Offenbarkeit*). So Heidegger's theology without being could still only be written against the backdrop of the dimension of Being itself: '[a]lthough God is not and need not be thought from being as His essence or foundation, the *dimension of Being* opens up access to the advent, the experience, the encounter with this God' (Derrida 1989a: 59). For Derrida, Heidegger's theology 'within and without being' even seems to belong within the metaphysical, negative theological tradition of designating being as the threshold (*parvis*) beyond which lies the naked hyperessential presence of God: 'Is this a theological, an onto-theological, tradition? A theological tradition?' (Derrida 1989a: 59).

Heidegger's attempt to counter the kind of representative thinking that sees God as the *causa sui* and reaches its culmination in the epoch of modern techno-science ends up – as Jean-Luc Marion has controversially shown (Marion 1991: 41) – turning Him into an instrument or tool at the beck and call of an anterior ontology. It can thus be confirmed that his attempt to distance himself from the principle of reason that produces both theology and technology still finally remains within the orbit of *causa efficiens* and *ens creatum*, on the one hand, and *phusis* and *technē*, on the other. Yet it is possible that the logic of originary technicity could offer a means of re-inventing Heidegger's critique of metaphysics and the ontotheological and technological projects that are its products. Derrida's consistent argument is that it is simply impossible to speak of God without setting in motion the logic of supplementation – whether we call it the yes, the promise or originary technicity – and this has important consequences not just for Heidegger but for his critics Lévinas and Marion as well. If

Heidegger's concept of a theology without being is contingent on a prior revelation of Being, then the early Lévinas's ethical critique imagines a purely empirical relation to an absolutely heterological other (Derrida 1978c: 79–195) whereas Marion's theological account presumes an absolutely non-predicative relationship with God (Derrida 1989a). The concept of originary technicity compromises every attempt to establish the extra-linguistic heterological purity of God by demonstrating that such a concept is the product of a metaphysical or ontotheological decision that is clearly anything but pure. There is an important sense in which Heidegger and his main critics cannot help but remain within the ontotheological tradition of being, in other words, precisely because they believe they can escape from it into an unmediated experience of God without or beyond being. This suggests that the post-Heideggerian attempt to overcome ontotheology by positing an ever-more absolute and essentialist heterogeneity between being and non-being is a naïve dream, to paraphrase Derrida in 'Violence and Metaphysics' (Derrida 1978c: 79–153) and that the ontotheological project can only be circumvented from within the interiority of the language of being. Now a theology of originary technicity might offer one means of overcoming the ontotheological project to reduce non-being to an instrument of being because – far from positing an impossibly absolute concept of God as non-being – it folds a divine non-being that exceeds every concept of instrument back into being itself as its condition of possibility. So my hypothesis is that a theology after technics might ultimately lead to a *more* radically heterogeneous concept of God than ontotheological concepts of an external God beyond or without being (who is nevertheless always put to work in the service of human *ratio*) because it would posit God as the experience of a non-human, non-living and even non-being alterity right at the heart of human being. Could originary technicity perhaps be one name for that impossible Heideggerian post-ontotheological theology, the one in which the word 'being' would not even figure?

Contemporary theology

Second, let me consider some contemporary theological approaches to the question of technology. It is possible to identify at least four basic Christian or quasi-Christian theological approaches to the question of 'modern technology' – and the label here is not insignificant – which run the gamut from total rejection to wholesale embrace. First, it is always possible to identify a simple anti- or counter-technological approach in Christian theology that seeks to reject what it sees as the nihilism of contemporary technology in favour of a valorization of faith or creation as sacred: John Paul II's encyclical *Evangelium Vitae*, with its wholesale condemnation of abortion, birth control and artificial insemination would be the most obvious example of this. Second, Christian theology has engaged in what might be called a more constructive critique with technology that does not simply reject it outright but seeks to redeem it by anchoring what it sees as its atomistic liberalism in a transcendental theological value system: Graham Ward's recent attempt to develop an analogical theology of cyberculture in *Cities of God* (Ward 2000) is perhaps the most forceful and imaginative example of this approach. Third, Christian theology could more optimistically still advocate a kind of natural theology which sees human reason or mathematical truth as reflecting the created order of the world: the work of Richard Swinburne (1977), Arthur Peacocke and John Polkingthorne on the relationship between theology and science comes to mind here. Fourth and finally, Christian theology could simply accept the fact that modern technology spells the death of all gods (except, that is, the golden calf of late capitalism) and either give up the ghost entirely or embrace its new-found status as an atheology or virtual theology: the work of Don Cupitt (1995), Paul Virilio (1991) and, more radically, Mark C. Taylor's remarkable *About Religion: Virtual Economies of Faith* (1999) point the way in this direction.

Yet contemporary theological approaches to theology are, I think, no less enmeshed in metaphysical thinking than Heidegger's critique of ontotheology. It is first of all disappointing that almost all these approaches simply reduce the question of technology to discussions of birth control, films, the Internet and Las Vegas casinos as if technics were simply a matter of the latest gadgets. It is also significant that the theological approaches to theology I have just sketched also share – despite their numerous and apparently very stark theological differences – a common metaphysical assumption that originary technics is a basically empirical problem to be worked out in Aristotelian terms. The fact is that there is no essential difference between those at one end of the spectrum who see technology as an instrument of humanity that has got badly out of control and those at the other who see humanity as increasingly the instrument of a rampant technology, because both reduce it to a question of a determinate technology that can be interpreted according to the logic of being and non-being, user and tool. This means that there is a more or less declaredly ontotheological set of assumptions at work in all contemporary theological approaches to technology – no matter whether they see it as nihilistic or, to turn it upside down, as religious – and this is the repeated application of the anthropocentric logic of the *causa efficiens* to the divine.

So contemporary theological approaches to technology have an essential congruity and, to demonstrate this, we could consider the seemingly polar opposite positions of Graham Ward's analogical theology of cyberculture and Mark C. Taylor's 'death of God' theology of Las Vegas. Graham Ward attacks what he sees as a nihilistic cyberculture in which 'technology is no longer an aid, a tool, a prosthesis extending human capacity' (Ward 2000: 253). Ward addresses this situation not by re-thinking the traditional concept of technology as prosthesis – given that, as he himself admits, it can now function independently of human capacity – but by invoking the analogical God to put technology back in its 'proper' place: 'to redeem the situation means rethinking this analogical worldview with respect to its digital reduction and simulation; rethinking creation in terms of its creator: a creator who maintains and validates the reality of its standing' (Ward 2000: 254). Ward's emphasis on God the creator re-establishes the collapsing Aristotelian logic of user and tool and gives humanity the whip-hand over cyberculture once again: '[a]nalogically constituted, the Internet and the virtual communities it establishes could then supplement our social relatedness and we would employ the computer prosthetically' (Ward 2000: 255). Mark C. Taylor embraces Las Vegas as the place where 'the death of God is staged as the spectacle of the Kingdom of God on Earth' (Taylor 1999: 170). Taylor argues that Vegas represents something close to the Baudrillardian final stage of the sign in which technology ceases to become the simple tool or mimesis of the real and finally bears no relation to the real whatsoever. But Taylor's thesis still remains vulnerable to the charge that it is merely inverting the customary Aristotelian logic in which the original becomes the mimesis and the mimesis original: '[a]s image is embodied in reality and reality becomes a "matter" of image, art is realized in a world that is effectively transformed into a work of art' (Taylor 1999: 201). From this perspective, Ward and Taylor's approaches could almost be seen as the mirror image of each other.

Now Derrida's logic of originary technicity clearly cannot be reduced to a power struggle between empirical human beings and technological objects in some nominally 'modern' era because, as we have seen, it is nothing less than the generalized logic of supplementation that allows the determinate concepts of humanity and technology to appear as opposites or alternatives. It would, I think, require a re-evaluation of both the analogical redemption of technology imagined by Ward and the atheological embrace of technology envisaged by Taylor. Ward's appeal to God as the 'creator who maintains and validates the reality' of His creation gives rise to the Heideggerian anxiety that the divine is being posited purely and simply in order to shore up a collapsing anthropocentrism: God is called upon to re-establish the primacy of the human over the technological because as the uncreated creator He is the one user we can guarantee will not turn out to be just another tool. Taylor's valorization of technology as the 'Kingdom of God on earth' is similarly vulnerable to the charge of anthropomorphizing the divine because it simply transfers the ontological primacy of the human to the technological: God is no less a means of re-establishing the primacy of the human here even if here it is in the guise of the technological. The challenge for contemporary theological approaches to technology must be to move beyond arguments for or against what is too simply called 'modern technology', then, which one way or another end up repeating the ontotheological fallacy of putting God at the service of human *ratio*. This theology would neither seek to reproduce the ontotheological tradition nor leave it behind altogether but rather repeat it differently. Could a theology after originary technics – with the ensuing complication of everything that goes under the names of creator and created, living and non-living – answer the impossible desire for a theology of birth control, cyberculture and Las Vegas that is not *simply* the product of ontotheological thinking?

Julia Kristeva

Finally, I would like to go back to where we started and examine Julia Kristeva's concept of the sacred. It is Kristeva's argument, you will recall, that the sacred is a kind of secular mysticism or negative theology that sees the transcendental fantasies of the religious as the products of an immanent economy of desire. Kristeva's attempt to sacralize *psychē* is carried out at the expense of *technē*, which is generally but not exclusively relegated to its traditional secondary status. But, as we have already seen, the opposition between the terms becomes impossible to sustain as it stands because it depends on what we have called originary technicity. The introduction of originary technics is the ruin of Kristeva's concept of the sacred as 'unscathed' of technology – as we suggested earlier – but perhaps it might also be the making of a sacred after technics. This theology after technics helps us to police what may be a residual ontotheology within Kristeva's concept of the sacred which – I want to argue – still leads her to reduce this supposedly 'unthinkable outside' to a tool or instrument of human being.

Kristeva may be more accurate than she thinks when she describes the sacred as a kind of negative theology or mysticism. She identifies her own theological project, as we have already seen, with Meister Eckhart's famous prayer 'I pray God that He may free me of God'. It is Kristeva's argument that Eckhart's prayer represents a sacred attempt to move beyond religious fantasies of origin. But Eckhart's mysticism is vulnerable to the Derridaean charge that he is not really thinking the unthinkable at all but remaining within a recognizably Neoplatonic tradition: '[w]hen I said that God was not a Being and was above Being, I did not thereby contest His Being, but on the contrary attributed to Him *a more elevated Being*' (Derrida 1978a: 337n). If Eckhart appears to negate God's being, Derrida's well-known argument is that his negative theology remains a theology and his attempt to move beyond ontotheology is still at bottom ontotheological: 'the negative movement of the discourse on God is still a phase of positive ontotheology' (Derrida 1978a: 337n).

Kristeva's secular negative theological attempt to imagine an infinitely immanent sacred is potentially subject to the same criticisms as Eckhart's bona fide negative theological attempt to imagine an infinitely transcendental God. It is my contention that the sacred attempt to think the unthinkable – to pray God that He may free us of God – is prone to the suspicion that it predetermines the very alterity it seeks to innocently affirm. Kristeva affirms a wholly immanent transcendence – the pre-originary psychic economy that, as we have seen, paradoxically exceeds the subject from within – but this project is vulnerable to the charge that it is simply *internalizing* the ontotheological gesture of Eckhart. Kristeva's psychoanalytic analysis of the sacred always contains a more or less explicit anthropomorphism that calls the stability of the human into question only to re-identify it as the exclusive source of its own self-division. First, I would argue that *In the Beginning was Love* ([1985] 1987a) sees the split subject of psychoanalysis as paving the way for a non-violent ethical relationship with the other: '[i]ts vital efficacy is inseparable from its ethical dimension, which is commensurate with love: the speaking being opens up to and reposes in the other' (Kristeva 1987a: 61). But this raises the question of exactly *who* or *what* the other whom we must love and respect is and the answer is clear. More recently, in the book *Strangers to Ourselves* ([1988] 1991) she writes powerfully about the 'paradoxical community . . . made up of foreigners who are reconciled with themselves to the extent that they recognize themselves as foreigners'. If we are indeed strangers to ourselves, however, it is interesting to note that the stranger within is always figured as a *human* stranger and the paradoxical community it entails a *human* community: 'people ready-to-help-themselves in their weakness, a weakness whose other name is our radical strangeness' (Kristeva 1991: 195). Finally, as we have already seen, *Le féminin et le sacré* (1999a) completes the anthropomorphizing of this supposedly radical alterity by somewhat dogmatically and unwarrantedly identifying the sacred with *phusis* at the expense of *technē*. We have already seen that in this text the sacred must be identified with the feminine and against technoscience even when – as in the case of birth control or artificial insemination – the opposition becomes difficult to sustain. My concern here is that the sacred is being called upon to make safe a crumbling distinction between the human and the non-human and so, once again, God's existence is established ontotheologically on Reason's terms. The immanent theology of Kristeva is no less susceptible to the charge of reducing the alterity of the sacred to an instrument of being than the transcendental theology of Eckhart. This psychoanalytic attempt to valorize human being as sacred would be just as vulnerable to a theology of originary technicity, I think, as the ontotheological attempt to valorize the sacred as a supreme or elevated being. So a theology after originary technics would seek to radicalize Kristeva's psychoanalytic concept of the human's pre-subjective openness to other humans by stressing its constitutive openness to the non-human as well. Why, for example, does Kristeva restrict her immanent theology of alterity to the human? Is it still possible to insist that the human has no ethical relation to the non-human whether animal, machine or divinity? Does Kristeva's secular negative theology remain vulnerable to the objection that the supposedly radical heterogeneity of the sacred merely conceals a secret ontotheology, a closet hyper-essentialism?

Conclusion

Julia Kristeva's desire for a 'beginning before the beginning' is, as she rightly suspects, an impossible one. It is already too late. *Technē* has always already started. If originary technicity is a kind of fall, though, it is an inevitable one that we do not have to approach tragically but affirmatively and – nothing rules this out – even theologically. Originary technicity, I have suggested, does not necessarily bring Kristeva's theology to a closure but offers it a future after ontotheology because it offers a new purchase on the relationship between being and non-being. The logic of originary technics makes possible a negative theological check on all attempts to situate the sacred against the ontological horizon that does not necessarily incur the accusation that it is merely re-instating ontology at a higher level. This logic helps theology resist the ontotheological drive to transform the sacred into an instrument or tool of being – Freud famously notes in *Civilization and its Discontents* how 'Man has, as it were, become a kind of prosthetic God' (Freud 1961: 38) – by making possible a concept of the sacred as a radical alterity within being that can never be reduced to a piece of *technē*. Now this theology after technics offers a future for Kristeva's secular negative theology because strangely it fulfils more completely than her own psychoanalytic project the critique of a modernity in which 'life ... has itself become an object, a product of the work of chemists, surgeons and genetic engineers serving power-hungry men and women' (Kristeva 1987a: 62). In other words, a theology after originary technics is paradoxically the only way of affirming Kristeva's desire for 'a non-place beyond the grasp of the original *technē*'.

Part IV

Futures

This concluding Part focuses in more detail on the future(s) of negative theology after modern French philosophy. It returns to Derrida's reading of negative theology. Its argument is that the *via negativa* is a priori open to a future that cannot be determined but only – more or less violently – decided. If we cannot determine a priori what form negative theology's future might take, however, it remains possible to consider what our attitude to the arrival of that future should be. The Part examines the stance we must take towards that future in more detail by examining Derrida's recent work on hospitality. This paves the way for the argument that Derrida's reading of negative theology constitutes not simply an act of hospitality, but a critique of contemporary concepts of hospitality and, most importantly, a new model for hospitality. In conclusion, it is suggested that one way of saving negative theology's future might be to apply it to contemporary political situations such as immigration, asylum-seekers or human and non-human rights.

6 Derrida and the 'passage to the totally other'

Jacques Derrida writes of negative theology in the concluding section of 'Sauf le nom (Post-Scriptum)': 'to let passage to the other, to the totally other, is hospitality' (Derrida 1995a: 80). It was with Derrida's reading of negative theology that we began this book and it is with Derrida that we must conclude. He argues, as we saw in Chapter 1, that negative theology is not simply a specific historical or theological phenomenon to be used or dispensed with at will by believers or non-believers, but a privileged name for the relation to the other as absolutely other that constitutes the basis for all responsible thought and action. His controversial thesis is that the *via negativa* constitutes an example of the deconstructive attempt to exceed the horizon of metaphysical or ontotheological thought and to think the other as absolutely heterogeneous to being. Derrida suggests that negative theology is a form of 'paradoxical hyperbole' that breaks free from its Neoplatonic Christian perimeters in the name of a God who is progressively a supreme being, a God beyond being, before finally becoming an alterity beyond God Himself. The *via negativa* affirms the advent of an absolute other in a future that will never arrive as such in the sense of a teleological goal that can be realized but which – in its very infinitude and unconditionality – constitutes the inescapable condition of all responsible ethical, religious and political decision-making in the present. This constant insistence that the future is essentially unknowable in Derrida perhaps produces an understandable sense of anti-climax among regular readers of his work – why can't he give us some more specific idea about what form it is going to take? – but any attempt by Derrida to offer a futurology would inevitably be just another way to project the present into the future and thereby shut down its unknowability. If Derrida's work on negative theology offers no predictions about the future, however, I would argue that it does raise the question of what our attitude towards that future must be and its most recent answer seems to be that the future must be welcomed in the spirit of a certain *hospitality*. My concluding chapter will explore this intriguing argument as it develops across a range of texts from Derrida's writings on hospitality to his work on theology. What is Derrida's particular concept of hospitality?

Should negative theology be welcomed, in Derrida's words, as a form of hospitality towards the other? Finally, and most importantly, if negative theology constitutes a form of hospitality, then what does that tell us about its own future(s)? In this final chapter, I want to suggest that Derrida's reading of negative theology is an *act* of hospitality, a *critique* of classical notions of hospitality but perhaps most importantly of all a privileged *example* for a new mode of hospitality as letting 'passage ... to the totally other'.

Derrida and inheritance

I want to preface this chapter, however, with a few words on Derrida's concept of the legacy or inheritance of negative theology. Derrida has turned to a generalized concept of inheritance in recent years to explain the relationship between his own work and philosophical and/or theological tradition (Bennington 2000: 34–46). The concept of inheritance Derrida develops is not, I want to suggest, essentially a relationship to the *past* but an affirmation of the *future*. This idea of inheritance is not simply a work of mourning that is performed out of respect for the dead, so to speak, but an act of welcoming or hospitality towards something that is still to come. Let me explain.

First, I want to explore what Derrida understands by inheritance. Derrida argues in an essay on Nelson Mandela's attitude to the parliamentary tradition of democracy that inheritance is not simply an act of conservation or fidelity with respect to tradition but something that necessarily involves an element of transgression or violence as well. Derrida's position is that inheritance does not involve slavishly reproducing the tradition one inherits in its most visible or monolithic forms but rather respecting the logic or force that produces that tradition in the first place even 'to the point of turning it back on occasion against those who claim to be its holders' (Derrida 1987b: 17).

Second, Derrida goes on to argue in *Specters of Marx* ([1993] 1994) that the legacy or inheritance is never a self-identical given in the sense of a unified corpus that can be handed down, part and parcel, from one intentional consciousness to another. It is an essential feature of an inheritance that its meaning should not be immediately legible or transparent but in some sense reserved or secret. Its meaning cannot simply be given or received by one subject or another – despite conservative claims to the contrary – but has to involve an act of interpretation, a hermeneutical duty to decode, determine or decide: '*one must* filter, sift, criticize, one must sort out amongst several different possibles that inhabit the same injunction' (Derrida 1994: 16). If it were possible to inherit a tradition wholly and completely, so to speak, then the question of duty, fidelity or responsibility to it would not arise at all and the inheritance would merely become a philosophical version of a hereditary condition: 'we would never have anything to inherit from it . . . we would be affected by it as by a cause – natural or genetic' (Derrida 1994: 16).

Third, this generalized concept of the legacy leads Derrida to a thesis on what we might call *ontological inheritance* where being itself is redefined as inherited. It is Derrida's argument, as we have already seen at length, that subjective identity is inscribed within an originary situation, gift or affirmation of language or tradition that shapes it, whether we acknowledge the fact or not. Derrida argues that the response to this ontological inheritance should be neither blind adherence as if its meaning were transparently clear and inescapable (the conservative error) or an equally blind rejection as if it could be left behind with, as it were, a single bound (the liberal mistake) but an act of interpretation or decision-making that seeks to do justice – however impossibly – to both responses. Derrida's position is that the only way to be faithful to tradition is to avoid knee-jerk acceptance or denial – which are, in his view, both forms of irresponsibility – by *inventing* new modes of being faithful in the absolute absence of any guarantees that they will ever actually succeed. If we were to borrow an argument from his recent seminar on perjury, we could say that the *acolyte* or follower always contains – and not simply etymologically – the possibility of the *anacoluthon* or failure of following. The conservative logic of inheritance whereupon our duty is to faithfully reproduce the immemorial past is transformed into a deconstructive logic of inheritance whereupon our duty is to invent a potentially infinite future. There is a sense in which the past to which we are seeking to be faithful paradoxically lies in front of us as an ambiguous and bottomless resource to be reinvented. This is why Derrida defines inheritance not as a bequest that has been passively received in its entirety – whether or not we choose to see it as that – but as an ongoing task that will never be exhausted. For Derrida, then, it would seem that inheritance is not so much a legacy from the *past* as paradoxically the welcoming of the *future*:

> Inheritance is never a *given*, it is always a task. It remains before us just as unquestionably as we are heirs of Marxism, even before wanting or refusing to be, and like all inheritors, we are in mourning. In mourning in particular for what is called Marxism. *To be*, this word in which we earlier saw the word of the spirit, means, for the same reason, *to inherit*. All the questions on the subject of being or of what is to be (or not to be) are questions of inheritance. There is no backward-looking fervour in this reminder, no traditionalist flavour. Reaction, reactionary, or reactive are but interpretations of the structure of inheritance. That we *are* heirs does not mean that we *have* or that we *receive* this or that, some inheritance enriches us one day with this or that, but that the *being* of what we are *is* first of all inheritance, whether we like it or know it or not.
>
> (Derrida 1994: 54)

Finally, and most pertinently for our discussion, Derrida goes on to consider this paradoxical concept of inheritance in his reading of negative theology. I think the concept of inheritance is a highly appropriate figure for Derrida's relation to the *via negativa*. It is possible to argue that Derrida's reading of negative theology is not simply an *act* of inheritance, nor even a particularly apposite *example* of inheritance, but an attempt to recognize the *via negativa* as in some sense a *model* for the logic of inheritance he is evolving. Derrida himself *inherits* negative theology, I would argue, not in the sense of a visible or legible bequest from the past that he chooses to accept or spurn but as a non-unified corpus that requires hermeneutical filtering, selecting, criticizing, and so on. He is an authentic inheritor of negative theology in the sense that he seeks to invent a means of being faithful to negative theology that respects both the logic and the form of the legacy. If Derrida's reading of negative theology is an *example* of what he means by inheritance – although almost any one of his texts would serve just as well – its greater claim to privilege perhaps lies in the suggestion that the negative theological tradition itself could be described as a model of inheritance. Derrida's essay 'Sauf le nom' suggests, for example, that Angelus Silesius offers a powerful reflection on the paradoxical logic of inheritance in his enigmatic text *The Cherubinic Wanderer*.

> *Nothing lives without dying*
> God himself, If he wants to live for you, must die:
> How do you think without death to inherit your own life? (1: 33)
> – Has anything more profound ever been written on inheritance? I understand that as a thesis on what *inherit* means (to say).
>
> (Derrida 1995a: 82)

What does Derrida mean here? I would argue that negative theology axiomizes the logic of inheritance Derrida traces in *Specters of Marx* and contemporaneous texts in a way that other Christian concepts of temporality apparently do not (Bennington 2000: 140).[1] It offers the same paradoxical temporality of life and death, continuity and rupture, conservation and invention. It is only possible to be faithful to Christ by seeking – without any way of knowing beforehand whether you will ever be successful – to repeat the irruptive force or violence of His original act of sacrifice. The key point to grasp here is that the work of mourning for the dead is once again transformed into the affirmation of future life. There is an important sense in which the responsibility to *receive* the past as an inheritance once again goes hand in hand with the responsibility to *welcome* the future as what always remains to be done in that inheritance. This raises the interesting prospect that negative theology's *legacy* – to us, to Derrida, and to modernity more generally – may in fact be nothing other than a form of *hospitality*: 'to let passage to the other, to the totally other, is hospitality'. In the next section, I want to explore Derrida's reading of hospitality in more detail.

Derrida and hospitality

I want, then, to give a brief summary of Derrida's reading of hospitality as it has appeared in a range of disparate texts including 'Le mot d'acceuil' ([1997] 1999c), 'Cosmopolites de tous les pays, encore une effort!' ([1997] 2001c), 'Pas d'hospitalité' (1997c) and 'Hostipitality' (2002c). It is helpful to see Derrida's work within the context of a more or less explicit 'political turn' in his work in recent years with a corresponding weight of work on classical juridico-theologico-political concepts of law, justice, friendship, forgiveness and cosmopolitanism among others (Bennington 1994; Beardsworth 1996; de Vries 2002a). It is possible to detect a series of related if not exactly identical moves or gestures in all these texts that need to be carefully unpacked if we want to understand what Derrida is saying. First, Derrida argues for a generalized and unconditional concept of hospitality that exceeds its classical status as an ethical or political concept. Derrida's argument is that hospitality must be understood as a primordial relationship or welcoming of the other as *absolutely* other that opens ethics, politics, and being more generally. If Derrida insists upon this originary and unconditional element of hospitality, however, he goes on to argue that hospitality must still inevitably be conditioned by certain ethical, political or juridical limits such as laws, rights, borders and conventions which limit its infinite dimension. The argument is that the concept of hospitality is constituted by a contradictory and absolutely irreconcilable double injunction to be both unconditional and conditional at the same time. There is a sense in which hospitality exists in an irresolvable tension between its status as an *unconditional* or hyperbolic welcome that opens itself absolutely and without question to the other regardless of who they are or might be and its status as a *conditional* welcome that is extended within certain established ethical, political or juridical limits. This tension produces a concept of hospitality that is perpetually and necessarily – rather than empirically or accidentally – vulnerable to the possibility of its own perversion as non-hospitality or hostility. Finally, and most importantly, Derrida is at pains to argue that – far from destroying or paralysing it – this aporia is the condition of any hospitality worth the name. Let me unpack this argument in a little more detail.

Hospitality

Jacques Derrida introduces his reading of hospitality in a number of texts and contexts but his most detailed analysis of the concept occurs in the essay 'Le mot d'accueil' (1999c). It is here that Derrida introduces the idea that hospitality originarily involves a general or unconditional dimension that exceeds its status as an ethical right or juridico-political duty. He presents this reading in the form of a complex and affirmative appreciation of Emmanuel Lévinas's seminal text *Totality and Infinity* ([1961] 1969). He begins with Lévinas's famous argument that the arrival of the other in a singular face-to-face relation constitutes the opening of ethics as such. Lévinas argues that it is through this face-to-face relation that the subject comes into existence as originarily responsible for the other. Lévinas's argument is that this originary responsibility to the 'other in me', so to speak, establishes ethics as first philosophy prior to the dimensions of ontology, totality and thematization. Derrida argues that Lévinas's text is, among other things, an important and unrecognized treatise on *hospitality* to the other. Derrida's thesis is that Lévinas's text contains within it a crucial but almost unnoticed affirmation of a moment of welcome that opens up the face-to-face relation to the infinite other in which ethics famously begins. If hospitality opens the face-to-face relation, then hospitality is the condition of everything that the face-to-face relation then makes possible, namely, ethics, subjectivity, and so on. More paradoxically, we might say that we are *originarily* hospitable to the other in the sense that our subjectivity exists purely on the basis that it has already welcomed the other into its interiority: *to be* means *to welcome*. The originary welcome of the other is absolutely unconditional (I do not pre-exist the other, I do not decide whether or not to welcome the other because he is already inside me, I cannot know in advance who or what the other will be or what welcoming him will entail) and this unconditionality forms the basis for all Derrida's work on hospitality. There is an important sense in which unconditional hospitality entails an absolute openness to the other regardless of who they might be, then, whether they are a refugee or a charlatan, whether they deserve or abuse my hospitality, whether they respect my domestic space or blow my house down. This unconditional hospitality to the other regardless of who or what they might be has, however, to be permanently open to the possibility of perversion or abuse as non-hospitality or hostility if it is to be unconditional in the first place. Now this means that an unconditional hospitality to the other cannot be upheld in isolation – without risking its own abuse, negation or exploitation – and so the question arises of the extent to which it can be organized or translated into a conditional hospitality to the other in legal or political terms. For Derrida, as we will now see, genuine hospitality involves the negotiation between a double or contradictory injunction to be both unconditional and conditional at the same time.

Hospitality's double injunction

Derrida goes on, then, to compare the unconditional concept of hospitality as the ethical relation to the other as such and the conditional concept of hospitality as the legal, institutional or political relation to specific others. It is a question that is all the more urgent in an era of repeated and depressingly familiar scare-stories and controversies about *sans-papiers*, asylum seekers, economic migrants, and so forth. He is specifically concerned with establishing the *relationship* between the unconditional and the conditional modes of hospitality and whether the two are mutually exclusive, compatible, or capable of synthesis. He traces the history of the concept of hospitality from its origins in the biblical city of refuge through Kantian notions of cosmpolitanism to Lévinas's idea of the welcome of the face of the other in the essay 'Cosmopolites de tous les pays, encore une effort!' (2001c). His conclusion is that the concept of hospitality is constituted by a contradictory injunction to be *both* unconditional *and* conditional, universal and particular, absolute and relative at the same time. Derrida's essay 'Pas d'hospitalité' (1997c) states quite explicitly that hospitality involves both an unconditional imperative to welcome the other absolutely, unreservedly and without question regardless of who they may be and a conditional imperative to welcome the other within the boundaries of ethical, juridical, economic and political exigencies:

> [T]here will be an *antinomy*, an insoluble antinomy, a non-dialectizable antinomy between, on the one hand, the *law* of hospitality, the unconditional law of an unlimited hospitality (to give to the arrivant a sense of his at-home [*chez-soi*] and of his self [*son soi*], to give his own, our own, without asking for his name, nor for compensation, nor placing the slightest condition upon him) and on the other hand, the *laws* of hospitality, the conditioned and conditional rights and duties that define the Greco-Latin, even Judaeo-Christian, tradition, all rights and all philosophy of rights until Kant and Hegel, in particular, across the family, the civil society and the State.
> (Derrida 1997a: 73)

On the one hand, hospitality must involve a dimension of infinitude or unconditionality no matter what context it takes place within otherwise it would simply be the exercise of a legal or administrative rule without responsibility. Derrida makes tactical use of Kant's categorical imperative to describe this dimension but – contrary to the suggestions of Mark Dooley and Michael Hughes (Derrida 2001a: xi) – he makes clear that the concept of unconditional responsibility is an infinite task rather than the simple fulfilment of a duty or debt in accordance with a regulative ideal (Derrida 1997a: 77). Derrida's argument is that hospitality necessitates an unconditional welcome to the arrivant over and above any ethical, political and juridical obligation and regardless of who or what might actually arrive:

> We say, yes, *to the arrivant*, before all determination, before all anticipation, before all *identification*, whether or not they are a foreigner, an

immigrant, whether they are invited or uninvited, whether or not the arrivant is a citizen of another country, a human being, animal or divine, living or dead, masculine or feminine.

(Derrida 1997a: 73)

On the other hand, unconditional hospitality must take place within certain conditional contexts – which inevitably limit its infinite demand – otherwise it would merely be the affirmation of a utopian or transcendental concept without practical application and as such would be perpetually open to abuse. Derrida shows how Kant's concept of the universal right to hospitality nonetheless remains limited to citizens of other states, to the right of visitation rather than access and to a larger politico-juridical arrangement between citizens and states (Derrida 1999a: 87). Derrida's argument makes clear that, to be effective, hospitality has to involve a certain concept of sovereignty, certain concepts of boundary and propriety and certain criteria about who or what is welcome:

There would be no effective unconditional law if it did not have to become effective, concrete, determined, if its being did not have-to-be [*devoir-être*]. It would risk becoming abstract, utopic, illusory and thus turn into its opposite.

(Derrida 1997a: 75)

What, to summarize, is the relationship between the unconditional and conditional dimensions of hospitality? Derrida stresses that genuine hospitality depends upon both unconditional and conditional hospitality because reliance on one alone would produce a situation of violence or pervertibility. If we could paraphrase Kant here, we might say that a pure unconditional hospitality would be empty whereas a limited conditional hospitality would be blind so genuine hospitality needs both dimensions in order to exist. The crucial point to grasp is that Derrida sees absolutely no question of choosing between or resolving the contradictory injunction of the conditional and the unconditional in dialectical terms because they exist in a relationship of undecidability. There is a crucial sense in which hospitality depends upon *maintaining* the tension between the two – so far as this is actually possible – if it is not to succumb to the respective violences of prudential bureaucracy, on the one hand, and absolute ethical purism, on the other. This leads Derrida to the characteristic conclusion that the essential undecidability of hospitality does not destroy or paralyse it but rather licenses a 'mad' hospitality, 'impossible' hospitality or hospitality of lesser violence (Derrida 2002a: 360). For Derrida, this form of hospitality – which is extended in an instant of madness where no norms, guarantees or obligations apply – is the only way of genuinely welcoming the other.

Hospitality without criteria

Finally, Derrida's argument goes on to analyse this new concept of hospitality without criteria in more detail. He will argue that genuine hospitality depends upon an *acknowledgement* of the a priori undecidability between hospitality and the perversion of hospitality rather than the attempt to disguise that undecidability by resorting to prior ethical norms or juridical rules. It is only through acknowledging the inability to determine in advance whether its outcome will be ethical or non-ethical that the chance of a hospitality that genuinely attains a less violent relation to the other can emerge.

Derrida takes as his starting point Lévinas's famous argument in *Totality and Infinity* about the arrival of what he calls the third party into the face-to-face relation (Lévinas 1969: 213). He traces Lévinas's argument that the face to face with the other is affected by the arrival of a third party in the form of another other, that is, an other who is other than me or who is other than my other. He argues that, for Lévinas, the arrival of the third party is the moment where the absolutely singular ethical relation begins to be translated into the field of law, politics and ontology more generally because it opens the question of establishing a basis of comparison, calculation and judgement upon the competing claims of the different others (Derrida 1999a: 32). The discussion begins to move beyond simple commentary, however, when Derrida argues that the singular face-to-face relation is affected *originarily* by the presence of the third party and with it the arrival of the political. There is a sense in which the presence of the third party in the face-to-face relation – the recognition of the existence of another other outside that relation who also makes claims upon me and requires me to triangulate my responsibility – paradoxically perpetuates *and* violates the ethical responsibility brought into being by that relation. This inseparability of the ethical and the non-ethical at the point of origin in the form of the third party is paradoxically the condition for any genuine ethical thought or action worth the name.

Derrida's classic thesis here is that the presence of the third party in the face-to-face relation is both a condition of possibility for the ethical relation in the sense that it protects its purity and a condition of impossibility for the ethical relation in the sense that it interrupts or compromises that purity. On the one hand, he argues – both with and through Lévinas – that the insertion of the third party into the singular ethical relation with the other raises the question of how that singularity might be generalized or institutionalized in a wider sense as law, society or politics. Derrida goes beyond Lévinas's own text to suggest that the introduction of the third party is actually necessary to protect against a potential singular absolutism or exclusivity within the ethical relation that could contain the possibility of violence: 'For the absence of the third would threaten with violence the purity of ethics in the absolute immediacy of the face to face with the unique' (Derrida 1999a: 32). On the other hand, he argues that the presence of the third party inevitably compromises the purity of ethics even in the act of protecting its purity by interrupting or violating the fidelity or responsibility to the other promised in the face-to-face relation. Derrida also argues that the third violates the opening of ethics by translating its singularity into the realm of law, calculation, and, through them, ontology, representation and thematization: 'It is true that the protecting or mediating third, in its juridico-political role, violates in its turn, at least potentially, the purity of the ethical desire devoted to the unique' (Derrida 1999a: 33). The larger point of Derrida's argument here is that the purity of ethics in the form of the singular relation to the other exists in a *constitutive* relation with the impurity of ethics in the form of the competing rights of the third party. There is a constitutive sense in which the ethical requires the presence of the non-ethical in order to *sustain* the purity of its own ethical demand and yet – by the same token – the presence of the non-ethical is the *contamination* of the purity of that ethical demand. This leads Derrida to the radical conclusion that the *perfectibility* of ethics as the Good or the Just and so on is a priori inseparable from and dependent upon the *pervertibility* of the ethical as Radical Evil, perjury and so forth:

> An intolerable scandal: even if Lévinas never puts it this way, justice commits perjury as easily as it breathes; it betrays the 'primordial word of honour' and swears [*jurer*] only to perjure, to swear falsely [*parjurer*], swear off [*abjurer*] or swear at [*injurier*]. It is no doubt in facing this ineluctability that Lévinas imagines the sigh of the just: 'What do I have to do with justice?'
>
> Henceforth, in the operation of justice one can no longer distinguish between fidelity to oath and the perjury of false witness, and even before this, between betrayal and betrayal, always more than one betrayal. One should then, with all requisite analytical prudence, respect the quality, modality, and situation of these breaches of the sworn word, of this 'primordial word of honour' before all oaths. But such differences would never efface the trace of the inaugural perjury. Like the third who does not wait, the proceedings that open both ethics and justice are in the process of committing quasi-transcendental or originary, indeed, pre-originary, perjury. One might even call it *ontological*, once ethics is joined to everything that exceeds and betrays it (ontology, precisely, synchrony, totality, the State, the political, etc.). One might even see here an irrepressible evil or a radical perversion, were it not that bad intentions or bad will might be absent here, and were its possibility, at least the haunting of its possibility, a sort of pervertibility, not also the condition of the Good, of Justice, Love, Faith, etc. And of perfectibility.
>
> (Derrida 1999a: 34)

What are the implications of Derrida's argument here? It is crucially important to be clear about what he is and isn't arguing. Derrida is certainly not contending that there is no difference between the ethical and the non-ethical, nor that we should affirm good and evil alike as if they had the same value, but that any avowedly ethical thought or action whatsoever necessarily rather than accidentally contains the possibility of being non-ethical. Derrida's entirely characteristic point is that the only possibility for a genuine ethics lies in the suspension of all possible criteria according to which a 'better' or 'worse' ethical outcome could be determined by the decision-maker in advance. If ethics were simply a matter of applying a prior juridical rule or philosophical norm, Derrida's now familiar response would be that ethical responsibility would be reduced to nothing more than a complacent act of bureaucratic or official administration. The ethical decision that Derrida canvasses for is a performative act of invention – taken in the absence of any criteria according to which it will be judged ethical or not – rather than a constative application or description of a prior set of categories. This ethical decision that takes place in the radical absence of any guarantees of its own ethical status is a decision of *lesser* violence because it acknowledges its own prescriptive force and stands in comparison to the ethical decision that believes itself to be a simple description of justice and that opens itself to the *worst* violence of all. For Derrida, genuine ethics needs to be offered in the full awareness of its own violence, illegality and pervertibility if it is to avoid the still worse violence that is good conscience, a sense of fulfilled duty or of having unquestionably described or acted out of justice. In Hent de Vries's account, genuine ethics must involve a compromise or calculation with the *necessary possibility* of the worst if it is to stand any chance of avoiding the *certainty* or *actuality* of the arrival of the worst:

> In this history, in order to mitigate the propensity towards radical evil, that other curvature in the order of things, one must run the risk of indispensable yet disposable errors, that is to say, idolatries and blasphemies. To risk less is to risk the worst. What's more, to risk less than the worst is to risk the worst of the worst, the evil of evil, more radical than radical evil: the indifference of indecision or, worse still, the complacency of good conscience.
>
> (de Vries 2002a: 398)[2]

Jacques Derrida's reading of hospitality, to summarize, seeks to affirm a general, infinite and unconditional responsibility to the arrivant that overflows the – still necessary and unavoidable – limitations of the Pauline, Kantian and even Lévinasian readings of the concept. It generalizes hospitality as the pre-ethical relation to the other *per se* because it is only through the hospitable *welcome* of the face that takes place before the appearance of the face itself that the ethical relation can begin. It infinitizes hospitality as a responsibility that must precede and exceed every ethical, juridical or political exigency if it is to avoid collapsing into the ethical graveyard of duties, quotas, obligations, federal or international agreements on asylum, economic migration, and so forth. If the ethical right to hospitality remains absolutely transcendent of empirical law, however, it risks the very ethical irresponsibility it seeks to escape from and so the situation arises where we have to undertake a calculation or compromise between the unconditional and the conditional, or more precisely, to uphold the unconditional *within* the conditional. Derrida reverses the traditional problematic of hospitality, then, whereby I must decide how much I can open myself, my interests or my interior space to the exteriority of the other so that it rather becomes a question of to what extent I am entitled to limit, to interiorize or conditionalize what is already open, exterior, unconditional. The decision of genuine hospitality is a negotiation between the unconditional and the conditional demands of hospitality with no guarantee of a successful outcome. This hospitality can only avoid the violence of transcendental purism, on the one hand, and juridical bureaucracy, on the other, by acknowledging the lesser violence or groundless of its own decision-making. For Derrida, then, genuine hospitality consists in the a priori absence of any means of determining its own hospitable status, in the absence of any guarantees about whether it is really hospitable or not, of whether it is ever being hospitable enough. In Derrida's account, this 'mad' hospitality, 'impossible' hospitality or hospitality of lesser violence is the only chance of a hospitality that genuinely welcomes the arrivant:

> This impossibility *is necessary*. It is necessary that this threshold not be at the disposal of a general knowledge or a regulated technique. It is necessary that it exceed every regulated procedure in order to open itself to what always risks being perverted (the Good, Justice, Love, Faith – and perfectibility, etc.) This is necessary, this possible hospitality to the worst is necessary so that good hospitality can have a chance, the chance of letting the other come, the *yes* of the other no less than the *yes* to the other.
>
> (Derrida 1999a: 35)

Derrida, hospitality and negative theology

I now want to consider Derrida's concept of hospitality in the light of his reading of negative theology. It has already been suggested that negative theology's legacy to modernity may be a mode of hospitality and I want to pursue this unlikely and surprising thought in the remainder of this chapter. First, I think that Derrida's reading of negative theology is a *gesture* of hospitality in the specialized sense he develops in the essays above. Second, my argument will be that Derrida's reading also locates within negative theological discourse on God a surprising discourse on hospitality that overflows existing historical theologico-philosophical concepts of hospitality as refuge, universal fraternity, cosmopolitanism, religious or political tolerance of the other, and so on. Finally and more generally, my conclusion will seek to show that negative theology's religious hospitality could pave the way for a generalized ethical or political hospitality that welcomes the divine, the human and the animal alike. In Derrida's account of hospitality, I want to argue that we will be able to locate one possible future for the *via negativa*. Let me expound my argument in more detail.

Derrida's hospitality to negative theology

First, I want to briefly sketch Derrida's reading of negative theology in the light of his concept of hospitality. My hypothesis is that Derrida offers a reading of the *via negativa* that is 'hospitable' on a number of levels beyond the ordinary sense of a generous, receptive or even creative response. It is quite possible, of course, to see the gesture of reading *per se* – irrespective of whether any *particular* reading is considered to be generous or mean-spirited – as a form of hospitality in the generalized sense that Derrida describes (Bennington 2000: 35). It could be argued, for instance, that reading itself is hospitable in the sense that it is constituted by an originary and unconditional welcome of an other – language – that begins before I open a book as the condition of its intelligibility and that does not end when I finish it because it can never be definitively communicated or received as such. More precisely, however, my contention is that Derrida's reading of *negative theology*, in particular, can only be properly understood and critically evaluated as an attempt to extend the general and unconditional hospitality described above.

Derrida offers a reading of negative theology that is not simply hospitable in the banal sense of being commendably receptive to a mode of thought that is foreign to it, I think, but in the more radical sense of letting itself be surprised or overtaken by what is absolutely other within that thought. He seeks, as we saw in Chapter 1, to detach the *via negativa* from its official theological and philosophical history or content (Neoplatonism, Christian revelation, and so forth) and generalize it as a discourse on an essentially indeterminable alterity (Derrida 1995a: 71) that overflows any idea we may have of it. Second, Derrida's reading of negative theology could be described as hospitable in the sense that no-one – least of all he himself – can claim mastery, propriety or ownership over this concept of the *via negativa*. Derrida's reading insists that negative theology or – to be more precise – the trial of alterity that passes under that name is central to all responsible thought worthy of the name whether Christian or non-Christian, theological or non-theological (Derrida 1995a: 83). Finally, and perhaps most crucially of all, Derrida makes clear that his thought is *originarily* rather than secondarily hospitable to negative theology in the sense that the openness to the other that passes under the name of the *via negativa* has always and already been made welcome within that thought as the condition of its possibility. From Derrida's perspective, we might even say that *to think* means *to be hospitable to negative theology*: 'I trust no text that is not in some way contaminated with negative theology, and even among those texts that apparently do not have, want, or believe they have any relation with theology in general' (Derrida 1995a: 69). The basic and originary *hospitality* to what passes under the name of negative theology described here is the irreducible condition of any intentional response to the *via negativa* whatsoever, whether it be theological or atheological, faithful or transgressive, receptive or aggressive. This gesture of general hospitality towards negative theology within Derrida's text raises the question, however, of what exactly he is being hospitable towards under the name of the *via negativa*. What precisely is Derrida welcoming when he says 'Bienvenue!' to negative theology?

Negative theology and hospitality

Second, then, I would like to consider Derrida hospitality towards negative theology a little more widely. It will be my larger contention in the remainder of this chapter that Derrida is hospitable to negative theology as *nothing other* than a distinct mode of hospitality in itself. Derrida's hospitality to negative theology consists, that is, in welcoming the *via negativa* as an *example* – albeit in a refined sense of that term – of the generalized hospitality he has written about over the past few years. The unconditional surprise that arrives under the venerable guise of the *via negativa* is an idea of the welcome that exceeds historical or current concepts of hospitality. This concept of negative theology offers one way in which the name of the *via negativa* might be saved for the future.

Derrida, as we have already seen, makes the striking claim towards the end of his essay on negative theology 'Sauf le nom' that '[t]o let passage to the other, to the totally other, is hospitality' (Derrida 1995a: 80). It is an enigmatic and surprising claim in this context because Derrida never really follows up the suggestion of an identity between negative theology and hospitality – as opposed to Judaism and hospitality (Derrida 1999a) or Islam and hospitality (Derrida 2002a) – either in this essay or subsequently. Derrida's texts actually contain many compelling arguments to support the *opposite* claim, namely, that negative theology is in historical and philosophical contradiction with the concept of hospitality as letting 'passage to the other, to the totally other'. First, as we saw in Chapter 1, Derrida consistently criticizes negative theology in texts like 'Différance' and 'How to Avoid Speaking' as a rarefied ontotheological discourse on God that welcomes the other very much on its own Neoplatonic or Aristotelian terms (Derrida 1982a: 6). More pointedly, negative theology clearly remains of a piece with a tradition of Christian theological or philosophical hospitality that Derrida is at pains to differentiate from the concept of hospitality he is developing. Negative theology is consistently identified in Derrida's texts, as we saw in Chapters 3 and 4, with a worryingly exclusive or hierarchical concept of Christian fraternity or community that stretches from Pseudo-Dionysius (Derrida 1989a: 24) to Augustine (Derrida 1995a: 40) and beyond. Finally, and perhaps most worryingly of all, we have seen how Derrida continually takes negative theology to task for making possible a contemporary geo-political project of Christian hegemony under the guise of international law (Derrida 1995a: 78). If Derrida sees negative theology as hospitable to the other only on the basis that this other is male, Christian and ontotheological, to put it crudely, then it is obviously impossible to square it with his definition of hospitality as an unconditional welcome 'whether or not the arrivant is a citizen of another country, a human being, animal or divine, living or dead, masculine or feminine' (Derrida 1997a: 73).

Derrida's reading of negative theology certainly acknowledges that it has given rise to terrible and violent parodies of hospitality – who could deny it? – but once again the purpose of his interpretation is to locate a set of different resources within it to counter its official history. It is my contention that Derrida's reading of negative theology contains within it the possibility of a different idea of hospitality. He certainly makes some very bold claims on behalf of the *via negativa* in the essay 'Sauf le nom' that seem calculated to differentiate it from the Augustinian, Kantian and even Lévinasian concepts. First, he contends that negative theology contains within it the possibility of an application that goes beyond the theologico-political concept of a universal fraternity or community of Christians. Negative theology, he suggests, makes possible a concept of universality without implying what he sees as the homogenous and totalizing implications of Augustinian concepts of community, fraternity or charity by achieving what he calls a 'gathering together of singularities' (Derrida 1995a: 46), the paradoxical universalization of singularization formalized as 'tout autre est tout autre' [every other is absolutely other] (Derrida 1995a: 74). More pointedly still, Derrida raises the possibility that negative theology might also offer a prospect of a universal peace that goes beyond the Kantian cosmopolitical concept of a juridical arrangement between the citizens of sovereign states in his *Definitive Article in View of Perpetual Peace*. For Derrida, negative theology is the chance of 'another treaty of universal peace' that exceeds an international law that is still too much the instrument of nation–states and superstates (Derrida 1995a: 81). Perhaps most intriguingly of all, however, negative theology is shown to correct a lingering humanism – which insists that our hospitable relation to the other must always be a relation to *another human being* – that dominates the tradition of hospitality up to and including the Lévinasian concept of the face-to-face relation (see Llewelyn 1991). If hospitality is to be truly unconditional, then it cannot be restricted to a fraternity, to the citizens of sovereign states or even ultimately to human beings: 'I would not yet speak of human, nor even anthropotheocentric, community or singularity, nor even of a *Gevier* in which what is called "animal" would be a mortal passed over in silence' (Derrida 1995a: 81). The tantalizing prospect being held out for us in 'Sauf le nom', then, is of negative theology as a non-totalizing, non-juridical and even ultimately non-anthropomorphic hospitality to the other. This concept of negative theology is constantly spoken of in the future tense by Derrida as a chance, a passage, a possibility, something that, appropriately enough, cannot yet be spoken of: '[w]ould there be a voice for that? A name?' (Derrida 1995a: 83). We clearly need to put some flesh on the bones of these – on the face of it – rather vague and general claims about community, universality and anthropomorphism before we go any further. To what extent is Derrida able to justify his claim that negative theology represents a mode of unconditional hospitality?

Negative theology as generalized hospitality

Finally, then, I want to consider exactly what Derrida might mean by describing negative theology as a future form of hospitality. He writes, as we already know, that: '[t]o let passage to the other, to the totally other, is hospitality' (Derrida 1995a: 80). I want to consider this assertion in some detail. Derrida does not really elaborate upon this enigmatic claim in the remainder of the text but there are enough clues scattered here and there to enable us to fill in some of the blanks in his account. If we want to understand what Derrida means, we will need to situate his discussion of negative theology not simply in the context of his discussions of hospitality but of a range of analogous concepts such as ethics, the gift, sacrifice, and so on (Derrida 1992a; 1995b). For Derrida, I eventually want to argue that negative theology's future may, if you will pardon the apparent tautology, be as a gesture of hospitality towards the essential unknowable and unpredictable arrival of the future itself.

First, Derrida's reading of negative theology as a mode of generalized hospitality depends on a productive ambiguity in the verb 'to let' or 'laisser' as it appears in the phrase 'to let passage to the other'. He offers some clues about how to understand this notion of 'letting' earlier in the essay. He argues, as we have already seen, that negative theology represents an excess or hyperbole within the European ontotheological tradition that generalizes its theological discourse on the Neoplatonic God into a respect for an absolute alterity beyond all determination:

> – On the one hand, this negation, as reaffirmation, can seem to double bolt the logocentric impasse of European domesticity (and India in this regard is not the absolute other of Europe). But on the

other hand, it is also what, working on the *open* edge of this interiority or intimacy, *lets* [*laisse*] passage, *lets the other be.*

(Derrida 1995a: 78)

What does it mean, then, 'to let the other be'? His argument is that negative theology 'lets the other be' because it progressively resists any attempt to determine that alterity as either God the supreme being, God beyond being, God without being or even God as such. But Derrida goes on to identify an ambiguity in the French verb 'laisser' that complicates any simple English translation of the phrase:

> [h]ow are they going to translate it? By 'to leave', as in the phrase that won't be long in coming when we will shortly have to go our separate ways (I leave you, I am going, I *leave*) or else 'to let'?
>
> (Derrida 1995a: 78)

Derrida draws attention to the problem that the verb 'laisser' can be translated into English as *both* to leave, to say goodbye to, or even to abandon ('Je vous laisse', for example, means 'I must leave you') *and* to let, to leave alone, to permit or allow something to be or do itself ('laisse-le faire' means 'let him do it himself'). Derrida's argument is less interested in resolving this ambiguity one way or another than in maintaining it as an indispensable characteristic of what he calls that 'serene indifference' or *Gelassenheit* that characterizes the negative theological relation to the other from Eckhart to Heidegger:

> – Here we must have recourse to the German idiom. Silesius writes in the tradition of the *Gelassenheit* that, as we noted above, goes from Eckhart, at least, to Heidegger. It is necessary to leave all, to leave every 'something' through love of God, and no doubt to leave God himself, to abandon him, that is, at once to leave him and (but) let him (be beyond being-something).
>
> (Derrida 1995a: 78–9)

The concept of *Gelassenheit* is not simply an ascetic sacrifice or renunciation of all worldly goods in the name of God, in other words, but an infinite or unconditional indifference that even abandons God as a nameable object. There is a paradoxical sense in which to let God be Himself is – if we want to avoid any suspicion of idolatry, egotism or narcissism – to leave or abandon any proper name or concept of God whatsoever. This leads Derrida to the important conclusion that the serene indifference to everything *excluding* God ultimately leads to the indifference to everything *including* God. For Derrida, as we will now see, negative theology's singular relation to God as the absolute other is inseparable from a certain non-singularity or substitutability with any other.

Second, then, I would argue that Derrida's reading of negative theology as a gesture of hospitality depends on the hypothesis that it extends the same unconditional welcome to *any* other whatsoever. He continually stresses throughout 'Sauf le nom' that negative theology's affirmation of the radical and infinite alterity of God is in principle attributable to any alterity at all, whether human or non-human, sentient or non-sentient. He formalizes this argument in a number of recent texts in the simultaneously simple and almost unthinkable difficult proposition 'tout autre est tout autre' or 'every other is absolutely other' (Derrida 1995a: 73–6). He canvasses for what we have paradoxically called a *universalization* of *singularization* here in which absolute singularity is only thinkable on the basis of an – on the face of it contradictory – equivalence with other equally absolute singularities. It is tempting to describe 'tout autre est tout autre' as the single most challenging idea in Derrida's recent work – prompting as it has the usual predictable accusations of relativism, on the one hand, and transcendentalism, on the other – precisely because it asks us to imagine singularity and universality together at the same time. It is possible, of course, to describe deconstruction *in general* as nothing other than the attempt to think through the aporetic relationship between the singular case and the universal structure that makes it simultaneously possible and impossible. If I were pushed to identify anything so problematic as a 'unifying theme' in Derrida's thought, it would probably be the logic of originary trace, repetition or supplementation that both allows a singular case to be marked and recognized as a singularity and loses or erases that singularity in the same gesture. Deconstruction insists without contradiction that everything is both absolutely 'different' in the sense that it is a radical alterity that cannot be gathered under any unifying genus or identity and at least partially 'the same' because it exists within a more or less recognizable but essentially non-unified network of originary trace or différance. But the formula 'tout autre est tout autre' only begins to appear in Derrida's work around the time of the so-called 'ethical turn' in texts such as *The Gift of Death* (1992) and 'Le mot d'accueil' ([1997] 1999c). Derrida develops, as we have already seen in this chapter, a concept of hospitality as a 'mad' or hyperbolic decision of lesser violence between the irreconcilable imperatives of the unconditional and the conditional, the singular and the universal, the ethical and the political, and so on. Derrida's argument is that the *singular* relation to the other in which ethics begins – such as Abraham's relation to God in *The Gift of Death* or the face-to-face relation in 'Le mot d'accueil' – is *universalized* at the point of origin by the presence of *another other* – such as the figure of Isaac or the third party – who *simultaneously* protects *and* destroys that relation by opening it to the field of law, justice and the community. The response I give to the singular other is rendered (im)possible by its originary multiplicity or substitutability as an infinite number of other singular others to whom I am also obliged to give a response. There is no way in which we can legitimately evaluate or adjudicate between the competing claims of the other and third party – or the dimensions of the ethical and the political that spring from them – because their apparent oppositionality is the product of the kind of originary chiasmus or complication we have traced throughout this book. This leads to a situation whereby responsibility to any one singular other always necessarily involves an inherently *unjustifiable* sacrifice of my responsibility to all the other singular others:

> I cannot respond to the call, the request, the obligation, or even to the love of another, without sacrificing to him the other other, the other others [*sans lui sacrificer l'autre autre, les autres autres*]. Every other is absolutely other [*tout autre est tout autre*].
> (Derrida: 1995b: 68)

Derrida's reading of negative theology as hospitality, then, is underwritten by the infinite responsibility where 'tout autre est tout autre'. He consistently argues that its relation to the *divine other* is only possible on the basis of this inescapable relation to *another other*, to all the other others: 'one should say of no matter what or no matter whom what one says God or some other thing' (Derrida 1995a: 73). His position is that negative theology's *theological* hospitality to God, so to speak, makes possible a *generalized* hospitality that is serenely indifferent to the other whether it be divine or human, animal or mineral:

> The other is God or no matter whom, more precisely, no matter what singularity, as soon as any other is totally other [*tout autre est tout autre*]. For the most difficult, indeed the impossible, resides there: there where the other loses its name or can change it, to become no matter what other.
> (Derrida 1995a: 74)

His argument goes on to reconceptualize this paradoxical conjunction of singularity and universality in terms of a logic of exemplarity that has important implications for any attempt to translate or generalize negative theology into a wider field. If every singular case is thinkable only on the basis of a universal structure that both protects and erases its singularity, Derrida then argues that every singularity necessarily contains within it the possibility of a certain *exemplarity* whereby the name of God can become the *example* of an infinite number of other names:

> Each thing, each being, you, me, the other, each X, each name, and each name of God can become the example of other substitutable Xs. A process of absolute formalization. Any other is totally other [*Tout autre est tout autre*]. A name of God, in a tongue, a phrase, a prayer,

> becomes an example of the name and of names of God, then of names in general.
>
> (Derrida 1995a: 76)

Derrida wants to argue that God's name is 'exemplary' not in the classic sense of a historical particularity that can be subsumed under some universal category such as the Kantian concept of the ethical but because its singularity necessarily contains within it the possibility of an essentially open-ended multiplication or substitution by the other(s). Derrida's argument is a variation on his suggestive claim that I am originarily hospitable in the sense that any singular identity is absolutely contingent upon a relation to the other and that this relation is, in turn, dependent upon the presence of the third party and so on to infinity. The upshot is that God's name can thus become the example of a potentially infinite and non-totalizable string of names such as justice, love or the good and *mutatis mutandis* – although interestingly he doesn't really elaborate on this point – such names can also become examples of God. This logic of exemplarity helps to explain how he can set up negative theology as an example of hospitality – or is hospitality an example of negative theology? – while avoiding the ever-present charge – mentioned in Chapter 1 – of merely recruiting it to the cause of some abstract or universal idea of the ethical such as is found in Kant or, differently, Lévinas.

What does Derrida mean, to summarize, by describing negative theology as an 'example' of hospitality? First, negative theology fulfils – if only in one of its voices – the Derridaean definition of hospitality as an unconditional responsibility to the arrivant that infinitely exceeds any idea we may have of it. It seeks to let the other be without drawing it into the *chez-moi* of European domesticity or fraternity and Christian ecumenicism. Its discourse on the heterogeneity of God with respect to being ultimately leads it to surrender any attempt to determine the status or identity of its arrivant whether it be human or divine, animal or mineral, the absolutely other or all the other others:

> God without being, God uncontaminated by being – is this not the most rigorous definition of the Face of the Wholly Other?
>
> (Derrida 1999a: 112).

Second, negative theology meets Derrida's concept of hospitality because its unconditional welcome of the other – as unconditional – is open to pervertibility. To determine exactly what we are being hospitable to in advance – the just or the unjust, the one true God or the false idol, the asylum-seeker or the economic migrant – is to leave ourselves open to the irresponsibility of self-righteousness or ethical complacency. Negative theology functions as positive theology's bad conscience, so to speak, the sense of infinite responsibility which insists that our welcome does not do

God justice, that we never make Him welcome enough, that His arrival is always more foreign and surprising than we can possibly imagine or prepare for. If the *via negativa* avoids the dangerous charge of believing in its own sense of justice or propriety, it is because its unconditional sense of responsibility opens it to the problem or opportunity of its own potential pervertibility:

> I try to dissociate the concept of this pure hospitality from the concept of 'invitation'. If you are the guest and I invite you, if I am expecting you and am prepared to meet you, then this implies that there is no surprise, everything is in order. For pure hospitality or a pure gift to occur, however, there must be an absolute surprise. The other, like the Messiah, must arrive whenever he or she wants.
> (Derrida 1999b: 70)

Finally, and most importantly, however, I would like to propose that negative theology is an example of hospitality in the sense that it must ultimately take the form of a *decision*, negotiation or compromise between this *unconditional* demand for hospitality and the *conditional* contexts of politics, law and institutions in which that demand takes place. The decision of genuine hospitality has to involve both unconditional and conditional dimensions if hospitality is not to be elevated to some absolutely unaccountable purism, on the one hand, or reduced to a legalistic bureaucracy of treaties and quotas, on the other. This raises the question that the true test of negative theology's status as a form of hospitality will precisely be the extent to which it can mediate between the irreconcilable demands of the ethical and the political, the other and the third, God and the *sans-papier* or asylum seeker. What form – if any – would a law or politics of negative theology take? Does negative theology have anything meaningful to say about immigration policy, xenophobia, the *sans-papiers*, asylum seekers? To what extent could the *via negativa* contribute towards a reinvention of the politics of hospitality? In the final section of this chapter, I want to sketch one possible future for negative theology as a politics of hospitality.

New arrivals?

I want to conclude this final chapter, then, by considering whether negative theology could contribute towards a future ethics or politics of hospitality. It is necessary to begin by pinpointing as precisely as we can the relationship *between* an ethics and politics of hospitality. Second, I will consider the extent to which the new form of hospitality we have encountered in and through negative theology can intersect with the existing ethical and juridical perimeters of hospitality as encountered in, for example, immigration and asylum policy. Finally, we will consider to what extent this relation constitutes one of the new – and necessarily surprising – futures for negative theology I have been canvassing for throughout this book. This project is obviously fraught with difficulties in an era when the proximity of theological and secular forms of hospitality seems to offer nothing but violence from Israel to Northern Ireland, from Algeria to French *lycées* (Derrida 1999a; Derrida 2001b: 77; 2002a: 301–8). In summary, my argument will be that negative theology does not offer a way of *eliminating* this violence – an illusion which is, as we have already seen, open to the possibility of the worst violence of all – but of *minimizing* it by raising the possibility of a hospitality without any theological or secular foundation.

The politics of hospitality

First, I want to explore the precise relation between an ethics and politics of hospitality. Derrida explores in 'Le mot d'accueil', as we have already seen, the passage from an *ethics* to a *politics* of hospitality. He differentiates his position from Kant's construal of the relationship between the ethical and the political in terms of categorical imperatives and hypothetical maxims, and Lévinas's understanding of it in terms of the relation between the other and the third or the Saying and the Said. He canvasses for an *aporetic* rather than an *idealist* or *dialogic* relationship between the two because – as his discussion of the other and the third shows – the ethical is already contaminated by the political as its condition of possibility. His argument is that the relationship between the ethical and the political is essentially undecidable, in other words, because they inhere in each other at their supposed point of origin. If the ethical does not exist in a pure or transcendental state – whether it be as the good, the categorical imperative or the face of the other – then it cannot be used as a regulative ideal or foundation to deduce what we should then think or do in the field of politics. What if, Derrida invites us to consider, this impossibility does not represent a lack or a failure but an *opportunity* to develop a concept of ethical and political responsibility without the 'assurance of an ontological foundation' (Derrida 1999a: 21)?

Derrida characteristically argues that ethico-political responsibility is *transformed* rather than *paralysed* by this impossibility, in other words, precisely because the absence of any rules or foundations about what to do or think gives it something to take responsibility for. It is clear that Derrida is canvassing for a concept of responsibility – or inheritance, or giving, or hospitality, for the list can be extended indefinitely – as constituted by a moment of more or less illicit or violent *reinvention* with respect to the law. His argument moves from what we might call a constative understanding of ethico-political responsibility which simply describes a pre-existent state of justice, then, to a performative understanding where it must invent the conditions according to which it will be considered to be just or not. The possibility of any genuine hospitable thought lies in deciding – in the full knowledge of its own violence and illegitimacy – where the line between the ethical and the political should be drawn in any given case. There is an important sense in which the hospitality of lesser violence Derrida canvasses for, which seeks to maintain the undecidability between the ethical and the political so far as possible, can be contrasted with a hospitality of greater violence latent in Kant and even Lévinas, which seeks to essentialize or hierarchize the distinction between the two. This hospitality of lesser violence maintains the chiasmus between the ethical and the political by insisting upon the capacity of the ethical to be politicized even in its supposedly singular purity and the capacity of the political to be interrupted by an unconditional ethical imperative despite the seemingly overwhelming demands of *realpolitik*. For Derrida, Lévinas's late Talmudic reading 'Au-delà de l'État dans l'État' (1996) points the way towards a form of hospitality that affirms this invagination of the other and the third, the ethical and the political, the unconditional and the conditional:

> Once again, beyond the State *in* the State, beyond law *in* the law, responsibility held hostage to the here-now, the law of justice that transcends the political and the juridical, in the philosophical sense of these terms, must bend to itself, to the point of exceeding and obsessing it, everything that the face exceeds, in the face to face or in the interruption of the third that marks the demand for justice as law.
> (Derrida 1999a: 110)

Negative theology and the politics of hospitality

Furthermore, and more importantly, I want to consider to what extent negative theology could contribute to this particular reading of the politics of hospitality. It is impossible to raise such a question without bearing in mind the enormous importance that Christian theology more generally accords to the concept of hospitality. Hospitality is used as a means of illustrating God's love (Luke 15. 22–24; 1. Pet. 4. 8–10), of exhorting Christians to lead a virtuous life (Luke 14. 12–14; Rom. 13. 9–13) and of exemplifying the practice and pedagogy of preaching the gospel (Matt. 10. 9–16). Hospitality's significance is extended into recognizably political language and territory, however, in Paul's proclamation to the Ephesians that they are no longer foreigners [*xenoi*] but 'fellow citizens with the saints and members of the household of God' (Eph. 2. 19–20). More generally, Derrida has shown how we can trace the fallout of this Pauline concept of universal community from Kantian cosmopolitanism to the present geopolitical monoliths of the nation–state, the superstates of the USA and the EU and what is commonly and unproblematically referred to as 'the international community' (Derrida 1995a: 78). If negative theology undoubtedly plays its own small part in contributing to this theologico-secular concept of universal community, the question remains of whether this is the only politics of hospitality we can imagine for it. What if negative theology represents a politics of hospitality that – according to the logic developed above – *transcends* contemporary concepts of fraternity, community and democracy from *within*?

Derrida advances precisely this possibility in the final pages of 'Sauf le nom'. He emphatically denies that negative theology could ever form the ethical or theological *basis* for a politics on the grounds that such an assured foundation would immediately deprive the political of all responsibility and turn it into a mechanical act of administration or application (Derrida 1995a: 81). But he is clear that negative theology's singular ethical or theological demand does not simply remain *above* politics because – like hospitality – it must *bend* to, or *collapse* into, the political at the same time: 'there would no more be any "politics", "law" or "morals" *without* this possibility, the very possibility that obliges us from now on to place these words between quotation marks. Their sense will have trembled' (Derrida 1995a: 81).

Derrida argues, in other words, that negative theology adheres to the exact same structure of 'transcendence in immanence' (Derrida 1999a: 99) with respect to the competing demands of the ethical and the political, the other and the third, the unconditional and the conditional, that we have been tracing in the case of hospitality. Derrida's argument is that negative theology's identity is given in *neither* the transcendental imperative to address God as the absolute other beyond all possible determination *nor* the empirical institutions and structures which it has generated but in the aporetic oscillation or 'trembling' between the two. If the *via negativa* has a meaningful contribution to make to any current debates on hospitality, then, it is not to sponsor this or that position, but to *uphold* the basic undecidability between the ethical and the political, to stop, in other words, the ethical from ossifying into the *merely* ethical and the political into the *merely* political. The *via negativa* has to respect both the pragmatic, judicial conditions in which any ethics of hospitality must take place if it has to have any force and the moment of infinitude or unconditionality that any politics of hospitality must not lose sight of if it is not to merely accede to the prudential demands of *realpolitik*. There is no alternative to this position if we do not want to succumb to the dangerous illusions of valorizing the purity of the ethical or the religious over the political, on the one hand (the theologized politics at work in Algeria, Northern Ireland and a certain strand of Lévinasian Zionism stand as warnings here), or upholding the authority of the political at the expense of the ethical or the religious on the other (the ongoing 'affaire des foulards' that forbids Muslims from wearing their veils in *lycées* or on identity cards on the grounds of the 'laïcité' or religious non-alignment of the French state is one small but telling example of this process). This position has to take the form of an 'impossible' decision which – as we well know – has to be taken in the absence of any preconceived course of action and in the full knowledge of its own possible pervertibility:

> I cannot think the notion of the way without the necessity of deciding there where the decision seems impossible. Nor can I think the decision and thus the responsibility there where the decision is already possible and programmable. And would one speak, could one only speak of this thing? Would there be a voice [*voix*] for that? A name?
>
> (Derrida 1995a: 83)

What form, however, might this decision take in practice, in reality, in that mythical land that politicians call the 'real world'? I think we have to be very cautious about translating Derrida's work on hospitality into concrete examples even if this does provoke the usual accusations of political quietism or irresponsibility from *soi-disant* 'radical' intellectuals. It is difficult to imagine how the unconditional hospitality to every other as absolutely other of which he speaks could be reduced to a finite number of illustrations – however compelling they may appear – without violating everything that is at stake in it. But on the other hand we have consistently shown how unconditional hospitality *must* be subjected to such a reduction to certain examples – irrespective of its violence – if it is to have any effectivity at all. If we are to avoid the greater violence of ethical purism, we have to succumb to the lesser violence of choosing some cases over others even as we acknowledge that every case exemplifies every other case. Let me conclude by identifying one or two possible examples while keeping in mind this necessary substitutability.

First, I would note that Derrida himself cites the examples of refugees, asylum seekers, *sans-papiers*, immigration and xenophobia as obvious, massive but no less inescapable contexts for his work. It goes without saying that the logic of hospitality expounded in his recent ethical, political and religious work has important implications for asylum policies that seem increasingly driven by the worst kind of political expediency and posturing. If no-one is suggesting that unconditional hospitality is possible, the maintenance of an idea of an infinite responsibility serves as a salutary means of interrupting the ruthless pragmatism of legislation like the British Government's Nationality, Immigration and Asylum Act 2002, for example, which was drawn up on the explicit *presumption* that the majority of asylum claims will always be fraudulent.[3] What concept of hospitality, after all, prides itself upon not being a 'soft touch' for immigrants who are yet to apply, on the speed by which it processes their imaginary applications, on compulsory English lessons and citizenship tests, and so-called 'accommodation centres' outside the European Union?

Moreover, Derrida has personally drawn attention to the 'hypocritical and perverse' (Derrida 2001a: 12) distinction between political asylum and economic migration that now forms the basis for all European legislation upon immigration. It is arguably this distinction more than any other that is responsible for the current controversy about immigration in Europe and the ensuing paranoia about 'bogus' asylum claimants. Political asylum is extended only to those who can prove that they are the victims of persecution in their country of origin rather than economic migrants seeking to gain economic advantage from residence in their host country. If we maintain the unconditional appeal to hospitality, however, we can again begin to question the expediency at work within a set of conditions that welcomes only those who can prove, so to speak, that they are not seeking to be welcomed. We might again ask what form of hospitality welcomes someone on the condition that they can expect no economic gain from their stay. What form of hospitality goes on to *stigmatize* the same political refugee for the welfare dependency it condemns him to, or for working illegally as a means of avoiding that dependency?

Finally, and perhaps most radically, however, I would like to return to Derrida's tantalizing idea towards the end of 'Sauf le nom' that negative theology raises the possibility of a community that could no longer simply be identified as human (Derrida 1995a: 81). It may be that even the thought of an unconditional hospitality to the asylum seeker or the illegal worker may not be unconditional enough. He raises the possibility that negative theology's status as a welcome to something that is absolutely heterogeneous to any identity – even ultimately a theological identity – might enable us to correct a lingering humanism within contemporary concepts of hospitality. Derrida has consistently identified, as we have already seen, a latently theological anthropocentrism within the concept of the universal community that stretches from Augustinian fraternity through Kantian cosmopolitanism to Lévinasian ethics. Derrida's criticism of Lévinas, for example, is that the identification of *language* as the basis for the relation to the other immediately restricts responsibility only to linguistic beings such as human beings and removes it from non-linguistic ones such as animals, plants, minerals and machines (Cadava *et al.* 1991: 112–13). Lévinas's emphasis on language not only compromises the radical nature of his critique of ontology but appears to deny the possibility of any ethical relation to non-human forms of life such as animals or even non-living matter such as technical objects or artificial intelligence. If we interpret Lévinas's emphasis on language more generously to encompass verbal and non-verbal communication – as Simon Critchley has recently suggested – then perhaps we can avoid this bias against the animal but even this extension would leave out the question of our ethical relation to technology (Critchley 1999: 80n). To what extent – and particularly in the context of debates surrounding animal rights, biogenetics and artificial intelligence – is it still defensible to limit the right of hospitality to an essentialized concept of the human and thereby exclude the non-human, animal, technological, or even divine?

Conclusion

Jacques Derrida, to summarize, enables a reading of negative theology as a spirit of generalized hospitality towards what is to come. He sees negative theology, to put it more precisely, as an example of the *parvis*, threshold or doorway that all responsible thought keeps opens to the absolutely other. Negative theology's hospitality to a God who is absolutely other can be translated into a more general hospitality to the stranger who will never totally arrive or the community that will never completely gather itself into a unity. If this line of argument still sounds somewhat Lévinasian, it is with the important difference that the hospitality negative theology extends to the other cannot be limited to the human stranger, but must be extended to every other as absolutely other whether they be divine, animal, human or technological. The politics of genuine hospitality must take the form of a contingent *decision* within and between the unconditional demand for hospitality, on the one hand, and the political and legislative context in which that demand takes place, on the other. There can be no guarantees in advance that such a decision will ever turn out to be a just or felicitous one but, as we well know, the absence of such guarantees is precisely what makes it a decision as opposed to the implementation or administration of a predetermined course of action. This decision of hospitality must be taken in the full knowledge of its own *possible* perversion if it is to avoid the *actual* perversion of a present European politics of hospitality that, for example, now pays impoverished Eastern European and African countries to detain, and process the applications of, asylum seekers to the European Union. In this and other ways, Derrida saves the name of negative theology for the future.

7 Conclusion
Negative theology after modern French philosophy

This book has argued for the centrality of a certain negative theology to modern French philosophy. It has attempted to negotiate a pivotal position for the *via negativa* within continental thought while avoiding the twin pitfalls of simply philosophizing theology (in the vein of post-Kantian philosophy of religion) or theologizing philosophy (as epitomized by the current Neo-Thomist or 'post-secular' theological resurgence). My point of departure was Jacques Derrida's fascinating hypothesis that negative theology is neither simply a theologically articulated doctrine about God nor a philosophical discourse on propositional language but a privileged example of the relation to the other as absolutely other that characterizes all responsible thought and action. If Derrida's argument was to become more than a contentless speculation, however, it needed to be put to the test and this is what this book attempted to do in a series of individual essays or case studies on his theological and philosophical contemporaries. What conclusions, then, can we draw? How far is negative theology something that remains constitutively unthought within continental philosophy? To what extent is it possible to speak of a negative theology after modern French philosophy? In this conclusion, I would briefly like to summarize my argument and imagine some of its wider implications.

First, I argued that Derrida sees negative theology as one of the most remarkable manifestations of the originary self-difference or supplementation that constitutes the Western tradition in deconstruction (Derrida 1995a: 71). He contends that negative theology is a privileged example of the constitutive non-identity of every tradition with itself, whether it be Christian or non-Christian, theological or philosophical, historical or transcendental. If it is objected that negative theology is only one example of this problematic, and an example that can, as we saw in Chapter 6, be substituted with any another example, Derrida might reply that the *via negativa* is one of the 'best' examples precisely *because* it is the worst, the most proper because it is least proper, the least substitutable because it is the most substitutable (Derrida 1995a: 76; see also de Vries 1999: 93–4 on God as the example of the trace *par excellence*). Derrida's work posits a certain *generalized* negative theology, then, as a prioritized name for the necessary undecidability that constitutes the field in which all thought and action takes place irrespective of whether it is that of canonical negative theologians like Pseudo-Dionysius, Meister Eckhart or Angelus Silesius or philosophers such as Heidegger, Wittgenstein or Derrida himself. The quasi-transcendental concept of negative theology advanced in Derrida's work offers a privileged point of access into the problematic construction of contemporary theism and atheism as mutually exclusive or antagonistic discourses.

Second, then, I went on to test Derrida's thesis by examining the ambiguous place of negative theology in the work of a number of his theological and philosophical contemporaries. I sought to show that Certeau, Marion, Foucault and Kristeva all encountered this dimension of undecidability within the *via negativa*. My argument demonstrated how each of these readings *foreclosed* this dimension by prematurely identifying it as theological or atheological in origin. It is this determination to *decide* the identity of the *via negativa* one way or the other – whether as divine or secular, transcendental or immanent, theological or non-theological – that unites the otherwise very disparate thinkers in this book. The problem with these decisions is not that they are prescriptive as such – if everything Derrida says about negative theology holds, then there is no way of responding to it neutrally or innocently – but that they seek to subsume that violence under the guise of simple description. There is a sense in which every thinker in this book from Certeau to Kristeva – all of whom seek in one way or another to overcome or circumvent metaphysics – subsume their decision-making under an appeal to a ground that somehow exceeds the ravages of difference whether we call it the 'mystical postulate' (Certeau), 'Gxd without being' (Marion), 'the outside' (Foucault) or the 'sacred' (Kristeva). This kind of decision-making seeks to shut down what we have seen to be the defining characteristic of negative theology – its absolute openness to an unpredictable future – by locating it within a proper name, tradition or corpus that can then be either embraced or rejected according to will.

Finally, and most importantly, this book has argued that these decisions qua decisions are – whether they know it or not or believe it or not – always taken in the radical absence of any grounds whatsoever and so are permanently open to the possibility of future decisions. It has been my argument that the attempt to foreclose the identity of the *via negativa* cannot but fail because the dimension of undecidability that makes such decisions necessary and unavoidable also ensures that no decision can absolutely resolve it one way or the other. My argument has shown that the attempt to determine the identity of the *via negativa* always produces a residuum or remainder which it cannot contain. If contemporary French philosophy seeks to decide the identity of negative theology one way or another, it remains vulnerable to a series of structural surprises whereupon its constitutive exclusions return to haunt it in spectral form as the return of the repressed. On the one hand, Michel de Certeau and Jean-Luc Marion seek to affirm a purely theological identity for the *via negativa* but their texts continually open a more radically heterological dimension that exceeds this ultimately dogmatic act of identification. On the other hand, Michel Foucault and Julia Kristeva seek to co-opt the resources of the *via negativa* for historical archaeology or psychoanalysis but their texts continually reproduce the transcendental gestures they seek to historicize or psychoanalyse. The impossibility of reducing negative theology to a singular theological, philosophical or historical concept that can simply be deployed or dispensed with makes it possible to reinterpret the *via negativa* in the generalized or quasi-transcendental terms described by Derrida. There is a sense in which negative theology is central to modern French philosophy – not because of some more or less hidden theological or nihilistic agenda (Janicaud 1991; Milbank 1995) – but because it names an essential tension to which all thought must respond in order to be responsible (Derrida 1995a: 83). For Derrida, negative theology is central to all thinking worthy of the name – regardless of whether we choose to embrace or reject the historical *via negativa* – because it concretizes that negotiation between the finite and infinite, the conditional and the unconditional that characterizes the field for all responsible thought and action whatsoever (Derrida 1995a: 83–4).

What, to conclude, is the future of negative theology after modern French philosophy? It is impossible to say, appropriately enough, without betraying everything that is apparently at stake in it. It is hopefully now clear that to *predict* the future of negative theology – as if it had a share price on the stock market – is to spurn the very hospitality to the future *as* future that it offers us. Let me close, then, less with predictions than with some imaginary bets, wagers or guesses about the implications of the *via negativa* that exceed the boundaries of this book and my own competency. Derrida attempts to posit a certain negative theology at the heart of all thinking and, if he succeeds, then the result of this enterprise would have to be a massive and almost unimaginable re-invention of the relationship between the Christian and the non-Christian, the theological and the philosophical *et al.* as *originarily interrelated*. First, Derrida's concept of a generalized negativity would necessitate a complication of the relation between the Christian and the non-Christian. If Christianity is shown to be non-identical with itself in its own interiority, so to speak, then it is revealed as originarily open to the possibility of *other religions* and *the other of religion* in a far more unconditional sense than the traditions of tolerance, hospitality and ecumenicism allow. Christian identity, then, becomes a kind of non-fraternal, non-essentialized community in which its relation to itself will already be a relation to what is other than itself and vice versa. Christianity's historic relationship to what ostensibly lies outside it – whether we construe it as violent or non-violent, intolerant or tolerant, hegemonic or pluralist – would need to be thought of as both the effect of, and the response to, this originary openness or non-propriety. Second, and following on from this, Derrida's generalized concept of negative theology asks us to imagine the relationship between philosophy and theology in similarly non-monolithic, pluralized or fractal terms. The possibility being held out for us is a reading of the relationship between theology and philosophy where one can only obtain self-identical purity through a wholly contingent and inevitably violent act of exclusion of the other. This would mean that every moment in the history of the relation between theology and philosophy from the repeated attempts to institute or hierarchize the difference between them (scholastic theology, rational theology, the current neo-Thomist revival) to the no less repeated collapse back into a tragic or culpable indifference or complicity (idolatry, ontotheology, even the so-called theological turn) would have to be re-described as nothing less than the inevitable *rhythm* or *economy* of this more originary instability playing itself out endlessly. Finally, and most crucially, however, Derrida's negative theology asks us to see this necessary *fatality* within every concept of the Christian or non-Christian, the theological or philosophical or religious and secular as an ethico-political *opportunity*. To posit this radical undecidability at the heart of every distinction between the religious and the secular is not to *destroy* or neutralize them, this book has argued, but to *save* them by recovering resources that are underthought within them, questioning the automaticity of their conceptual purity or integrity and, most importantly, by transforming an ethics and politics of legalistic administration into one of infinite responsibility and decision-making, today, tomorrow and in the future. In this sense, negative theology's future will remain a matter of *decision*.

Notes

1 Derrida and 'saving the name'

1 Jacques Derrida was asked whether deconstruction was a form of negative theology by a member of the audience after the first oral delivery of 'Différance' as a lecture in 1968: 'It is the source of everything and one cannot know it. It is the God of negative theology.' He replied: 'It is and it is not. Above all it is not' (Derrida 1988b: 84).
2 Derrida writes:

> I ... am quite convinced of the need for a rigorous and differentiated reading of anything advanced under this title (negative theology). My fascination at least testifies to this, right through my incompetence: in effect I believe that what is called 'negative theology' (a rich and very diverse corpus) does not let itself be easily assembled under the general category of 'ontotheology to be deconstructed'.
>
> (1982b: 61)

3 Milbank argues: 'Derrida's written difference, defined by its possibility of surviving the death of every speaker, is necessarily a deferred difference, a difference that never arrives, that is therefore nothing, no-difference' (1997: 61).
4 George Orwell famously wrote his essay 'The Lion and the Unicorn: Socialism and the English Genius' (1968: 56) during the London Blitz of 1940.

2 Certeau's 'Yes, in a foreign land'

1 Jacques Derrida uses this phrase at the beginning of the essay 'A Number of Yes'. It can also be interpreted as 'yes, to the stranger', of course, but the context suggests the translation of 'l'étranger' as 'abroad' or 'a foreign country'.
2 Michel de Certeau was, according to his friend and collaborator Luce Giard, planning a new book with the provisional title of *Heterologies* at the time of his death and the posthumous collection published under that name in 1986 contains some of his work-in-progress.
3 Geoffrey Bennington criticizes a popular tendency in contemporary theory to reduce difference to a liberal value in (Bennington 1999: 103–23).
4 Certeau wrote about his experiences of Christian identity in Brazil and the USA in his essays 'Les chrétiens et la dictature militaire au Brésil' and 'Conscience chrétienne et conscience politique aux USA: Les Berrigan'. He is clearly interested in thinking forms of Christianity that resist the political status quo such as the actions of the Brazilian Marxist Christians against the military dictatorship and the Catholic anti-Vietnam War movement led by the Jesuit Priest Daniel

Berrigan. He tends to be much more critical – indeed almost to the point of prejudice at times – of Christian movements that he believes *sustain* the political status quo such as what he describes as the predominantly Irish, working-class and reactionary Catholic Church in the USA which lent its support to the right-wing 'Law and Order' platform of the Nixon administration in the late 1960s and early 1970s. It is my contention, however, that the radical thrust of Certeau's argument deprives him of the means of making such a sharp distinction between radical and conservative forms of Catholicism and thus between admired anti-war American Jesuits like Berrigan and disliked '*Irish Catholic Priests*: three words that pile together three sorts of conservatism' (Certeau 1987a: 161).

5 Certeau's account of the *volo* does not necessarily entail a metaphysics of the subject in the way Derrida suggests. He stresses that the *volo* cannot be traced back to any subject or object because it is ultimately just the modal condition of wanting itself (Certeau 1992: 169). See also Certeau's claim that the *volo* exceeds the Cartesian cogito (1992: 241).

6 Derrida argues that the gift is rendered impossible by the possibility of exchange in *Given Time 1: Counterfeit Money* (1992a) but this impossibility is exactly what enables us to recognize the absolute alterity of giving and thus the arrival of justice, responsibility, and so on. Certeau also argues that the gift is rendered impossible by the possibility of exchange but my feeling is that this impossibility is often simply a lack or absence for Certeau because, I would argue, he is unwilling to recognize the existence of the gift outside the exchange between subject and object. Graham Ward offers a different comparison of Derrida and Certeau's concepts of the gift in *Theology and Contemporary Critical Theory*:

> Revelation, the gift, for Derrida is always compromised because of this necessary involvement in exchange ... Certeau explores another direction – mediation as revelatory, as not only caught up in the exchange of signs but making that exchange of signs possible and salvific (that is, of eschatological significance.
>
> (Ward 1999: 193)

Ward's view is an important complement to my own but from my perspective it is rather too severe on Derrida (he does a lot more than 'compromise' the gift) and a bit too generous on Certeau (there is not much evidence in 'Believing and Making People Believe', say, that mediation is revelatory).

3 Marion and 'a paradoxical writing of the word *without*'

1 Marion's readings of Aquinas, Heidegger and Derrida have been criticized and developed by John Milbank, Laurence Hemming and Marion himself in the years since *God Without Being* was first published. Marion admits that Aquinas's discussion of God and *esse* is not idolatrous because, in Aquinas's reading, God's *esse* remains only analogically connected to the *ens commune* in his preface to the English edition of the book (Marion 1991: xxii–xviv). John Milbank also criticizes Marion's reading of Aquinas by stressing that Aquinas proposes an analogical rather than (as Marion suggests) a univocal, and thus ontotheological, relation between God and Being, and goes on to oppose Marion's theology of gift and donation to a theology of analogy and participation derived from Aquinas, and principally, Eckhart in 'Only Theology Overcomes Metaphysics' (Milbank 1995: 325–43). Laurence Hemming takes issue with Marion's argument that Heidegger constitutes a surreptitious 'double idolatry' by contesting that Heidegger proposes a temporal and phenomenal rather than (as Marion

assumes) an eternal and essential relation between God and Being in 'Reading Heidegger: Is God without Being?' (Hemming 1995: 343–51).
2 Marion's work has faced numerous accusations of illicitly blurring or conflating his phenomenology of givenness with a theology of God as giver since the publication of Dominique Janicaud's *La tournant théologique de la phénoménologie française* (Janicaud 1991). Derrida argues that Marion illicitly determines (and thus annuls) the anonymous and indeterminable content of the gift by attributing it to the Father in his book *Given Time 1: Counterfeit Money* (Derrida 1992a: 51–2). Graham Ward also maintains that a *volte-face* occurs in Marion's work where his philosophical project gives way to a dogmatic theological project in which that gift is decisively but uncritically named after God in his essay 'The Theological Project of Jean-Luc Marion' (Ward 1998: 229–40). Thomas A. Carlson, however, criticizes the view that there is an obvious distinction or *volte-face* between Marion's philosophical and theological treatment of the gift, preferring to argue that his phenomenology complements his theology and vice versa in his book *Indiscretion: Finitude and the Naming of God* (Carlson 1998: 190–238). Jean-Luc Marion has maintained that his philosophical and theological projects are strictly differentiated in his recent work *Etant donné: essai d'une phénoménologie de la donation*. Marion distinguishes between philosophical discourse on the phenomenological possibility of revelation and theological discourse on the specific existence, meaning and content of revelation (Marion 1997a: 325–43), but it could be argued that he blurs this distinction through his consistent recourse to theological revelation as a means of exemplifying philosophical concepts such as his argument that Christ is the saturated phenomenon *par excellence*.
3 Caputo argues that, for Derrida,

> it would not be necessary that the name spoken in praise by the mystical theologian imply an adequate comprehension of what it praises, but only that it would be 'significant' and that we would have an adequate understanding that we are praising this rather than that.
>
> (Caputo 1999: 190–1)

It is also significant that Marion never once addresses Derrida's crucially important point about the promise or call of repetition that makes prayer possible and impossible in his critique of 'How to Avoid Speaking'.
4 Derrida and Marion clarify the similarities and differences between their concepts of the gift in 'On the Gift: A Discussion between Jacques Derrida and Jean-Luc Marion, Moderated by Richard Kearney'. It is impossible to summarize this remarkable and extremely entertaining debate in any detail here. Marion describes a phenomenology of the gift in which the gift appears as a 'saturated phenomenon', in other words, a givenness that absolutely exceeds intention, causality and economy. Derrida counters with his own aporetic concept of the gift in which any attempt to identify the gift in phenomenological terms immediately re-inscribes it back into the economy that it supposedly exceeds and hence annuls it as gift. The debate tends to concentrate on the *phenomenological* rather than the *theological* possibility of the gift, however, and it is to be hoped that this latter question will be addressed more directly by the two thinkers at some point in the future. See also Jacques Derrida, *Given Time* (Derrida 1992a); Jean-Luc Marion, *Etant donné: essai d'une phénoménologie de la donation* (Marion 1997a) and John D. Caputo, 'Apostles of the Impossible: God and the Gift in Derrida and Marion' (Caputo 1999: 185–223).
5 Marion argues that negative theology constitutes 'first a rivalry (presence can be deconstructed without it), then a marginalization (deconstruction would not

forbid access to God, outside presence and without Being)' of deconstruction (Marion 1999: 22). Marion's reading of negative theology is formidable, but I would want to take issue with his seemingly historicist and period-based interpretation of deconstruction here. First, negative theology cannot be a 'rival' to deconstruction (in the sense that it pre-empts and challenges deconstruction) because, as we have seen, deconstruction cannot be understood as a period-based concept which comes 'after' negative theology and 'before' some new development but as the grounding incoherence upon which the Western philosophical tradition in its entirety depends. So negative theology cannot pre-empt or challenge deconstruction because it is already *in* deconstruction and any resemblance between the two can be accounted for by this simple fact. Second, negative theology cannot marginalize deconstruction (in the sense that it foils deconstruction's prohibition on God-talk) for the simple reason that, as we are beginning to see, deconstruction does not forbid access to God *per se*, merely the God who is philosophically conceived as presence or being. Deconstruction certainly calls into question the ability to gain access to God *within* presence or being but, as we have seen, it is concerned with *nothing other* than that which is outside being. The question of whether that *hyperousios* can be identified with God or not is a question that Derrida, at least, seems most concerned to leave in suspension. This, presumably, is why Derrida does not find negative theology's adoption of deconstructive strategies quite as devastating a blow to deconstruction as Marion seems to think he should: 'that is not surprising' (Caputo 1999: 47).

6 Simon Critchley gives what is, for me, the best currently available definition of the complex temporalities of the democracy to come in his review essay on Derrida's *Specters of Marx*:

> '*la démocratie à venir*' does not mean that tomorrow (and tomorrow and tomorrow) democracy will be realized, but rather that the experience of justice as the maintaining-now of the relation to an absolute singularity is the *à venir* of democracy, the temporality of democracy is *advent*, it is arrival happening now.
>
> (Critchley 1999: 154)

7 Carlson argues that Derrida's 'long-standing' position is that the God of negative theology remains within ontotheology. It is difficult to square this statement with his later claim about Derrida's argument in 'Sauf le nom': negative theology 'oscillate[s] between, on the one hand, an affirmation of the ontotheological injunction to speak the name of God in its truth, according to the true (hyper-) being of God and, on the other hand, the refusal of this injunction through a suspension or destruction of all positive (or negative) theses' (Carlson 1998: 214–20). If, however, we recognize that '*hyperousios*' can be interpreted in Blanchotesque terms as 'without being', and thus oscillates *in itself* between ontotheological and non-ontotheological positions, then Derrida's argument in this respect can be seen to be wholly consistent.

8 Derrida draws attention to an analogous undecidability between determined and general messianisms in 'Faith and Knowledge: The Two Sources of "Religion" at the Limits of Reason Alone':

> [t]he question remains open, and with it that of knowing whether this desert can be thought and left to announce itself 'before' the desert that we know (that of the revelations and the retreats, the lives and deaths of God, of all the figures of kenosis or of transcendence, of religio or of historical 'religions'); or whether, 'on the contrary', it is 'from' this last desert that we can glimpse that which precedes the first, what I call the desert in the desert.
>
> (Derrida 1998a: 21)

It is possible to argue that the logic of the without also impacts upon the distinction between determined and general messianisms so that every 'determined' messianism has to open itself to the possibility of repetition in alterity whereas every 'general' messianism cannot escape the possibility of the trace, and through it, history and context. See Jacques Derrida, *Specters of Marx* ([1993] 1994); John D. Caputo, 'The Messianic', in *The Prayers and Tears of Jacques Derrida* (Caputo 1997: 138–9) and the essays in James H. Olthius (ed.) *Religion With/out Religion: The Prayers and Tears of John D. Caputo* (Olthius 2002) for further discussion of the distinction between determined and general messianisms.

9 Caputo accuses Marion of a 'consummately dangerous political and ecclesiastical absolutism' in *The Prayers and Tears of Jacques Derrida* (Caputo 1997: 47). Kearney echoes Caputo's charge of a 'mystical-authoritarian hermeneutic' in his essay 'The God Who May Be' (Kearney 2001: 63). Scott David Foutz is more generous to Marion's defence of the primacy of the Bishop but there is a slight air of special pleading about his claim '[a]t the very least, we would all hope to say that our ecclesial leaders should be our best and most spiritually reliable exegetes and interpreters' ('Postmetaphysical Theology, A Case Study: Jean-Luc Marion', Foutz 1999).

4 Foucault and 'the thought from the outside'

1 Foucault expands on the dialectical status of negative theology in a 1964 debate with Philippe Sollers and the *Tel Quel* group. He defends Sollers against the charge of mysticism on the grounds that the term implies a dialectical element that is absent from Sollers's work:

> [t]hat is why the categories of spirituality, mysticism etc., do not appear to hold up. There is an ongoing effort, fraught with difficulty (even, and especially, in philosophy), to determine what thought is without applying the old categories, by attempting to bypass this dialectic of mind once defined by Hegel. Using dialectical thought to conceive of something that is newer than dialectics seems to me to be a completely inadequate analytical approach for what you [Sollers] are doing.
>
> (Carrette 1999: 74)

2 Derrida and Foucault's debate has been subject to numerous commentaries over the years. Foucault seeks to turn the tables on Derrida in his bad-tempered essay 'My Body, This Paper, This Fire' (1979b) and accuse *him* of being the closet transcendentalist: 'I will not say that it is a metaphysics, metaphysics itself or its closure which is hiding in this "textualization" of discursive practices' (Foucault 1979b: 28). Michael Sprinker, Peter Flaherty, Roy Boyne and other critics have followed Foucault's lead in attempting to paint the debate as a contest between the human sciences (Foucault) and traditional or idealist philosophy (Derrida), discourse and textuality, context and text (Sprinker 1980; Flaherty 1986; Boyne 1990). Derrida has to my knowledge never responded *directly* to Foucault or any other reader of his work but it is possible to construct the basis of a response from a reading of subsequent texts. To begin with, Foucault certainly misreads or misconstrues Derrida's critique on a number of counts. The central accusation is clearly based on a still common misreading of Derrida's claim that 'there is nothing outside the text' (Derrida 1976: 157–8) as advocating a position of a-historical idealism. This still common misinterpretation flies in the face of Derrida's repeated stress that he is not criticizing Foucault's 'intraworldliness' from some transcendental vantage point – 'I am not invoking an *other world*, an alibi or an evasive transcendence' (Derrida 1978e:

157–8) – but, as we have seen, from a point of quasi-transcendental undecidability *between* the historical and the transcendental. More importantly, the definition of history as the play or transition between finite structures and what exceeds them in the direction of infinity should put paid to any lazy attempts to see deconstruction as simply an attack on the inside, the factical or empirical from the vantage point of the outside, the ideal or transcendental.
3 See Jean-François Lyotard's *La Confession d'Augustin* (1998) for an alternative reading of the time of confession in Augustine.

5 Kristeva and 'the original *technē*'

1 Sigmund Freud writes:
> Long ago, [man] formed an ideal conception of omnipotence and omniscience which he embodied in his gods. To these Gods he attributed everything that seemed unattainable to his wishes, or that was forbidden to him. One may say, therefore, that these gods were cultural ideals. Today he has come very close to the attainment of this ideal, he has almost become a god himself... Man, has as it were, become a kind of prosthetic God.
> (1961: 38)

2 Jacques Derrida writes of Heidegger's claim that the essence of technology is nothing technological: '[t]his matrix statement remains, at least in one of its aspects, traditionally philosophical. It maintains the possibility of thought that questions, which is always thought of the essence, protected from any original and essential contamination by technology' (Derrida 1989b: 10).
3 Stiegler is the first contemporary philosopher to make explicit the logic of 'originary technicity'. See also Beardsworth (1996); Pearson (1997); Critchley (1999: 143–83); Clark (2000: 238–58) and Bennington (2000: 162–80) for important readings of the relationship between deconstruction and technics.
4 Richard Beardsworth argues that there is a 'ambivalence' towards originary technicity in Derrida's work that can be witnessed in the fact that his earliest texts analyse oppositional logic in technical terms as writing whereas his later ones analyse oppositional logic in quasi-religious terms as *khōra*, the yes or the promise (Beardsworth 1996: 145–57). Geoffrey Bennington criticizes what he claims to be Beardsworth's implicit suggestion that the two approaches can be opposed on the grounds that originary technicity necessarily precedes the established distinction between the religious and the technological (Bennington 2000: 204–5). Derrida has in fact said on a number of occasions that religion and technology are inseparable and we could support this with references to many other texts besides 'Faith and Knowledge' such as 'How to Avoid Speaking: Denegations' (1989a), 'Circumfession' (1993), 'Sauf le nom: (Post-Scriptum)' (1995a) and *Archive Fever* (1996).

6 Derrida and the 'passage to the totally other'

1 Geoffrey Bennington opposes the temporality of deconstruction to a metaphysical and particularly Christian concept of messianic or eschatological time in his excellent essay 'Is it Time?' (Bennington 2000: 128–40). Bennington argues that deconstruction enables a concept of infinite arrival that is distinct from the teleological concept of time in Judaic and Pauline accounts. It might be possible to take issue with the argument that Judaeo-Christian messianic time is simply teleological here. Derrida appears more willing to affirm or liberate the possibility of a non-teleological dimension within Judaic or Christian temporality as his

consistent tactical use of the language of negative theology, eschatology and messianism indicates. The essay 'Sauf le nom' seems to draw a direct parallel between the temporality of negative theology and the temporality of deconstruction around the figure of inheritance.
2 Derrida's argument that the ethical decision must open itself to the acceptance of the necessary possibility of violence in order to avoid the worst violence raises a number of questions that cannot be fully addressed here. It is possible to argue, for example, that if accepting the possibility of 'the worst' is the only means of stemming off 'the worst of the worst, the evil of evil, something more radical than radical evil' (de Vries 2002a: 398), then what we are opening ourselves to logically cannot be 'the worst' after all. It is crucially important that the decision of lesser violence does not itself become the vehicle for good conscience by taking its own minimal or moderate status for granted or by assuming too quickly what form the absolute worst will take.
3 This law was ostensibly an attempt to make the asylum process more efficient and to cut illegal immigration. It enabled the creation of 'accommodation centres' where asylum seekers can be housed for up to six months while their claims are considered. It also limited the appeals process, blocked all applications from European Union countries and compelled asylum seekers to have English and citizenship lessons while in the country. The initial result of the legislation was a 50 per cent cut in the number of asylum applications to Great Britain. In 2003, the British Government also announced proposals to set up new 'accommodation centres' outside the European Union and the first such centre was scheduled for opening in Albania by the end of the year.

Bibliography

Jacques Derrida

(1973) *Speech and Phenomena and Other Essays on Husserl's Theory of Signs*, trans. D. Allison, Evanston, IL: Northwestern University. Originally published as *La voix et la phénomène*, Paris: Presses Universitaires de France, 1967.

(1976) *Of Grammatology*, trans. G. C. Spivak, Baltimore, MD, and London: Johns Hopkins University Press. Originally published as *De la grammatologie*, Paris: Minuit, 1967.

(1978a) *Writing and Difference*, trans. A. Bass, London: Routledge & Kegan Paul. Originally published as *L'écriture et la différence*, Paris: Seuil, 1967.

(1978b) 'The Mystic Writing Pad: Freud and the Scene of Writing', in *Writing and Difference*, trans. A. Bass, London: Routledge & Kegan Paul, pp. 196–277. Originally published in 1967.

(1978c) 'Violence and Metaphysics', in *Writing and Difference*, trans. A. Bass, London: Routledge & Kegan Paul, pp. 79–195. Originally published in 1964.

(1978d) 'From Restricted to General Economy: A Hegelianism without Reserve', in *Writing and Difference*, trans. A. Bass, London: Routledge & Kegan Paul, pp. 251–300. Originally published in 1967.

(1978e) 'Cogito and the History of Madness', in *Writing and Difference*, trans. A. Bass, London: Routledge & Kegan Paul, pp. 31–63. Originally published in 1964.

(1978f) 'Structure, Sign and Play in the Discourse of the Human Sciences', in *Writing and Difference*, trans. A. Bass, London: Routledge & Kegan Paul, pp. 278–94.

(1982a) *Margins of Philosophy*, trans. A. Bass, Chicago: University of Chicago Press. Originally published as *Marges de la philosophie*, Paris: Minuit, 1972.

(1982b) 'Letter to John P. Leavey Jr.', in R. Detweiler (ed.) *Semeia: Derrida and Biblical Studies*, Chico, CA: Scholars Press.

(1982c) 'Différance', in *Margins of Philosophy*, trans. A. Bass, Chicago: University of Chicago Press, pp. 1–28. Originally published in 1967.

(1982d) 'Signature Event Context', in *Margins of Philosophy*, trans. A. Bass, Chicago: University of Chicago Press, pp. 307–30. Originally published in 1972.

(1986a) *Glas*, trans. J. P. Leavey Jr. and R. Rand, Lincoln and London: Nebraska University Press. Originally published as *Glas*, 2 vols, Paris: Denoël/Gonthier, 1974.

(1986b) *Parages*, Paris: Galilée.

(1986c) 'Pas', in *Parages*, Paris: Galilée, pp. 10–116.
(1987a) *The Postcard: From Socrates to Freud and Beyond*, trans. A. Bass, Chicago: Chicago University Press. Originally published as *La carte postale de Socrate à Freud et au-delà*, Paris: Aubier/Flammarion, 1980.
(1987b) 'The Laws of Reflection: Nelson Mandela, In Admiration', trans. M.-A. Caws and I. Lorenz, in *For Nelson Mandela*, New York: Seaver. Originally published in *Psyché: Inventions de l'autre*, Paris: Galilée, 1987.
(1988a) 'A Number of Yes (*Nombre de Oui*)', trans. B. Holmes, *Qui Parle* 2: 2: 118–33. Originally published in *Psyché: Inventions de l'autre*, Paris: Galilée, 1987.
(1988b) 'The Original Discussion of Différance', in D. Wood and R. Bernsaconi (eds) *Derrida and Différance*, Evanston, IL: Northwestern University Press.
(1988c) *Limited Inc*, trans S. Weber and J. Mehlman (eds) G. Graff, Evanston, IL: Northwestern University Press.
(1989a) 'How to Avoid Speaking: Denegations', trans. K. Frieden, in S. Budick and W. Iser (eds) *Languages of the Unsayable: The Play of Negativity in Literature and Literary Theory*, Stanford, CA: Stanford University Press. Originally published as 'Comment ne pas parler: denegations', in *Psyché: Inventions de l'autre*, Paris: Galilée, 1987.
(1989b) *Of Spirit: Heidegger and the Question*, trans. G. Bennington and R. Bowlby, Chicago: University of Chicago Press. Originally published as *De l'esprit: Heidegger et la question*, Paris: Galilée, 1987.
(1990) 'Force of Law: The "Mystical Foundation" of Authority', with original French text, trans. M. Quaintance, *Cardozo Law Review*, 11: 5/6: 920–1045.
(1991) 'Letter to a Japanese Friend', trans. D. Wood and A. Benjamin, in P. Kamuf (ed.) *A Derrida Reader: Between the Blinds*, New York: Columbia University Press. Originally published in *Psyché: Inventions de l'autre*, Paris: Galilée, 1987.
(1992a) *Given Time 1: Counterfeit Money*, trans. P. Kamuf, Chicago: University of Chicago Press. Originally published as *Donner le temps 1: La fausse monnaie*, Paris: Galilée, 1991.
(1992b) *The Other Heading: Reflections on Today's Europe*, trans. P.-A. Brault and M. B. Naas, Bloomington, IN: Indiana University Press. Originally published as *L'autre cap suivi de 'La démocratie ajournée'*, Paris: Minuit, 1991.
(1992c) 'Before the Law', trans. A. Ronell and C. Roulston, in D. Attridge (ed.) *Acts of Literature*, London: Routledge. Originally published as 'Prejuges: Devant la loi', in J. Derrida *et al.*, *La faculté de juger*, Paris: Minuit, 1985.
(1993) 'Circumfession', trans. G. Bennington, in G. Bennington and J. Derrida, *Jacques Derrida*, Chicago: University of Chicago Press. Originally published as 'Circonfession', in J. Derrida and G. Bennington, *Jacques Derrida*, Paris: Seuil; 1990.
(1994) *Specters of Marx: The State of the Debt, The Work of Mourning and The New International*, trans. P. Kamuf, New York: Routledge. Originally published as *Spectres de Marx*, Paris: Galilée, 1993.
(1995a) 'Sauf le nom (Post-Scriptum)', trans. J. P. Leavey, Jr., in T. Dutoit (ed.) *On the Name*, Stanford, CA: Stanford University Press. Originally published as *Sauf le nom (Post-Scriptum)*, Paris: Galilée, 1993.
(1995b) *The Gift of Death*, trans. D. Wills, Chicago: University of Chicago Press. Originally published as 'Donner la mort', in J.-M. Rabaté and M. Wetzel (eds) *L'éthique du don: Jacques Derrida et la pensée du don*, Paris: Transition, 1992.

(1995c) *Points . . . Interviews 1974–1994*, trans. P. Kamuf et al., Stanford, CA: Stanford University Press. Originally published as *Points de suspension . . .*, Paris: Galilée, 1992.
(1996) *Archive Fever: A Freudian Impression*, trans. E. Prenowitz, Chicago: University of Chicago Press. Originally published as *Mal d'archive*, Paris: Galilée, 1995.
(1997a) *De l'Hospitalité: Anne Dufourmantelle invite Jacques Derrida à répondre*, Paris: Calmann-Lévy.
(1997b) *Politics of Friendship*, trans. G. Collins, London: Verso. Originally published as *Politiques de l'amitié*, Paris: Galilée, 1994.
(1997c) 'Pas d'hospitalité', in *De l'Hospitalité: Anne Dufourmantelle invite Jacques Derrida à répondre*, Paris: Calmann-Levy, pp. 71–136.
(1998a) 'Faith and Knowledge: The Two Sources of "Religion" at the Limits of Reason Alone', trans. S. Weber, in J. Derrida and G. Vattimo (eds) *Religion*, Cambridge: Polity. Originally published as 'Foi et savoir', in J. Derrida and J. Vattimo (eds) *La Religion*, Paris: Seuil, 1996.
(1998b) *Resistances of Psychoanalysis*, trans. P.-A. Brault and M. Naas, Stanford, CA: Stanford University Press. Originally published as *Résistances de la psychoanalyse*, Paris: Galilée, 1996.
(1999a) *Adieu to Emmanuel Lévinas*, trans. P.-A. Brault and M. Naas, Stanford, CA: Stanford University Press. Originally published as *Adieu à Emmanuel Lévinas*, Paris: Galilée, 1997.
(1999b) 'Hospitality, Justice and Responsibility: A Dialogue with Jacques Derrida', in R. Kearney and M. Dooley (eds) *Questioning Ethics: Contemporary Debates in Philosophy*, London: Routledge.
(1999c) 'Le mot d'acceuil', in *Adieu to Emmanuel Lévinas*, trans. P.-A. Brault and M. Naas, Stanford: Stanford University Press, pp. 15–123. Originally published in *Adieu à Emmanuel Lévinas*, Paris: Galilée, 1997.
(2001a) *On Cosmopolitanism and Forgiveness*, trans. M. Dooley and M. Hughes, London: Routledge. Originally published as *Cosmopolites de tous les pays, encore une effort!*, Paris: Galilée, 1997.
(2001b) 'A Silkworm of One's Own', trans. G. Bennington, in H. Cixous and J. Derrida, *Veils*, Stanford, CA: Stanford University Press. Originally published as *Voiles*, Paris: Galilée, 1996.
(2001c) 'Cosmopolites de tous les pays, encore une effort!', in *On Cosmopolitanism and Forgiveness*, trans. M. Dooley and M. Hughes, London: Routledge, pp. 1–24. Originally published in *Cosmopolites de tous les pays, encore une effort!*, Paris: Galilée, 1997.
(2002a) *Acts of Religion*, ed. G. Andijar, New York and London: Routledge.
(2002b) *Echographies of Television*, trans. J. Bajorek, Oxford: Polity. Originally published as *Échographies de la télévision*, Paris: Galilée, 1998.
(2002c) 'Hostipitality', in G. Andijar (ed.) *Acts of Religion*, London: Routledge, pp. 358–420.

Michel de Certeau

(1984) *The Practice of Everyday Life*, volume 1, trans. S. Rendall, Berkeley, CA: University of California Press. Originally published as *L'Invention du quotidien 1: arts de faire*, Paris: Gallimard, 1980.

(1986) *Heterologies: Discourse on the Other*, trans. B. Massumi, Minneapolis: University of Minnesota Press.
(1987a) *La Faiblesse de croire*, L. Giard (ed.), Paris: Editions de Seuil.
(1987b) 'Extase blanche', in *La Faiblesse de croire*, L. Giard (ed.), Paris: Editions de Seuil, pp. 315–18.
(1987c) 'Lieux de transit', in *La Faiblesse de croire*, L. Giard (ed.), Paris: Editions de Seuil, pp. 227–52.
(1987d) 'La misère de la théologie', in *La Faiblesse de croire*, L. Giard (ed.), Paris: Editions de Seuil, pp. 253–66.
(1988) *The Writing of History*, trans. T. Conley, New York: Columbia University Press. Originally published as *L'Ecriture de l'histoire*, Paris: Gallimard, 1975.
(1990) *L'Invention du quotidien 1: arts de faire* (nouvelle edition), Paris: Gallimard.
(1992) *The Mystic Fable: The Sixteenth and Seventeenth Centuries*, vol. 1, trans. M. B. Smith, Chicago and London: University of Chicago Press. Originally published as *La fable mystique: XVI–XVII siècle*, Paris: Gallimard, 1982.
(1997a) 'How is Christianity Thinkable Today?', in G. Ward (ed.) *The Postmodern God*, Oxford: Blackwell. Originally published in *Theology Digest* 19, 1971, 334–45.
(1997b) *The Capture of Speech and Other Political Writings*, trans. T. Conley, Minneapolis: Minnesota University Press. Originally published as *La Prise de parole*, Paris: Gallimard, 1968.
(2000a) G. Ward (ed.) *The Certeau Reader*, Oxford: Blackwell.
(2000b) *The Possession at Loudun*, trans. M. B. Smith, Chicago: University of Chicago Press. Originally published as *La Possession de Loudun*, Paris: Gallimard/Julliard, 1970.
(2000c) 'The Weakness of Believing: From the Body to Writing, a Christian Transit', in G. Ward (ed.) *The Certeau Reader*, Oxford: Blackwell. Originally published in 1974.
(2002) *Michel de Certeau: Les chemins de l'histoire*, sous la direction de C. Delacroix *et al.*, Paris: Complexe.

Jean-Luc Marion

(1977) *L'Idole et la distance: Cinq études*. Paris: Grasset.
(1991) *God Without Being: Hors-Texte*, trans. T. A. Carlson. Chicago: Chicago University Press, 1991. Originally published as *Dieu sans l'être: Hors-Texte*, Paris: Presses Universitaires de France, 1982.
(1996) *La Croisée de visible*. Paris: Presses Universitaires de France.
(1997a) *Etant donné: essai d'une phénoménologie de la donation*. Paris: Presses Universitaires de France.
(1997b) 'Metaphysics and Phenomenology: A Summary for Theologians', trans. A. McGeoch, in G. Ward (ed.) *The Postmodern God: A Theological Reader*. Oxford: Blackwell. Originally published in *Bulletin de Litérature Ecclésiastique* 94, 3, 1993, 189–206.
(1999) 'In the Name: How to Avoid Speaking of "Negative Theology"', trans. J. L. Kosky, in J. D. Caputo and M. J. Scanlon (eds) *God, the Gift and Postmodernism*, Bloomington, IN: Indiana University Press.
(2001) 'The Saturated Phenomenon', trans. B. G. Prusak, in D. Janicaud *et al.* (eds) *Phenomenology and the 'Theological Turn'*, New York: Fordham University

Press. Originally published as 'Le phénomène saturée', in D. Janicaud *et al.* (eds) *Le tournant théologique dans la phénoménologie française*, Paris: Presses Universitaires de France, 1991.
(2002a) *Prolegomena to Charity*, trans. S. Lewis, New York: Fordham University Press. Originally published as *Prolegomènes de la charité*, Paris: Editions de la différence, 1986.
(2002b) *In Excess: Studies of Saturated Phenomena*, trans. R. Horner and V. Berraud. New York: Fordham University Press. Originally published as *Du surcroît*, Paris: Presses Universitaires de France, 2001.

Michel Foucault

(1961) *Folie et déraison: Histoire de la folie à l'âge classique*, Paris: Plon.
(1965) *Madness and Civilisation: A History of Insanity in the Age of Reason*, trans. R. Howard, New York: Random House. Abridged translation of *Folie et déraison: Histoire de la folie à l'âge classique*, Paris: Plon, 1961.
(1972) *The Archaeology of Knowledge*, trans. A.M. Sheridan Smith, London: Tavistock. Originally published as *L'Archáeologie du savoir*, Paris: Gallimard, 1969.
(1979a) *The History of Sexuality 1: An Introduction*, trans. R. Hurley, Harmondsworth: Penguin. Originally published as *L'Histoire de la sexualité I: La volonté de savoir*, Paris: Gallimard, 1976.
(1979b) 'My Body, This Paper, This Fire', trans. G. Bennington, *Oxford Literary Review* 4: 1: 5–28.
(1984a) *The Use of Pleasure: The History of Sexuality*, vol. 2, trans. R. Hurley, Harmondsworth: Penguin. Originally published as *L'Histoire de la sexualité II: L'usage des plaisirs*, Paris: Gallimard, 1984.
(1984b) *The Care of the Self: The History of Sexuality*, vol. 3, trans. R. Hurley, Harmondsworth: Penguin. Originally published as *L'Histoire de la sexualité III: Le souci de soi*, Paris: Gallimard, 1984.
(1987a) 'Maurice Blanchot: The Thought from the Outside', trans. J. Mehlman and B. Massumi, in *Foucault/Blanchot*, New York: Zone Books. Originally published as 'Maurice Blanchot: la pensée du dehors', *Critique*: 229, 1966.
(1987b) 'Michel Foucault as I Imagine Him', in *Foucault/Blanchot*, New York: Zone Books.
(1991) *The Order of Things: An Archaeology of the Human Sciences*, trans. A. Sheridan, London: Routledge. Originally published as *Les mots et les choses: Un Archáeologie des sciences humaines*, Paris: Gallimard, 1966.
(1999a) 'A Preface to Transgression', in J. Carrette (ed.) *Religion and Culture by Michel Foucault*, Manchester: Manchester University Press, pp. 57–71.
(1999b) 'The Prose of Acteon', in J. Carrette (ed.) *Religion and Culture by Michel Foucault*, Manchester: Manchester University Press, pp. 75–84.

Julia Kristeva

(1982) *Powers of Horror: An Essay on Abjection*, trans. L. Roudiez, New York: Columbia University Press. Originally published as *Pouvoirs de l'horreur: Essai sur l'abjection*, Paris: Editions de Seuil, 1980.
(1984) *Revolution in Poetic Language*, trans. M. Waller, New York: Columbia University

Bibliography

Press. Originally published as *La révolution du langage poétique: l'avant-garde à la fin du XIX siècle*, Paris: Editions de Seuil, 1974.

(1987a) *In the Beginning was Love: Psychoanalysis and Faith*, trans. A. Goldhammer, New York: Columbia University Press. Originally published as *Au commencement était l'amour: Psychoanalyse et foi*, Paris: Hachette, 1985.

(1987b) *Tales of Love*, trans. L. S. Roudiez, New York: Columbia University Press. Originally published as *Histoires d'amour*, Paris: Denoël, 1983.

(1989) *Black Sun: Depression and Melancholia*, trans. L. S. Roudiez, New York: Columbia University Press. Originally published as *Soleil noir: Dépression et mélancholie*, Paris: Gallimard, 1987.

(1991) *Strangers to Ourselves*, trans. L. Roudiez, New York: Columbia University Press. Originally published as *Étrangers à nous-mêmes*, Paris: Fayard, 1988.

(1995) *New Maladies of the Soul*, trans. R. Guberman, New York: Columbia University Press. Originally published as *Les nouvelles maladies de l'âme*, Paris: Fayard, 1993.

(1999a) With Catherine Clément, *Le féminin et le sacré*, Paris: Stock.

(1999b) *Le génie féminin 1: Hannah Arendt*, Paris: Fayard.

(2000) *Le génie féminin 2: Mélanie Klein*, Paris: Fayard.

(2002a) *Le génie féminin 3: Collette*, Paris: Fayard.

(2002b) 'Athée en éveil', *Actualité des religions* 41: 50–4.

Works by other authors

Ahearne, Jeremy (1995) *Michel de Certeau: Interpretation and its Other*, Cambridge: Polity.

Aquinas (1964–75) *Summa Theologica* (Latin and English version), New York: McGraw-Hill.

Aristotle (1984) *The Complete Works of Aristotle*, J. Barnes (ed.), Princeton, NJ: Princeton University Press.

Barnett, Stuart (ed.) (1998) *Hegel After Derrida*, London and New York: Routledge.

Baudrillard, Jean ([1976] 1993) *Symbolic Exchange and Death*, trans. I. H. Grant, London: Sage.

Bauerschmidt, Frederick Christian (1996) 'The Abrahamic Voyage: Michel de Certeau and Theology', *Modern Theology* 12: 1, 1–26.

Beardsworth, Richard (1996) *Derrida and the Political*, London: Routledge.

Bennington, Geoffrey (1994) *Legislations: The Politics of Deconstruction*, London: Verso.

—— (1999) 'Inter-', in Martin McQuillan *et al.* (eds) *Post-Theory*, Edinburgh: Edinburgh University Press.

—— (2000) *Interrupting Derrida*, London: Routledge.

Bernauer, James W. (1990) *Michel Foucault's Force of Flight: Towards an Ethics for Thought*, London: Humanities.

Boyne, Roy (1990) *Foucault and Derrida: The Other Side of Reason*, London: Unwin Hyman.

Bradley, Arthur (2001) 'Without Negative Theology: Deconstruction and the Politics of Negative Theology', *The Heythrop Journal* 42: 2, 133–47.

—— (2002) 'Thinking the Outside: Foucault, Derrida and Negative Theology', *Textual Practice* 16: 57–74.

Buchanan, Ian (2000) *Michel de Certeau: Cultural Theorist*, London: Sage.
Bulhof, Ilse N. and ten Kate, Laurens (eds) (2000) *Flight of the Gods: Philosophical Perspectives on Negative Theology*, New York: Fordham University Press.
Cadava, Eduardo *et al.* (eds) (1991) *Who Comes After The Subject?*, London: Routledge.
Caputo, John D. (1993) 'On Not Knowing Who We Are: Madness, Hermeneutics and the Night of Truth in Foucault', in J. D. Caputo and M. Yount (eds) *Foucault and the Critique of Institutions*, Philadelphia, PA: Pennsylvania University Press.
—— (1997) *The Prayers and Tears of Jacques Derrida: Religion without Religion*, Bloomington, IN: Indiana University Press.
—— (ed.) (1999) *God, the Gift and Postmodernism*, Bloomington, IN: Indiana University Press.
—— (ed.) (2001) *Questioning God*, Bloomington, IN: Indiana University Press.
—— (ed.) (2002) *The Religious*, Oxford: Blackwell.
Carabine, Deirdre (1995) *The Unknown God: Negative Theology in the Platonic Tradition: Plato to Eriugena*, Amsterdam: Eerdmans.
Carlson, Thomas A. (1998) *Indiscretion: Finitude and the Naming of God*, Chicago: University of Chicago Press.
Carrette, Jeremy (ed.) (1999) *Religion and Culture by Michel Foucault*, Manchester: Manchester University Press.
—— (2000) *Foucault and Religion: Spiritual Corporality and Political Spirituality*, London and New York: Routledge.
Chopp, Rebecca S. (1997) 'From Patriarchy into Freedom: A Conversation between American Feminist Theology and French Feminism', in G. Ward (ed.) *The Postmodern God: A Theological Reader*, Oxford: Blackwell.
Cixous, Hélène (1981) 'The Laugh of the Medusa', trans. K. and P. Cohen, in Isabelle Courtivron (ed.) *New French Feminisms*, Brighton: Harvester Press.
Clark, Timothy (2000) 'Deconstruction and Technology', in N. Royle (ed.) *Deconstructions: A User's Guide*, Basingstoke: Palgrave.
Corbin, Michael (1974) *Le chemin de la théologie chez Thomas d'Aquin*, Paris: Beauchesne.
Coward, Harold and Foshay, Toby (eds) (1992) *Derrida and Negative Theology*, Albany, NY: SUNY.
Critchley, Simon (1992) *The Ethics of Deconstruction: Derrida and Lévinas*, Edinburgh: Edinburgh University Press.
—— (1999) *Ethics-Politics-Subjectivity*, London: Verso.
Cupitt, Don (1982) 'Kant and the Negative Theology', in B. Hebblethwaite and S. Sutherland (eds) *The Philosophical Frontiers of Christian Theology*, Cambridge: Cambridge University Press.
—— (1995) *The Last Philosophy*, London: SCM.
Damascius (1987) *Des premiers principes: Apories et résolutions*, French trans. M. C. Galpérine, Paris: Verdier.
Descartes, René ([1641] 1986) *Meditations on First Philosophy*, trans. J. Cottingham, Cambridge: Cambridge University Press.
De Vries, Hent (1999) *Philosophy and the Turn to Religion*, Baltimore, MD, and London: The Johns Hopkins University Press.
—— (2002a) *Religion and Violence*, Stanford, CA: Stanford University Press.
—— (ed.) (2002b) *Religion and Media*, Stanford, CA: Stanford University Press.
Dews, Peter (1995) *The Limits of Disenchantment: Essays on Contemporary European Philosophy*, London: Verso.

Dosse, François (2002) *Michel de Certeau: Le marcheur blessé*, Paris: La Decouverte.
Eagleton, Terry (1990) *The Ideology of the Aesthetic*, Oxford: Blackwell.
Eliot, T. S. (1963) *Collected Poems 1909–1962*, London: Faber.
Fiske, John (1988) 'Popular Forces and the Culture of Everyday Life', *Southern Review* 21: 3: 288–306.
Flaherty, Peter (1986) '(Con)textual Contest: Derrida and Foucault on Madness and the Cartesian Subject', *Philosophy of the Social Sciences* 16: 157–75.
Foutz, Scott David (1999) 'Postmetaphysical Theology, A Case Study: Jean-Luc Marion', *Quodlibet, Online Journal of Christian Theology and Philosophy* 1: 3 www.quodlibet.net/marion.shtml (accessed 15 November 2000).
Freud, Sigmund ([1927] 1975) *The Future of an Illusion*, trans. J. Strachey, New York: Norton.
—— ([1929] 1961) *Civilisation and its Discontents*, trans. J. Strachey, New York: Norton.
Frow, John (1990) 'Michel de Certeau and the Practice of Representation', *Cultural Studies* 5: 1: 52–60.
Gasché, Rodolphe (1986) *The Tain of the Mirror: Derrida and the Philosophy of Reflection*, Cambridge, MA: Harvard University Press.
Geffré, Claude (ed.) (1991) *Michel de Certeau ou la différence chrétienne*, Paris: Cerf.
Habermas, Jürgen ([1981] 1985) 'Modernity – An Incomplete Project', trans. S. Ben-Habib, in H. Foster (ed.) *Postmodern Culture*, London: Pluto Press.
Haraway, Donna (1991) *Simians, Cyborgs and Women: The Reinvention of Nature*, London: Free Association Press.
Hart, Kevin (1989) *The Trespass of the Sign: Deconstruction, Theology and Philosophy*, Cambridge: Cambridge University Press.
—— (1997) 'Jacques Derrida: The God Effect', in Phillip Blond (ed.) *Beyond Secular Philosophy: Between Philosophy and Theology*, London and New York: Blackwell.
Hegel, G. W. F. ([1807] 1977) *Phenomenology of Spirit*, trans. A. V. Miller, Oxford: Oxford University Press.
Heidegger, Martin (1969) *Identity and Difference*, trans. J. Stambaugh, New York: Harper & Row.
—— (1980) *Séminaire de Zurich*, French trans. D. Saatdjian and F. Fédier, in *Poésie* 13. Paris.
—— (1991) *The Principle of Reason*, trans. R. Lilly, Bloomington, IN: Indiana University Press.
—— (1997) *The Question Concerning Technology and Other Essays*, trans. W. Lovitt, New York: Harper & Row.
—— (1998) *Pathmarks*, trans. W. McNeill, Cambridge: Cambridge University Press.
Hemming, Laurence (1995) 'Reading Heidegger: Is God without Being?', *New Blackfriars*, Special Issue on Jean-Luc Marion's *God Without Being* 76: 343–51.
Hill, Leslie (1990) 'Julia Kristeva: Theorizing the Avant Garde', in J. Fletcher and A. Benjamin (eds.) *Melancholia and Love: The Work of Julia Kristeva*, London: Routledge.
Hobson, Marian (1998) *Jacques Derrida: Opening Lines*, London and New York: Routledge.
Horner, Robyn (2001) *Rethinking God as Gift: Derrida and Marion at the Limits of Phenomenology*, New York: Fordham University Press.
Irigaray, Luce ([1977] 1985) *This Sex Which is Not One*, trans. C. Porter, Ithaca, NY: Cornell University Press.

Janicaud, Dominique (1991) *Le Tournant théologique de la phénoménologie française*, Paris: L'éclat.

Jantzen, Grace M. (1995) *Power, Gender and Christian Mysticism*, Cambridge: Cambridge University Press.

Jardine, Alice (1981) *Gynesis: Configurations of Women and Modernity*, Ithaca, NY: Cornell University Press.

Kant, Immanuel ([1781] 1998a) *Critique of Pure Reason*, trans. P. Guyer and A. W. Wood, Cambridge: Cambridge University Press.

—— ([1791] 1998b) *Religion Within the Boundaries of Mere Reason*, trans. A. Wood and G. di Giovanni, Cambridge: Cambridge University Press.

Kearney, Richard (1980) *Heidegger et la question de Dieu*, Paris: Grasset.

—— (1984) *Dialogues with Contemporary Continental Thinkers*, Manchester: Manchester University Press.

—— (2001) 'The God Who May Be', in J. D. Caputo *et al.* (eds) *Questioning God*, Bloomington, IN: Indiana University Press.

Kearns, Cleo McNelly (1993) 'Kristeva and Feminist Theology', in C. W. M. Kim, S. M. St Ville and S. M. Simonaitis (eds) *Transfigurations: Theology and French Feminists*, Minneapolis: Augsburg Fortress.

Kierkegaard, Søren (1985) *Kierkegaard's Writings*, 20 vols, XII: *Philosophical Fragments*, trans. H. and E. Long, Princeton, NJ: Princeton University Press.

Law, David R. (1994) *Kierkegaard as Negative Theologian*, Oxford: Clarendon Press.

Lévinas, Emmanuel ([1961] 1969) *Totality and Infinity: An Essay on Exteriority*, trans. A. Lingis, Pittsburgh: Duquesne University Press.

—— ([1982] 1998) *Of God Who Comes to Mind*, trans. B. Bergo, Stanford: Stanford University Press.

Llewelyn, John (1991) 'Am I Obsessed by Bobby? (Humanism of the Other Animal)', in Robert Bernasconi and Simon Critchley (eds) *Re-Reading Lévinas*, Bloomington, IN: Indiana University Press.

Louth, Andrew (1980) *The Origins of the Christian Mystical Tradition: From Plato to Denys*, Oxford: Clarendon.

Lyotard, Jean-François ([1979a] 1984) *The Postmodern Condition: A Report on Knowledge*, trans. G. Bennington and B. Massumi, Manchester: Manchester University Press.

—— ([1979b] 1985) *Just Gaming*, trans. W. Godzich, Minneapolis: University of Minnesota Press.

—— ([1983] 1988) *The Differend: Phrases in Dispute*, trans. George van Den Abeele, Manchester: Manchester University Press.

—— ([1991] 1994) *Lessons on the Analytic of the Sublime*, trans. E. Rottenberg, Stanford, CA: Stanford University Press.

—— (1998) *La Confession d'Augustin*, Paris: Galilée.

McGinn, Bernard (1991) *The Foundations of Mysticism: Origins to the Twelfth Century*, London: SCM.

MacIntyre, Alisdair (1981) *After Virtue: A Study in Moral Theory*, London: Duckworth.

Malebranche, Nicholas (1992) 'Entretiens sur la metaphysique, sur la religion et sur la mort', in *Œuvres*, Paris: Gallimard.

Meister Eckhart (1981) *The Essential Sermons, Commentaries, Treatises and Defense*, trans. E. Colledge and B. McGinn, New York: Paulist Press.

Merleau-Ponty, Maurice (1964) *Le Visible et l'invisible*, Paris: Gallimard.

236 Bibliography

Milbank, John (1995) 'Only Theology Overcomes Metaphysics', *New Blackfriars* Special Issue on Jean-Luc Marion's *God Without Being* 76: 895: 325–43.

—— (1997) *The Word Made Strange: Theology, Language, Culture*, Oxford: Blackwell.

Mortley, Raoul (1986) *From Word to Silence*, vol. 2, *The Way of Negation: Christian and Greek*, Bonn: Hanstein.

Nancy, Jean-Luc ([1990] 1991) *The Inoperative Community*, trans. Peter Connor *et al.*, Minneapolis: University of Minnesota Press.

—— (1993) *The Birth to Presence*, trans. B. Holmes *et al.*, Stanford, CA: Stanford University Press.

Olthius, James (2002) (ed.) *Religion With/out Religion: The Prayers and Tears of John D. Caputo*, New York and London: Routledge.

Orwell, George (1968) 'The Lion and the Unicorn: Socialism and the English Genius', in S. Orwell and I. Angus (eds) *Collected Essays, Journalism and Letters*, vol. 2, *My Country Right or Left 1940–43*, New York: Harcourt.

Pearson, Keith Ansell (1997) *Viroid Life: Perspectives on Nietzsche and the Transhuman Condition*, London: Routledge.

Plato (1961) *The Collected Dialogues*, E. Hamilton and H. Cairns (eds), Princeton, NJ: Princeton University Press.

—— (1967) *Timaeus, Critias, Cleitophon, Menexenus, Epistles*, trans. R. G. Bury, London: Heinemann.

Plotinus (1991) *The Enneads*, trans. S. MacKenna, Harmondsworth: Penguin.

Pseudo-Dionysius the Areopagite (1980) *The Divine Names and the Mystical Theology*, trans. J. D. Jones, Wisconsin: Marquette University Press.

Rorty, Richard (1984) 'Deconstruction and Circumvention', *Critical Enquiry* 11: 18, 1–23.

Salusinszky, Imre (1987) *Criticism in Society: Interviews with Jacques Derrida et al.*, London: Methuen.

Schrag, Calvin O. (2002) *God as Otherwise than Being: Towards a Semantics of the Gift*, Evanston, IL: Northwestern University Press.

Shelley, Mary ([1818] 1985) *Frankenstein, or The Modern Prometheus*, Harmondsworth: Penguin.

Sikka, Sonya (1997) *Forms of Transcendence: Heidegger and Medieval Mystical Theology*, New York: SUNY.

Smith, James K. A. (2002) *Speech and Theology: Language and the Logic of Incarnation*, London and New York: Routledge.

Solignac, Aimé (1990) *Dictionaire de Spiritualité*, vol. 15, Paris: Beauschesne.

Spivak, Gayatri Chakravorty (1988) *In Other Worlds: Essays in Cultural Politics*, London: Routledge.

Sprinker, Michael (1980) 'Textual Politics: Foucault and Derrida', *Boundary* 2: 8: 75–98.

Steiner, George (1989) *Real Presences*, London: Faber.

Stiegler, Bernard (1994) *La technique et le temps 1: La faute d'Epiméthée*, Paris: Galilée.

—— (2001) 'Derrida and Technology: Fidelity at the Limits of Deconstruction and the Prosthesis of Faith', in T. Conley (ed.) *Jacques Derrida and the Humanities*, Cambridge: Cambridge University Press.

Swinburne, Richard (1977) *The Coherence of Theism*, Oxford: Clarendon.

Tambling, Jeremy (1990) *Confession: Sexuality, Sin and the Subject*, Manchester: Manchester University Press.

Taylor, Mark C. (1999) *About Religion: Virtual Economies of Faith*, Chicago: Chicago University Press.
Turner, Denys (1995) *The Darkness of God*, Cambridge: Cambridge University Press.
Virilio, Paul (1991) *L'écran du désert: Chroniques du guerre*, Paris: Galilée.
Von Balthasar, Hans Urs (1982) *The Glory of the Lord: A Theological Aesthetics*, Edinburgh: T & T Clark.
Ward, Graham (ed.) (1997) *The Postmodern God: A Theological Reader*, Oxford: Blackwell.
—— (1998) 'The Theological Project of Jean-Luc Marion', in P. Blond (ed.) *Post-Secular Philosophy: Between Philosophy and Theology*, London and New York: Routledge.
—— (1999) *Theology and Contemporary Critical Theory*, 2nd edn, 2000, London: Macmillan.
—— (2000) *Cities of God*, London and New York: Routledge.
—— (ed.) (2001) *The Blackwell Companion to Postmodern Theology*, Oxford: Blackwell.
Westphal, Merold (2001) *Overcoming Ontotheology: Towards a Postmodern Christian Faith*, New York: Fordham University Press.
Wyschogrod, Edith (1990) *Saints and Postmodernism: Revisioning Moral Philosophy*, Chicago: University of Chicago Press.
Žižek, Slavoj (2001) *On Belief*, London and New York: Routledge.

Index

abjection 151–2
acolyte 191
Agape 88, 92
agathon/khōra 103–4
alterity: Certeau 51, 64; Christianity 56;
  divine 120; faith 79; God 19;
  humanity 184–5; justice 170; Lévinas
  179; madness 19; negative theology
  201–2; non-Christian 57; philosophy
  20; repetition 3; sacred 177–8; *see also*
  other
apophatic theology: Aquinas 15;
  Derrida 90–1; Eckhart 16; individual
  136–7; negative theology 21; politics
  110; third way 37, 121; transcendence
  of God 14, 82
aporia 27, 109–10
Aquinas, Thomas 15–16, 84–5
arche-writing 25, 26–7, 168–9
Argentinian military dictatorship 163–4
Aristotle 84–5, 86, 167, 175, 181
artificial insemination 154, 162
asylum policy 209–10, 213
Augustine, Saint 97, 144–7, 158, 203
Austin, J. L. 71
auto-immunization 172–4

Bataille, Georges 116
Baudrillard, Jean 76
Bauerschmidt, Frederick Christian 59,
  76
Beardsworth, Richard 169, 193,
  225[5]n4
being 22, 177, 179–80; *see also* without
  being
belief: Certeau 58–9, 60–1, 63, 75–7;
  Christianity 77–8; faith 171;
  psychoanalysis 164; secular 164
Bennington, Geoffrey 190, 192, 193,
  201, 220[2]n3, 225[5]n4,
  225–6[6]n1
Bernard of Clairvaux 21
Bernauer, James 116, 136, 137
Berrigan, Daniel 220–1[2]n4
Bin Laden, Osama 176
biodeterminism 160, 162–3, 175
biotechnology 159, 160–1, 168
birth control 162–3
Bishop 106, 110–11, 224[3]n9
Blair, Tony 41
Blanchot, Maurice: Derrida 103;
  Foucault 115, 136; literature 116,
  117; Pseudo-Dionysius 118–19;
  without 4, 81, 99
body/technology 159
Bonaventure, Saint 21
Bourdieu, Pierre 71, 74
Brazilian Christianity 220–1[2]n4
Buchanan, Ian 70, 72
Bulhof, Ilse 17, 22
Bush, George W. 41, 42

Callas, Maria 165
Caputo, John D.: continental
  philosophy 20, 83; deconstruction 7;
  Derrida 38, 94–5, 222[3]n3; Foucault
  116, 136–7, 224[3]n9; Marion 37,
  106; messianism 3
Carlson, Thomas A. 120, 223[3]n7
Carrette, Jeremy 116, 120, 137
Catholic Church 105–6, 116–17, 154
Certeau, Michel de 49–50; alterity 51,
  64; belief 58–9, 60–1, 63, 75–7;
  'Believing and Making People
  Believe' 69–70, 72–3, 78; *The Capture
  of Speech* 50; Christianity 4, 52, 53–5,
  57–61, 64; Derrida on 65–7, 77;
  Descartes 75; deviance 70, 71;

'Extase blanche' 51; God 51, 52, 54; *Heterologies* 220[2]n2; heterology 50–1, 53, 56, 57; 'How is Christianity Thinkable Today?' 51, 52, 53–5, 80; *kenosis* 60; 'Lieux de transit' 55; Marxism 72; *The Mystic Fable* 50, 62, 64–5; mystical speech 3, 62–3, 66, 217; mysticism 52, 61; negative theology 52; *The Practice of Everyday Life* 50, 52–3, 54, 69–71, 73, 74–5; religious/secular 51–2; 'The Scriptural Economy' 71; 'Signature Event Context' 75; *société récitée* 72, 76, 77–9; speech acts 75; Teresa of Avila 20; *via negativa* 1, 17, 49, 218; *volo* 62–3, 66, 221[2]n5; 'The Weakness of Believing' 55–7, 63; yes 64, 65, 80
Christian theology 4, 180–1
Christianity: alterity 56; belief 77–8; Brazil 220–1[2]n4; Certeau 4, 52, 53–5, 57–61, 64; heterology 56; historical authority 79; hospitality 203; Incarnation 160–1; madness 129–30; mysticism 62, 71, 120, 130, 152–3, 157–9; negative theology 13–15, 17, 44; Neoplatonism 13–14; phenomenology 88–9; plurality 53–4, 60; postmodernity 59; repetition of Christ's absence 53–4, 55
Cixous, Hélène 21
Clément, Catherine 1, 150–1, 164
Colossians, Epistle to 88
community 203, 211, 214
confession 115, 117, 143–8
cosmopolitanism 195, 203, 211
Coward, Harold 20
Credo 153
Critchley, Simon 214, 223[3]n6
cultural materialism 140
Cupitt, Don 17–18, 181
cyberculture 181–2

Damascius 13, 15
De Vries, Hent 1, 3, 7, 20, 176, 193, 199
Debord, Guy 165
decision-making: aporia 109–10; Cartesian 78; Derrida 191; ethics 199; hospitality 209; metaphysics 217; negative theology 219; politics 109; violence 226[6]n2
deconstruction 23–4; aporia 27; Caputo 7; Derrida 22–8, 79–80, 166–7, 169–70, 220[1]n1; negative theology 33; ontotheology 97; technology 167–70; theological turn 35–6; truth 107
Deleuze, Gilles 1
democracy 109
Derrida, Jacques: apophatic theology 90–1; *arche*-writing 25, 26–7, 168–9; Blanchot 103; on Certeau 65–7, 77; *Circumfession* 147; 'Cogito and the History of Madness' 123–6; confession 144–8; 'Cosmopolites de tous les pays' 193, 195; critics 35–6; decision-making 191; deconstruction 22–8, 79–80, 166–7, 169–70, 220[1]n1; *différance* 25, 29–30, 85–6, 87; 'Différance' 28, 35–6, 95–6, 179, 202; *The Divine Names* 14–15; donation 89; Eckhart 36; ethical turn 206; 'Faith and Knowledge' 151, 170–2, 176, 223[3]n8; faith/knowledge 176; Foucault 123–4, 146; 'From Restricted to General Economy' 28; *The Gift of Death* 206; *Given Time* 77; *Glas* 131; God's name 11–12; *Of Grammatology* 75, 77; 'A Hegelianism without Reserve' 132; Heidegger 179, 225[5]n2; history 127–8; hospitality 189–90, 193–200; 'Hospitality' 193; 'How to Avoid Speaking: Denegations' 28, 30–5, 89–93, 92–3, 96, 100, 104, 107, 144–5, 173, 179, 202; *hyperousios* 34, 36–7, 95–8, 100; ineffable 31–2; inheritance 190–3; justice/perjury 198; *khōra* 102–3, 171, 174; *laisser* 205; madness 123–4, 126–7; Marion 37, 81–3, 93–5; Marxism 191, 220–1[2]n4; messianic 28, 38–9; metaphysics of presence 23–4, 26, 81; 'Le mot d'accueil' 193–4, 206, 210; negative theology 1–2, 21, 28–30, 37–8, 41–2, 44, 101–2, 107–11, 216–17, 220[1]n2; 'A Number of Yes' 4, 61–5, 66–7, 77, 173, 220[2]n1; ontotheology 31; other 19, 42–3; 'Pas' 99; 'Pas d'hospitalité' 193, 195; political turn 193; *The Postcard* 99–100; Pseudo-Dionysius 36–7, 89–93; religion 1, 60, 172–3; salvation 6; 'Sauf le nom (Post-Scriptum)' 1–2, 11, 22, 28–9, 33–5, 37, 40, 93, 98, 100–4, 108,

Index

Derrida, Jacques *continued*
144–8, 189, 192, 202, 203, 206, 212, 214, 226[6]n2; Silesius 37; *Specters of Marx* 39, 78, 103, 190, 192, 223[3]n6; *Speech and Phenomena* 39–40; *Of Spirit* 179; subject 20–1; technicity, originary 166–70, 181–3, 225[5]n4; technology 156; text 25–6; third way 93–5, 108; transcendental contraband 142; *via negativa* 2–3, 22, 28–9, 42–4, 103–4, 203; 'Violence and Metaphysics' 28, 180; without 98–9, 111; writing 168–9
Descartes, René: decision-making 78; Foucault 125–7; madness 126–7; *Meditations on First Philosophy* 124, 125, 137; subject 20, 58, 70, 75
deviance 4–5, 70, 71, 128–9
dialectics 132–3
Diana, Princess of Wales 162, 165–6
différance 25, 29–30, 85–6, 87
difference 55, 61–2
discourse 134, 140, 141, 144
donation 89, 93, 94, 104, 221[2]n6, 222[3]n2, 222[3]n4
Dooley, Mark 195

Eckhart, Meister: apophatic/kataphatic theology 16; Augustine 97; Derrida 36; God 16, 17, 22, 36; prayer 158, 183–4
Eliot, T. S. 28
empirical/transcendental 129
Ephesians 211
ethics: De Vries 199; decision-making 199; hospitality 200; Lévinas 19, 78, 85, 180, 214; purity 197–8; violence 226[6]n2
Eucharist 105, 106–7
exteriority: deviance 128–9; Foucault 118–19, 133, 217; interiority 116, 121–2, 127, 133, 200; transcendental 121–2

face-to-face relations 197–8, 203–4
faith 79, 84, 171, 173, 176
Falwell, Jerry 61
fantasy 153, 158
fidelity 61–2, 67–8
Foligno, Angele de 1, 157–8
Form, Platonic 12, 13
Foshay, Toby 20
Foucault, Michel: *Archaeology of Knowledge* 133–5, 138–40; Blanchot 115, 136; Christian negative theology 17; confession 115, 143–4; critiques of 136–8; Descartes 20, 125–7; deviance 4–5; discourse 140, 141; exteriority/interiority 118–19, 133, 217; *Folie et déraison* 123–4, 132, 133–4, 143, 148; *Histoire de la folie* 131; historical a priori 138–42; history 127–8; *History of Sexuality* 115, 143, 146, 148; identity politics 134; knowledge 1, 19–20; madness 1, 19, 115, 130–1; 'Maurice Blanchot: The Thought from the Outside' 116, 117–19, 122–3, 132, 139, 148; 'My Body, This Paper, This Fire' 224–5[4]n2; mysticism 117, 118–19; negative theology 116, 119–20, 133, 142, 149; 'A Preface to Transgression' 122; 'The Prose of Acteon' 122; reason/madness 127, 129; religion 116–17, 118, 129–30; structuralism 71, 127; transcendentalism 129, 139, 140; undecidability 127; *via negativa* 119–20, 137, 218
Frankfurt School 160
French Republicanism 163–4
Freud, Sigmund 152–3, 159–60, 169, 185, 225[5]n1

Gasché, Rodolphe 19
Gelassenheit 43, 205
genetic engineering 160
genetics 162–3, 168
gift: *see* donation
God: alterity 19; Aquinas 15–16; Certeau 51, 52, 54; creator 150, 182; death of 59–60; donation 104, 222[3]n2; Eckhart 16, 17, 22, 36; faith/philosophy 84; goodness 90; hospitality 211; *hyperousios* 4, 14–15, 90, 96, 223[3]n5; Kant 17; Marion 179; name 11–12, 63–4, 82, 86, 207–8; negative theology 30, 32; Neoplatonism 204; ontotheology 88, 178, 184; other 34–5, 51, 52, 54, 205, 212, 216; Pseudo-Dionysius 14–15, 22; technicity, originary 177; transcendence 14–15, 82; Unity/Trinity 82, 90; without being 97, 208
grand narratives 72

Index 241

Gulf Wars 41
Gxd without Being 81, 88, 92, 107, 217

handwriting/typewriting 167
Haraway, Donna 167
Hart, Kevin 7, 37, 38, 82, 96–7
Hegel, G. W. F. 99, 132
Heidegger, Martin: Being 22, 179–80; Derrida 179, 225[5]n2; Marion 87–9, 179; negative theology 44; nihilism 160; not-without 58; ontology 85, 87–9; ontotheology 18, 32, 84–5, 89, 177, 178–80; *The Principle of Reason* 178; *The Question of Technology* 178; technology 159, 166, 167
Hemming, Laurence 221–2[3]n1
heterology 53, 56, 57
Hildegarde of Bingen 157
history 127–8
Hitler, Adolf 164
Horner, Robyn 104
hostipitality 197–200; antinomy 195; asylum policy 209–10, 213–14; Christianity 203; conditional 195; decision-making 209; Derrida 189–90, 193–200; ethics 200; future 204; generalized 215; God 211; humanity 214; immigration 152, 209–10, 213–14; Lévinas 211; negative theology 192–3, 200–9, 211–14, 215; other 110, 202; pervertibility 208–9; politics of 210–11; unconditional 195, 196, 204, 208–9, 213; undecidability 196, 197; *via negativa* 201; violence 211
Hughes, Michael 195
humanism 169, 203–4
humanity 167, 168, 184–5, 214
Husserl, Edmund 24–5
hyperessentiality: *see hyperousios*
hyperousios: Derrida 34, 36–7, 95–8, 100; God 4, 14–15, 90, 96, 223[3]n5; Marion 95–8; negative theology 107; non-Christians 111; Pseudo-Dionysius 81, 87, 92, 93–4, 110; sacred 185; without 97; without being 223[3]n7

identity politics 134
idolatry 88
illusion 153, 159
immaculate conception 155, 159
immigration 152, 209–10, 213–14
Incarnation 160–1

individual 136–7
infant 151–2, 156–7
inheritance 190–3
instrumentalism 175
interiority: exteriority 116, 121–2, 127, 133, 200; historical 121–2; reason 128–9
Irigaray, Luce 21
Islam 41, 174, 212

Janicaud, Dominique 19, 89, 218, 222[3]n2
Jantzen, Grace 17, 120, 130
Jesus Christ 53–4, 55, 64, 88, 105
John of the Cross, Saint 17, 118, 120
John Paul II, Pope 41, 42, 176, 180
John the Evangelist, Saint 61
jouissance 156
Julian of Norwich 118, 130
justice 170, 198, 210–11

Kant, Immanuel: categorical imperative 195; cosmopolitanism 195, 203, 211; God 17; messianic 39; morality 84; sublime 20
kataphatic theology: Aquinas 15; Eckhart 16; Foucault 136–7; Pseudo-Dionysius 82–3; revealed nature of God 14; third way 37, 121
Kearney, Richard 23, 106
kenosis 53–4, 60, 64
khōra 25, 35, 36, 89, 102–4, 171, 174
Kierkegaard, Søren 18, 148
knowledge 1, 19–20, 176
Koresh, David 59
Kristeva, Julia: abjection 151–2; beginning 150, 185; *In the Beginning Was Love* 152–3, 155, 157, 160–1, 163, 184; Christianity 152–3, 157–8; Diana 165–6; 'Faith and Knowledge' 167; female subject 21; *Le féminin et le sacré* 1, 5, 150–1, 152, 161–2, 167, 184; Mary, mother of God 153, 154–6; *New Maladies of the Soul* 152, 155; *Powers of Horror* 151; psychoanalysis 151–2, 184; religion 152, 154–6; *Revolution in Poetic Language* 151; sacred 5–6, 156–9, 166–7, 183–5, 217; semanalysis 151, 153; *la société du spectacle* 165; *Strangers to Ourselves* 184; *Tales of Love* 152; *technē* 174, 175; technology 155–6, 159–60, 161–2; *via negativa* 218

Index

Labour, New 72
Lacan, Jacques 1, 50
laisser 205
language 90, 91
Larkin, Philip 155–6
Las Vegas 181, 182
Lautrémont, Comte de 152
Law, David 18
Lévi-Strauss, Claude 70, 71, 74, 75
Lévinas, Emmanuel: alterity 179; ethics 19, 78, 85, 180, 214; face-to-face relations 197–8, 203–4; hospitality 211; *hyperousios* 96; other 19; *Totality and Infinity* 194, 197
liberal democracy 164
Lisieux, Thérèse de (Saint Thérèse de l'Enfant Jesus) 58, 59, 61
logocentrism 75
Louth, Andrew 14
Luke, Saint 105, 211
Lyotard, Jean-François 20, 72, 76, 80

McGinn, Bernard 16
MacIntyre, Alasdair 76
madness: alterity 19; Cartesian thought 126–7; Christianity 129–30; Derrida 123–4, 126–7; Foucault 1, 19, 115, 130–1; negative theology 130; reason 127, 129; secular sources 130
Malebranche, Nicolas 80
Mandela, Nelson 190
Marion, Jean-Luc: Bishop 106, 110–11, 224[3]n9; denomination 94; Derrida 37, 81–3, 93–5; *différance* 85–6; eucharistic hermeneutics 106–7; God 179; *God without Being: Hors-Texte* 1, 87–9, 94, 104–5; Gxd without Being 81, 88, 92, 107, 217; Heidegger 87–9, 179; *hyperousios* 95–8; *L'Idole et la distance* 85–7, 94, 95; 'In the Name' 96; negative theology 22, 92, 104–7, 222–3[3]n5; nostalgia 85–6; ontotheology 84–5; Pseudo-Dionysius 3, 4, 81, 83–5, 89–90, 93–4; subject 121; theology 81, 88–9; third way 83, 93–5; *via negativa* 103–4, 218; without 98–9, 111
Marxism 72, 131, 191, 220–1[2]n4
Mary, mother of God 153, 154–6, 162–3, 163
maternity 155, 163
Matthew, Saint 211
May 1968 events 50

media 72–3, 168
memory 67–8, 169
Merleau-Ponty, Maurice 79
messianism 3, 28, 38–9, 223–4[3]n8
metaphysics 27–8, 84–5, 87, 217
metaphysics of presence, Derrida 23–4, 26, 81
Milbank, John 39, 218, 220[1]n3, 221[3]n1
morality 84
Mortley, Raoul 14, 22, 32
mysticism: Certeau 52, 61; Christianity 62, 71, 120, 130, 152–3, 157–9; Foucault 117, 118–19; secular 159, 183–5; subject 64, 120; technology of the self 120; worldly 136; yes 64–5
mystics 1, 17

name of God 11–12, 63–4, 82, 86, 207–8
Nancy, Jean-Luc 20–1
narcissism 156–7
National Socialism 160, 163–4
Nationality, Immigration and Asylum Act (UK) 213, 226[6]n3
negative theology: alterity 201–2; Certeau 52; Christianity 13–15, 17, 44; counter-metaphysical 84, 94; decision-making 219; deconstruction 33; Derrida 1–2, 21, 28–30, 37–8, 41–2, 44, 101–2, 107–11, 216–17, 220[1]n2; Foucault 116, 119–20, 133, 142, 149; futures 6–8, 189, 190, 218–19; God 30, 32; historical archaeology 130–3, 141–2; history of 2–3, 12, 21–2; hospitality 192–3, 200–9, 211–14, 215; *hyperousios* 107; madness 130; Marion 22, 92, 104–7, 222–3[3]n5; modernity 17–22; Neoplatonism 12–13, 40, 101–2; ontotheology 92–3; other 205; politics 104, 107–11; postmodernity 17–22; Pseudo-Dionysius 21, 44, 81–3, 89, 119; sacred 183–5; third way 83; undecidability 110
Neoplatonism 2, 12–14, 40–1, 101–2, 204
neo-structuralism 74
Neo-Thomism 39, 216
new historicism 140
Nietzsche, Friedrich 69, 84, 139
nihilism 160–1, 181–2
nostalgia 85–6

Index   243

One 13, 22
ontology 84, 85, 87–9, 168
ontotheology: deconstruction 97; Derrida 31; God 88, 178; Heidegger 18, 32, 84–5, 89, 177, 178–80; Marion 84–5; negative theology 92–3; *via negativa* 102
Orwell, George 41, 220[1]n4
other 206, 207; absence of 50; absolute 189, 193, 215, 216; Derrida 19, 42–3; divine 207; fusion with 152, 157; God 34–5, 51, 52, 54, 205, 212, 216; hospitality 110, 202; negative theology 205; singular/multiple 206–7; stranger 49; *see also* alterity

Paisley, Ian 59
Paul, Saint 88, 178, 211
Peacocke, Arthur 181
perjury 198
Peron, Eva 164
phallogocentrism 21
pharmakon 161, 172, 173
phenomenology 88–9
philosophy 23–4; alterity 20; continental 20, 83, 216; faith 84; French 1, 217–18; history 128; technology 167
phonocentrism 74–5
Pickstock, Catherine 39
Plato: Forms 12, 13; *khōra* 89; *Meno* 167; *Phaedo* 12; *Phaedrus* 24; *Timaeus* 32, 89
Plotinus 13, 22, 82–3
politics: apophatic theology 110; decision-making 109; immigration 152; narratives of 72–3; negative theology 104, 107–11; religion 59; sacred 163–4
Polkingthorne, John 181
Pollock, Jackson 152
positivism 169
postmodernity 17–22, 59, 60, 80
prayer 91, 158, 183–4
Proclus 13, 15
Propp, Vladimir 71, 74
Pseudo-Dionysius: Blanchot 118–19; Christian community 203; Derrida 36–7, 89–93; *The Divine Names* 32, 106; God 14–15, 22; *hyperousios* 81, 87, 92, 93–4, 110; identity politics 134; Marion 3, 4, 81, 83–5, 89–90, 93–4; mystical subject 120; mystical theology 86; *Mystical Theology* 3, 21, 32, 89; name of God 86; negative theology 21, 44, 81–3, 89, 119; prayer 91; third way 82, 83, 121; without 99
psychoanalysis 151–2, 158–9, 160–1, 163, 164, 184

Radical Orthodoxy movement 39, 59
rationalism/nihilism 160–1
reason 127, 128–9, 152–3, 171, 172–4
refugees 213–14
religion: auto-immunization 174; Derrida 1, 60, 172–3; Foucault 116–17, 118, 129–30; genetics 162–3; illusion 159; Kristeva 152, 154–6; Marxism 131; politics 59; reason 152–3, 171, 172–4; sacred 162; secular 51–2, 171; technology 160, 164–5, 170–6; tele-technoscience 172; violence 174
repetition 3, 53–4, 55, 65, 66–7, 68
reproductive technologies 154

sacralization 165
sacred: alterity 177–8; feminine 159; *hyperousios* 185; Kristeva 5–6, 150–1, 156–9, 166–7, 183–5, 217; negative theology 183–5; originary technicity 175–6; politics 163–4; religion 162; secular mysticism 159; *technē* 151; technology 164–5, 166, 175
salvation 6, 41
Saussure, Ferdinand de 25
scriptural economy 74–5
sculptor image 82–3
secularism 51–2, 130, 159, 164, 171, 183–5
semanalysis 151, 153
sexuality 144, 150–1, 155–6
Shelley, Mary 175
signified/signifier 121
Silesius, Angelus 34, 44; Derrida 37; *Gelassenheit* 205; inheritance 192; without 4, 81, 99; yes 63, 64
Smith, James K. A. 104
société récitée 72, 76, 77–9
Sollers, Philippe 117, 224[4]n1
speech/writing 24–6, 61–2, 75, 146; mystical 3, 62–3, 66, 217
Spivak, Gayatri Chakravorty 38
Steiner, George 76
Stiegler, Bernard 168, 169, 176, 225[5]n3

stranger/other 49
structuralism 70, 71, 74, 127–8, 131
subject: Cartesian 20, 58, 70, 75;
   Derrida 20–1; female 21; Marion 121; mystic 64, 120; transcendental 58, 70; will of 66
subjectivity 70, 117, 151
sublime 20
suicide bombers 174
superessentiality: *see hyperousios*
supplementation, logic of 179
Swinburne, Richard 181

Tambling 144
Taylor, Mark C. 181, 182
technē 150–1, 159, 162, 174, 175
technicity, originary: Aristotle 181; Derrida 166–70, 181–3, 225[5]n4; God 177; sacred 175–6; theology 185
technology: auto-immunization 172–4; body 159; deconstruction 167–70; Derrida 156; faith 173; Heidegger 159, 166, 167; humanity 167, 168; Kristeva 155–6, 159–60, 161–2; originary 162; philosophy 167; poison/cure 161, 172, 173; quasi-transcendental 174; radicalization 166; religion 160, 164–5, 170–6; reproductive 154; sacred 164–5, 166, 175; violence 174
technology of the self 120
Tel Quel 224[4]n1
tele-technoscience 172
Ten Kate, Laurens 17, 22
Teresa of Avila, Saint 17, 20, 118, 120, 130, 157
text 25–6
theiology 89, 91
theological turn 1–2, 11, 18–19, 35–6, 115, 152
theology: Christian 4, 180–1; contemporary 180–3; counter-metaphysical 86, 89; deconstruction 38–40; future 176–8; Marion 81, 88–9; medieval 15–17; metaphysics 84, 87; mystical 83, 86; postmodern 60; post-ontotheological 177, 180; technicity, originary 185
Thérèse de L'Enfant-Jesus, Saint *see* Lisieux, Thérèse de

third way 37, 82–3, 93–5, 108, 121
totalitarianism 162–5
tout autre est tout autre 206, 207
transcendence 13, 14–15, 82, 128, 131, 137; subject 58, 70
transcendentalism 121–2, 129, 134, 139, 140
transgression 117, 118, 119
transubstantiation 105
truth 86, 107
Turner, Denys 14, 22

undecidability: Foucault 127; hospitality 196, 197; metaphysics 27–8; negative theology 110; positivity/negativity 132; *via negativa* 217

veil-wearing 212
via negativa 16–17; absolute other 189; Certeau 1, 17, 49, 218; continental philosophy 216; Derrida 2–3, 22, 28–9, 42–4, 103–4, 203; Foucault 119–20, 137, 218; hospitality 201; Kristeva 218; Marion 103–4; ontotheology 102; transgression 118; undecidability 217; without 81
Villanova University 93–5
violence: confession 147–8; decision-making 226[6]n2; ethics 226[6]n2; hospitality 211; religion 174; technology 174
Virilio, Paul 181
volo 62–3, 66, 221[2]n5

Ward, Graham 60, 76, 181–2
without: Blanchot 4, 81, 99; Derrida 98–9, 111; *hyperousios* 97; Marion 98–9, 111; Pseudo-Dionysius 99; Silesius 4, 81, 99; *via negativa* 81
without being 97, 223[3]n7
Wittgenstein, Ludwig 44, 71
writing 24–6, 62, 146, 167, 168–9

yes: Certeau 64, 65, 80; divine/Nietzschean 66, 69; mystic 64–5; originary 65, 67, 68, 90; pre-originary 173; repetition 65, 66–7, 68; Silesius 63, 64

Žižek, Slavoj 53

CPSIA information can be obtained
at www.ICGtesting.com
Printed in the USA
BVHW03*0042160518
516350BV00007B/99/P